On Assignment in the Wild

More Midlife Adventures

Gary G. Ruhser

Jean C. Beyer Ruhser

Photography by the authors.

Front cover
Top photo: Lake Agnes, Boundary Waters Canoe Area Wilderness
Bottom Photo: Alamo Lake, Arizona

Back cover
The authors: Jean and Gary

We are indebted to our daughter, Gayle C. Edlin, an excellent writer in her own right, for her talented work in putting together the covers of all our books from our ideas, words, and photos.

This book is dedicated to our daughters,
Gayle and Janis,
with heartfelt thanks for their constant love
and support.

And to our granddaughter, Jayne,
who was born after many of these adventures,
and thus, missed out on hearing about them
at the time.

Table of Contents

INTRODUCTION – Falling in love with fieldwork

In 1990, when Gary set off to work on a US Forest Service crew in the Boundary Waters Canoe Area Wilderness, and Jean drove out to Idaho to help reintroduce five young Peregrine Falcons to the wild, little did we anticipate how much we would come to treasure doing fieldwork. The next year, Gary joined Jean in Peregrine work as described in our earlier book, *Seven Summers with Peregrines: Finding Midlife Adventures*. A map of the United States hangs on a wall in our home, with 20 little yellow flags marking the geographical locations of our fieldwork adventures. Eight of those flags mark the hack sites where we worked with The Peregrine Fund to release a total of 65 young Peregrine Falcons in Idaho, Montana and Wyoming in the 1990s.

But, what about all the other flags, the ones scattered in two corners of Colorado, one each in Arizona, Texas, and Minnesota, with others in northeastern Wyoming, and in Wisconsin? These commemorate fieldwork for Greater Sage-Grouse, Ring-necked Pheasants, Bald Eagles, Aplomado Falcons, the aforementioned Boundary Waters, Sharp-tailed Grouse, and more general bird surveys of several types. These stories remain to be told, some of them in the book before you.

Jean's teaching job in the Biology Department of the University of Wisconsin-La Crosse was not very secure; without a Ph.D. degree, she was dependent on being offered contracts when a faculty member had release time for research or went on sabbatical, or when the courses she could teach were over-enrolled. Many of her teaching contracts were issued for one semester at a time and were only part-time. Four times in the more than 20 years of her teaching career at UW-L, she received no contract there at all. One of those four spring semesters, Jean was called to teach at Winona

State College (now Winona State University), but in two springs, she found fieldwork opportunities.

Gary had quit his engineering job in 1991 to do Peregrine reintroduction work, and, until he returned to full-time engineering in 1997, he was self-employed as a consulting engineer for a variety of employers in several different locations. Thus, both of us had periods free from our usual careers, when we could undertake fieldwork projects.

Part One in this book is the story of Gary's work on a crew in the Boundary Waters during the summer of 1990, when he fully enjoyed camping and canoeing in that wilderness area. The crew's work included rehabilitating portages and campsites, planting trees, representing the Forest Service in visitor contacts, and performing maintenance work to ensure the natural characteristics of the area in spite of it being the most visited wilderness area in America.

In Part Two, Jean writes of spending four and a half months in Arizona as a Bald Eagle Nestwatcher in 1993. As a grantee for Arizona Game and Fish Department, she camped in primitive conditions from late winter into early summer, observing and recording data on two pairs of desert-nesting Bald Eagles. She, and her three Bald Eagle Nestwatch partners, were also tasked to prevent human intrusion into the vicinity of the nests, so the reproductive and hunting behavior of the nesting eagles would not be disturbed.

Part Three takes place on a barrier island off the Gulf coast of Texas in 1997, where Jean worked as a Hack Site Attendant for young, captive-bred Aplomado Falcons. Reintroduction of this species was patterned after the hacking procedures that had worked so well in the recovery of Peregrine Falcons. Punishing working conditions included the summer heat and humidity, and the difficult "commute" between the mainland and the island. Island wildlife, such as alligators, poisonous snakes, scorpions, feral hogs, and ants—lots of ants—were challenging neighbors.

The final portion of this book, Part Four, describes Gary's nine years as a volunteer for the Wyoming Wildlife Federation and the Wyoming Game and Fish Department. In the early spring each year, 2001-2009, he spent a week or two in northeastern Wyoming, driving the back roads, exploring National Grasslands, and accessing private ranchlands with permission, to search for the leks (display grounds) of Sharp-tailed Grouse and Greater Sage-Grouse. Once a lek was located, Gary counted the male grouse displaying, and the number of females visiting the lek to choose a mate. Each year, he reported his data to both agencies.

Part One – Gary

Boundary Waters

Minnesota

1990

Prologue

As a corporate engineer with 23 years of representing my company, I recorded the following note in my personal journal after checking into my motel during yet another business trip:

August 8, 1989 4:41 PM – Upon my arrival at my room in the La Baron Motel in Dallas, Texas, as I dejectedly stand looking out the solitary room window with one leg cocked up on the air conditioner, having just arrived after three air flights through four airports and a long rental car drive through this huge city, as I stare out over the cluttered, packed, endless maze of buildings, cars, trucks, humanity, and ugly flat black and brown roofs stretching out endlessly into the industrial haze, I think to myself the choice: You can either keep doing this for another 20 years or you can paddle off into the Boundary Waters Canoe Area next summer as a volunteer wilderness ranger – seems terribly fundamental what the choice should be.

Introduction

Prior to 1990 I think most of my friends and relatives would probably have declared me to be a "normal" citizen, a decent man, not prone to being a rebel, a good husband and father, a successful and gainfully employed corporate engineer, providing a respectable home for his family on a farm in Wisconsin. But some of those classifications, at least as viewed casually from the outside, began to fall apart in the summer of 1990.

On a Sunday morning in early June, daughter Janis made me French Toast for my parting breakfast, and both loving daughters bid me a fond farewell, filled with good wishes for my future plans. As I drove north 300 miles to Cook, Minnesota, in my Ford pickup truck, the back filled with all the possessions I would need for the next eight weeks, I was filled with a mixture of trepidation and curiosity for what lay ahead. I was an introvert headed for an eight-week long extrovert experience as a voluntary member of a six-person Boundary Waters Rehabilitation Crew. It was a wind-driven rainy day with low, dense clouds racing over the hilltops and casting intermittent showers over my two-lane concrete escape path to the North Country. The windshield's blurry vision, knocked back and forth by the wipers contributed to my general malaise, depression, and wandering dark thoughts.

A six-hour drive allows ample time for thought and I tried, again, to make sense of what I was embarked upon, if it was the right and best action to be taking at this stage of my life. I was born into a poor, but respected, German rural farm family in Northwest Iowa, was President of my high school class, and Salutatorian. I married my childhood sweetheart, Jean, at age 21, graduated from Iowa State University at 22, became a father at 24. Jean and I had by 1990 been married 25 years, both daughters were in college, and the house and farm mortgages were both paid off. So, what was I doing driving away from my heritage and from all we had accomplished together?

Jean and I were separating, a "trial" separation for the summer. We were counting on and trusting our daughters to believe in us and in themselves, in spite of Janis's friends telling her, "Oh, yeah. They are getting a divorce all right." I had engaged in hard, stressful negotiations with several Vice-Presidents regarding my continued employment at the company where I had worked for over 20 years. Future employment was contingent upon their and my compliance with the complex agreement we had struck. I was angry about that agreement. As the summer wore on, I would find myself returning to smoking, a habit I had quit 27 years earlier. Amongst my new young friends that summer, I would develop a fondness for whiskey and its inebriating aftereffects. Late one night in midsummer I would stay out of reach of two drunken, violent men as they wrestled, arms thrashing and grabbing, and crashed into furniture, upsetting it, and repeatedly threw one another onto the floor, thuds echoing around the interior of a small cabin in the wilderness near the Canadian border. And on that first night in Cook, away from home in the North Country of blue lakes, tall forests, and adventure, I would share my bedroom with Elaine, an attractive young woman about the same age as my daughters. It was to be a summer of life-altering experiences.

The Forest Service mobile home at the edge of Cook, MN, which we used as our dormitory during time off

Unloading our canoes in the Moose River parking lot for the portage and paddle journey to Lake Agnes

Work Tour 1, Days 1 through 10

The preceding paragraphs are all true. But, ….what is truth? There is often more to the story. Truth often has many layers. Taken out of context, truth can be misleading. And so, below I will present to you a broader picture of my summer of 1990 and a clarification of the misimpressions you may now harbor based only on the short introduction above.

In the late 1980's as our older daughter, Gayle, progressed into college and our younger one, Janis, neared the end of high school, a certain amount of re-evaluation and restlessness set in for both Jean and me, not too unusual at this life stage when adults ask themselves whether their careers are adequately fulfilling, or whether there are any unmet goals or dreams that deserve to be attended to in the post-childrearing stage of adulthood, when retirement is still "way out there" in the future. I was finding engineering challenging, interesting and a good way to make a living, but what about my boyhood dream of becoming a wildlife ranger? Jean believed teaching was the right career for her, and biology was the subject she still loved teaching, but what about her feeling that she ought to be doing biology, as well as teaching it? Should we perhaps be living more varied lives NOW instead of waiting for retirement, NOW while we were still active and healthy, NOW when we could have some new adventures? Was it possible for us to find some kind of outdoor, environmental work that we yearned for, that would benefit the natural world? Our summer plans for 1990 would begin to provide some answers to these issues.

After an extensive amount of research, analysis, discussion, and a thorough review of our financial and health status, as well as an assessment with our daughters about how our near-term plans for 1990 might affect them, we decided to use the summer of 1990 as a testing grounds to determine our future vocational and avocational goals. Jean decided to apply to be a Hack Site Attendant for the summer in the Rocky Mountains for the reintroduction of Peregrine Falcons being conducted by The Peregrine Fund. (See our book, *Seven Summers with Peregrines, Finding Midlife Adventures.*) With Jean's biology background, she was easily accepted by The Peregrine Fund and she spent that summer in a beautiful hack site overlooking Hells Canyon in Idaho. As an engineer with no biology training in my resume, I did not want to adversely affect her acceptance by applying with her, so I sought my own summer activity and was accepted to be a member of a six-person rehabilitation crew working in the Boundary Waters Canoe Area Wilderness (BWCAW) for the Superior National Forest, with my base location in Cook, Minnesota. Jean and I were both elated to be accepted for these jobs.

As I drove toward Cook that first day, along with the complex thoughts alluded to above, I had a wide-ranging array of memories of the recent history of how I got to this point, of preparations for this journey, of the weather conditions during this drive. I could see cattle along the road and on the rolling pastures of Wisconsin adjoining US Highway 53. The cattle were wet from the nearly constant showers of rain, brisk winds pelting them with droplets, some were grazing on soaked grasses, some were lying down, chewing their cud, water running gently off their furry hides. I could envision wolves and deer in the North Country I was headed toward being in the same conditions and I wondered if I could be as content as these animals appeared to be when I found myself in their same situation: no building to take shelter in, no protection from the winds and cold temperatures other than from whatever I would carry on my back or in the canoe. I realized the wild and domesticated animals do it all the time, that is their life. As I continued driving, I said to myself, "If they can, I can. And I will."

Included in the application for this job was a precautionary statement that described the project task as "hard and strenuous work under primitive and arduous conditions." I acknowledged that, and signed my completed application form anyway. Then I attached the required physical examination signed by my physician, which certified to the extent required by the lawyers that a doctor believed, based on his examination of my heart and health, that I shouldn't die from my efforts expended to satisfy the Forest Service's work requirements. It seemed fair and a wise precaution on the part of the Superior National Forest. My main concern was my temperamental lower back and associated joints and muscles which had plagued me on occasion. Frankly, an earlier diagnosis while I was yet in my 30's from my local medical clinic that I had degenerative arthritis of my lower back, was one of my prime motivators for my future plans. I wanted to climb mountains and paddle rivers while I was able to, not wait until the normal retirement age, and I worried I might be in a wheel chair by then, or otherwise unable to physically engage in an active lifestyle in the great outdoors.

As I continued my travel northward, I found I had tensed up, gripped the truck steering wheel harder, grimaced, and tightened my focus as I reflected on the road blocks which my employer had put in my path to this point. Noting that I had actually attained an acceptable compromise to continue my employment while still being able to engage in my chosen manner of environmental volunteerism in the Boundary Waters, I relaxed my grip on the wheel and willed my body to relax and enjoy the drive.

My goal had been to request and be granted an unpaid leave of absence from the company to allow Jean and I to trial-run our new life goals without immediately risking my future employment and health insurance coverage. Leaves of absence were granted on occasion among Jean's collegiate peers and in the post-graduate academic world. But they were just barely being recognized in 1990 for their benefit of educational and personal development in the corporate world in which I worked. A small number of professional societies, such as the American Society of Heating, Refrigerating and Air-Conditioning Engineers, of which my company was an active participant, were advocating the benefits of employees volunteering for the betterment of communities, but that did not translate into any acceptance of such a policy at my company.

I went for the gold (I knew some fundamentals about negotiating tactics) and initially asked for 10 weeks leave of absence. Fortunately for me, my immediate superior was a supporter of my goals and had spent some pleasant vacations enjoying the Boundary Waters of northern Minnesota. Without his support any requests solely on my part to upper management would likely have been permanently rejected. Predictably (I understood the company culture, at my level we were still wearing sport coats, ties, and dress shirts daily. You might say my company was a stuffy, very conservative 1980's corporation.), even with my boss's gentle support, my request was still rejected outright. I was not surprised. I countered that a different corporation in the city granted up to six weeks leave to new mothers or fathers. Even our company granted some leave to cope with severe medical problems, including alcoholism, but none were allowed for "good," "essential" employees. Official letters, counter-proposals went back and forth as my own calendar counted down to when I was to report to the Superior National Forest and engage in my work contribution to an environmental cause. Classified as a Volunteer while there I would not be "paid" as such, nor be termed as an "employee." I would be granted twelve dollars a day by the Forest Service for my physical effort and this amount was deemed as coverage of my expenses to be there, namely food to eat and transportation to get there. This meant I would pocket a whopping twelve dollars a day volunteering in the BWCAW, instead of approximately 20 times that amount per day, which I could earn as a gainfully employed full-time engineer! During one meeting with my immediate vice-president, he facetiously suggested the company could grant a leave of absence to me. All I had to do was sign up for military service. I was 46 at the time.

In the end, perhaps due to my obstinance, persistence, and intransigence, and after five weeks of negotiations through my boss (my immediate superior) and with three vice-presidents of the company, my boss's boss and two levels of bosses above my boss, we came to an agreement. I would be granted two weeks leave of absence, I would take all of my remaining three weeks of vacation, during two of my five-day time off periods from working for the Forest Service I would come back to the office 300 miles away from Cook and put in a 40-hour work week during those days, and I would call in once a week to my boss for consultation in case a particular company situation developed that would specifically need my knowledge and verbal input. This would give me seven weeks of time that I could devote to the Forest Service. And…. I was told by upper management to NEVER ask for this again.

With minor exceptions, the job assignments for myself and the crew I worked with at the Forest Service, took the form of seven days on a work tour in the Boundary Waters, followed by five days off, and this twelve-day pattern would repeat four times, thus matching the seven-week time allocated by my corporate leaders. I will characterize that schedule in this book by the terminology "Work Tour" during which time I am engaged with my fellow crew members in living and working in the Boundary waters wilderness, and by the term "Time Off" during which time I have no obligation to the Forest Service, but on two of those periods I will be obligated to put in a 40-hour week at my engineering job.

At the start of Work Tour 1, on June 3,1990, I had completed my six-hour drive north and pulled up and parked on the shoulder of Highway 53 just outside of town where I took a picture of the green and white Highway sign identifying Cook, Minnesota, with a population of a surprisingly even number, 800. I hopped out and took several pictures of the small town that would be my mailing address for the summer. On the assumption this would be a momentous summer, I intended to fully document it as an amateur photographer and had brought along two 35mm single-lens reflex cameras, one filled with color negative film, the other filled with color slide film. In my backpack was a spiral-bound blank notebook. I intended to fill the notebook with daily journal entries.

Instructions received by mail, advised me to stop in at the Ranger Station, easy enough to find in a small community where the Forest Service was one of the major employers. There I could locate further information on where I could spend nights while in Cook, as well as the time to report for duty the following morning. As my arrival was on a Sunday, the Ranger Station was closed, but there was information inside the entryway with a map showing where to find the Forest Service house trailer in which I could spend that night, and any other nights when I wasn't out on the lakes or portages with my fellow crew members.

I followed the map to the northeast edge of town, in a quiet older residential area, bounded to the east by railroad tracks and by low-lying ground beyond, which was covered by head-high stagnant water-loving brush. I parked in front of the mobile home, which the forest Service owned and used as housing for its temporary summer workers. The trailer was brown and white, long and narrow, and was fixed upon its own town lot, and was surrounded by a broad lawn and wood-frame houses on adjacent lots. I grabbed my small backpack, jacket, cameras from the truck seat and walked in, no locks needed, no knocking on the door necessary, I was automatically an "occupant." Once inside I was warmly greeted by Derek, Blaine, and Ginger. They were there as I was, all on the first evening of their summer employment, eager to know what would happen tomorrow, and what our roles would be. Each of the three was about 20 years younger than me, but they seemed to have no reservations because of our age differential. We each shared briefly how we had come to be there at this point in our individual lives. Derek was disaffected by his career and social situation and had come to seek an alternative path in his vocational and life goals. Blaine was a college student and was there strictly to bolster his resume as he pursued a degree in the environmental field. Ginger was an elementary teacher and this would be her "summer job." Meeting these earnest, well-meaning individuals gave me my first opportunity to practice my story line of how and why, as an obviously older person, I had come to join them in what was undeniably a well-used old house trailer, in a remote corner of Minnesota, willfully to become engaged in physical labor for a pittance of monetary reward. I briefly summarized my reasons for being there, they seemed to accept it at face value, and we moved on jointly to how to share the refrigerator, everyone's supper plans, bedding arrangements, and to convivial conversation.

Ginger, following her pattern of the previous summer, was staying in her private small camper trailer, parked in back of our mobile home. She was a summer employee of the US Forest Service, with suitably higher pay, unlike the other three of us who were classified as volunteers. Derek and Blaine had staked out the front bedroom of this two-bedroom trailer, so I gravitated to the opposite end of the trailer and discovered an unclaimed single bed in the bedroom there along with a second bathroom, staked out that bed as mine and tossed my pack and gear on it.

Each of us had driven over several hundred miles to get there and were tired after a long day. After some post-supper conversation, the Minnesota dark sky descended and we mutually decided it was time to get some sleep and prepare for an early rising the next morning. I turned off a few of the overhead lights as I went to my end of the trailer, cleared the bed of my stuff, prepped it for sleeping the night away, turned off the last light, rolled to my side and was promptly asleep, the old mattress and bedsprings under it actually feeling quite restful and good for my tired body.

Sometime shortly before midnight the overhead light in my bedroom snapped on and a soft feminine voice quickly said, "Oh! Scuse me," and the light snapped off. She proceeded to walk past my bed and cycle through the bathroom, which adjoined our shared bedroom, and as quietly as she could, slipped into the other single bed located inches away from mine. Her bed, the second bed in the bedroom, was on the other side of a custom-built, thin panel wall separating our beds, the wall about as long as the beds. The entry door to the bedroom was adjacent to the head of my bed. The entry door to the bathroom was on the opposite wall from our bedroom door but on the other side of the room near the foot of the second bed. Thus, we each had access to one bed in the room and had common and open access to the bathroom door which was located off her "half" of our bedroom.

The next morning, I would learn my bedroom partner was Elaine, a college student, and she was transient worker like the rest of us. It was Elaine's gear and bedding that had declared to me when I arrived that the other bed was already taken. Having been awakened from my deep sleep, I lay there for a while pondering customs, mores, and the passage of time, and what a difference a few decades can make. I could sense that my compatibility and acceptance by the younger generation I would be working and living with, would be contingent upon my ability to mentally reduce my age by about two decades and to join their relationship to the world around them. I would need to understand, emotionally

24

and socially, their mode of living and their acceptance of me while yet appearing physically as an adult with 20-25 years of life experience beyond theirs. But from my own perception of how Derek, Blaine, and Ginger had responded to me so far, I felt I could successfully share my life philosophy and make a two-way success, theirs and mine, out of this summer. They were unborn or still infants when I was already the age they had attained by 1990. They could not sense nor truly understand the world in which I existed when I was their age. When I was their age I could not legally smoke nor drink any alcoholic beverage nor be in a woman's room in the women's dormitory of the college I was then attending. In my hometown the only place one could buy hard liquor was in a state liquor store. Hugging between males and females whether in greeting or in parting was not done in public. The birth control pill was only just becoming known and used. Divorce was still shunned and living with a member of the opposite sex was much less common. In the engineering college I had attended, less than a handful of the graduates were women. No doubt, the outdoor jobs of the Forest Service in the 1960's were largely occupied by men, with women mostly working as secretaries and other office staff. I was subject to being drafted into the military and could not choose my future vocation without considering the military draft. The nation was being torn asunder by the Vietnam War and racial inequality. In large sections of the country, African Americans were still being required to use separate drinking and bathroom facilities, and to ride only in the back of the bus. Laying there I was stunned at the difference in our lives at the same age. Could I pass muster and live well and rightly with these good, ambitious, free-spirited young adults? Could I do the physical work the Forest Service would require? These thoughts whirled jack-hammer-like through my mind until in a quiet moment of reflection on where I actually was, in a comfortable bed of a dark room late at night, and with my own tiredness returning, I could hear and tell that my bedroom partner had fallen asleep. I rolled over and joined her, she in her half, me in my half of the bedroom. Not even a full day in, and already it was proving to be an interesting summer.

The next morning Elaine's alarm clock went off at 5:15 AM, shortly after the long freight train carrying fully loaded cars of iron ore clacked, clicked and rumbled through town a few blocks away. Its passage was a noisy one to this country boy and could be dimly felt through the floor and bedframe as subtle vibrations transmitted through the low-lying moist soils of the community. Elaine had already been working for the Forest Service the past few weeks and needed to be at the Ranger Station by 6:00 AM. I rolled out of bed 25 minutes later and took my shower when Elaine was done with hers. Being already aware in general terms of what my wilderness schedule would be in the coming weeks I knew hot running water was going to be a rare gift, and should be utilized when available.

Our schedule called for us to be at the Ranger Station at 7:30 AM. After my breakfast of an orange and donuts I joined Derek, Blaine, and Ginger in walking the 10 blocks to the Station. Along with others who were drifting in for the orientation session and a summer of work in the Boundary Waters, we were all greeted by Mike, the local Cook, MN Ranger Station contact who had approved our applications and arranged our work assignments. Mike introduced us to Ron, Jack, and Tom, part-time employees of the La Croix District who lived in the area, as well as Ginger, all of whom were "crew chiefs," reporting to Mike, and who would supervise one or more of us, the volunteers. For the first time we also met the other volunteers who would be working in the District: Chad, a recent high school graduate trying out a possible vocation and on his first job assignment away from his home in Northern Minnesota; Nikki and Greg, a young unmarried couple who had paddled down a remote river in Canada the previous summer and were using this assignment as "free housing" to avoid paying two month's rent on an expensive apartment, in order save up for their planned marriage in the future; Dan; and Sandy, both of whom were college students seeking outdoor experience and the opportunity to enhance their future job resumes. Elaine and Dan would be supervised by Tom and normally on assignment in the northeast part of the District. Sandy would be supervised by Ginger; the two of them would mostly be working in the Trout Lake area. Derek would be assigned to Jack and both would be patrolling the east end of Lac LaCroix and working out of the Ranger Cabin there. Blaine, Chad, Nikki, Greg, and I would be the "wilderness rehabilitation crew" working for Ron. His crew would be working on the campsites and portages of Lake Agnes, and also at Lac La Croix where our activities would periodically intersect with those of Jack and Derek.

Stewart, who was Mike's immediate supervisor, and David, another manager of the La Croix District, came to our meeting area to welcome us all to the District and to the job and to define their expectations for us. In addition, they explained the managerial details of work time versus time off and how and when we would be paid. Two videos were shown including the classic, "Path of the Paddle" by Bill Mason, both of which imbued us with a sense of the history and tradition of canoeing in the North Country. If the idea was to get us anxious to hop in a canoe and do some paddling, it worked. Within three hours of arriving at the Ranger Station we were loading five canoes on the trailer.

Paddling to Lake Agnes on the Moose River through a wide reed bed

Preparing to portage from Lake Agnes to Boulder Bay of Lac La Croix

Some of us did not realize what would occur this day and were given a few minutes to go across the street to a convenience gas station to grab some junk food for a noon meal. Mike led the way, our several vehicles following him, to Orr, MN, then we turned east onto the Echo Trail to the Hunting Shack River. We ten paddlers quickly unloaded the canoes and placed them in the clear, gently flowing waters of the river and paddled about 1½ miles down the river to Astrid Lake. It was a lovely day for paddling, warm, sunny, calm wind, few bugs. At Astrid Lake, we dined on our junk food at a camp site while Mike gave a short lecture on paddling safety and being aware of the water and potential dangers of working with hand tools in the wilderness.

Yes, for those of our readers unacquainted with rules and regulations of the BWCAW, power tools and wheels are prohibited. The good news is we wouldn't have to worry about lugging around heavy chain saws or the messy fuel to power them. No need to fear the rapidly spinning chain slicing through our jeans or boot leather and carving at our soft flesh underneath. In keeping with the tradition and silence of wilderness only hand tools can be used, some of them quite common to many of us like the axe, hatchet, bow saw, shovel, pick-axe, two-person crosscut saw, branch nipper; but other tools like the Pulaski, Sandvik, and Picaroon, were new to some of us. Still, used without caution, any of these hand tools can injure an individual as severely as a power tool.

After lunch we all paddled to the end of Pauline Lake to another typical wilderness camp site to examine its structure, cleanliness, orientation, and what could be done to improve it for future users. Next, we walked a 20-rod portage to Nigh Lake to understand overland transit of canoes between lakes or waterways. By this time, we had seen the fundamentals of our future in canoe country and easily paddled upstream to the trailer and vehicles to reload and drive back to Cook, arriving there about 4:00 PM. At the Ranger Station we were each issued our personal heavy canvas portage pack with straps for carrying on one's back, sleeping bag, foam sleeping pad, and life jacket and then dismissed until the next morning.

That late afternoon and early evening I cased the town for familiarity by driving around it and taking a long walk with a few of my new friends. Learning quickly from these less economically advantaged individuals and recognizing my current income level was equal to theirs for the next two months, I brought back a loaf of day-old bread for half price and tallied up my savings. It was the first of numerous worthy lessons I would learn from my young partners of the summer.

We four first residents of the trailer were all glad we already had our claims staked on the only four relatively-comfy objects that could be called beds, situated two each in two bedrooms. Because the next five people that arrived at the trailer as the day wore on would be sharing and bedding down in the living room. The Forest Service had thoughtfully provided two used army surplus folding camp cots, but the last three people would be relegated to whatever flat spare space could be found on the living room floor. It worked out well enough, lots of conversation, getting acquainted, laughter amongst the nine of us, three gals, six guys. A combination radio/cassette player was provided as part of the furnishings and was soon cranking out constant tunes as backdrop for the gabfest underway between individuals. It was a crowded dorm. But it was our dorm and we were all in this together.

Next morning, I awoke at 6:00 AM mentally anxious to put in a day's effort and to learn more about what we were to accomplish in and for the BWCAW. The implication yesterday was that we would all be going somewhere to do something, but as leadership is sometimes prone to do, few details of our actual work assignment were given in advance to us menial laborers. Following our late night of visiting, the five lifeless bodies strewn around the living room were still sound asleep at 7:10 AM. Derek assumed the responsibility for group cohesiveness and roused them out of their slumber. We drove to the Ranger Station in a light rain, several of us sharing our vehicles with others so that everyone arrived for our new day in a relatively dry condition. Mike started us off with one more lecture and revealed our task for the day. Then the crew chiefs led us to the equipment shed where we were each issued a canvas daypack, safety helmets, safety glasses, and leather gloves.

This would be a full group effort of all District volunteers plus several of the crew chiefs, no canoes required, and everyone piled into multiple vehicles. The five members of Ron's crew, of which I would always be one, rode with Ron in a large Chevrolet Suburban, easily accommodating the six of us plus a selection of hand tools and our personal gear. While the five of us had come to know a little about each other in the house trailer, riding with Ron for an hour to our destination was our first opportunity to learn more about our "boss," and he about us. Ron would be our leader, responsible for our safety and well-being while camping and paddling miles away from anyone else of authority. He would give us our assignments for 7-8 days in a row, and we would live and work together with him in wilderness settings. I think we all sensed we would either become a well-oiled, well-meaning team, or it would become an uncomfortable summer, and we all hoped for the best.

Ron was a barrel-shaped, stoutly constructed man, not tall, with twinkling observant eyes, and a sly little grin, that verged on evil, when he was joshing with you. He was in his mid-30's, about 10 years my junior, and had lived in northern Minnesota since he was a young boy. Ron had worked for some of the local resorts, had been a hunting guide. As a seasonal employee of the Forest Service for the past few years, he had managed other crews like ours, and, based on his stories during the drive, we felt he had the experience and knowledge we were looking for as our own personal "guide" for the summer.

In this vast north country of multitudinous lakes and seemingly endless forests, travel distance and travel time must always be taken into account when planning a day's activities. Ron drove to Orr on Highway 53, then east on Highway 23 to Buyck, then north on Highway 24 until he turned off onto County Road 424. After a few more miles, we arrived at the parking lot at the trailhead of the Herriman Lake Trail where we stopped. The distance from Cook to this trailhead was 45 miles and the transit time was about 1 ½ hours. Just coming and going can consume half of a modest work day. It had been raining intermittently all the way, but seemed to be winding down, so we ate our lunch in the vehicles before we grabbed the hand tools, daypacks, and whatever waterproof clothing we had with us, and trudged on up the trail.

Our assignment was to clear out the Herriman Lake Hiking Trail up as far as Dovre Lake, a distance of three miles. A lack of maintenance for a few years and several harsh winters had left it somewhat obscured and overgrown in sections of the trail. Ice can linger on these far north lakes sometimes until mid-May so when we arrived it was early in the recreational summer and few, if any, hikers had used it yet, an ideal time for us to be there and give it some deserved attention.

This would be our first opportunity to work with one another and assess more of each other's personality and work ethic. We each grabbed a few hand tools and set out on the trail, whacking, sawing, cutting, nipping, chopping as we went and gradually strung out in a moving line traversing down the trail attacking those obstructions that matched our tools in a continuing effort to clear the trail and make it convenient and easy to follow for future hikers. Strong young men grabbed heavy tools to match their self-perceived strength and preferences, two teamed up to man a two-person cross-cut saw and sawed trail gaps in eight deadfalls of 10 to 50-year-old trees that had fallen across the trail. Nikki and I each carried branch nippers and paired up to nip off and cut and remove brush and branches up to an inch or so in diameter. Teams and individuals leap-frogged one another in pursuit of obstacles matching their tools and exchanged complimentary wisecracks and precautionary comments about the rain or the bugs or the best method to drop a leaning tree.

The rain had generally ceased but one shower in mid-afternoon had me donning my waterproof jacket as others had done. Waterproof gear does well at keeping external water off you but, if you are engaged in heavy labor, it traps the condensation of your sweat on the inside of the clothing and you feel like you are inside a sauna. Our legs and feet though were rather defenseless against the wet grasses, brush, and water-laden leaves. We got soaked on the lower half of our extremities and, upon the moisture soaking through boot leather or jeans, it felt like we had been walking in a stream bed.

During our slog up the trail, I had several opportunities to walk alone and I relished the pines and glacial soils and unfamiliar bushes, so different from our Coulee Region farm fields and oak hillsides. I had my cameras in the day pack and took some pictures of the hard-working crew in action as well as some huge pink lady-slipper flowers. Common Yellow-throat warblers, White-throated Sparrows, and Veeries were in the trees and brush, singing their spring mating songs. I felt like these familiar birds were my cheerleaders.

After several hours of effort, blue waters hove into view and we made our goal of reaching Dovre Lake where all were entitled to a break and the fine scene in front of us. Mission accomplished, we all hiked back to the parking lot in a light-hearted mood despite being wet from the waist down and sweat laden from the waist up.

Ron's crew hopped into the Chevy Suburban he had checked out of the District inventory for this outing, and Ron proceeded to drive us all back to Cook. About half way there we witnessed the passage of a severe thunderstorm across our path south, the rumble of thunder, the intense flashes of lighting coursing from clouds to treetops. Then, with the storm to the east of us, we passed through its aftereffects and slowed down to maneuver cautiously over a one-inch depth of fresh hail beginning to melt on the roadway, crushing it with our tires. We were all glad to be in a solid vehicle and not camped out in tents in the path of that isolated storm.

During the drive we felt relieved to be done working for the day, while still excited about what we had accomplished. The physicality of meaningful work was beginning to set in and we were mutually coming down from an endorphin-driven high. Our conversations too were turning from the casual to the meaningful and all six of us got into quite a "fix the world" conversation. Opinions were given and exchanged, postulations were provided, solutions were proposed, a raft of subjects and examples were given voice: over-population, pollution, the growth of cities, fast cars, environmental concern, taxation, politics. What we discovered was, with small specific examples and exceptions, all six of us were in basic fundamental agreement on the big issues of the day. Suddenly, it occurred to me that I had been working in two different large corporations for 24 years and had never found five other individuals who were as aligned as these five "strangers" were to me in what I felt, believed, and advocated. I remember the feeling and the camaraderie we all sensed during the drive, based on our exchanged opinions, but it was not until years later, as I contemplated writing this book, that I pondered more deeply the reason. In the companies where I worked, several thousand individuals had come together because they were in pursuit of a livelihood. While any of us could find some individuals within the company who shared one or more of our interests, the philosophical orientation of thought was far from universal in the other employees we met. Whereas, for Ron and his crew of five, a great winnowing and sorting out of perspectives had already taken place merely from submitting our application and being accepted for the roles and work in which we now found ourselves. Who would sign up for and willingly apply to be here? Who would volunteer to be paid a pittance to work outdoors in primitive and arduous conditions? We did. And if a statistician or a sociologist were to analyze our commonalities, they would have discovered "average" people or a normal cross-section of Americans would not be here. We had self-selected to be a unique sub-group.

Back at the Ranger Station we were all dismissed by Mike, given one day off, and told to report back for our next assignment on Thursday morning. I'm sure this had more to do with the complexity of scheduling and workers needed on our next assignment and less to do with our performance on this day, but we who did the labor felt a sense of being rewarded. An awareness of what we could accomplish together and some group pride was beginning to creep into the crew. Even the Old Guy of the crew could sense we were beginning to click.

At the trailer, tossing our wet gear near our individual bed areas, we learned Greg and Nikki and one other volunteer were taking off and heading to quieter locales and some privacy for the evening. This gave the rest of us more room in which to hang or organize our belongings, to sort wet from dry, to think about nourishment. I chipped in $1.50 with the others and we purchased a pizza to share.

The radio/tape deck was turned on, loud, alternating between country or pop songs with some of the group sharing their favorites on tape. The Forest Service-supplied card decks got a work-out, some players drifting between that and deeper conversations, or questioning of others. I was not, and have hardly ever been, a game-player but it was fun and interesting to watch and listen to the others in between reading a bit in books I had brought. Elaine, Sandy, and I broke out for a discussion group about 11:00 PM and for an hour or more we plumbed our shared depths of Lao Tse, *The Aquarian Conspiracy* by Marilyn Ferguson, and *The Power of Myth* by Joseph Campbell. I am sure very few, if any, of my peers at the company I worked in could have joined our conversation. Sandy had spent some time at a Buddhist Monastery in Colorado the past January and I fell asleep that night admiring these young seekers of wisdom, so many of them seeking meaning beyond the materialistic. I had to admit to myself, I was on a similar path, albeit two decades beyond their stage of life.

Wednesday morning found everyone remaining in the dorm trailer, sleeping in, at least for a little while. After my shower and breakfast, I threw a few belongings in my truck and drove 47 miles to Ely, Minnesota, checking out the Pfeiffer Lake Campground on the way, just in case I needed a place to stay some night when in the area again. Lots of bunchberry, starflower, and foamflower were blooming. Ely has four times the population of Cook, plus it is a very cool and fun tourist town. There were a good number of summer visitors starting to come in, several streets were lined with canoe and outdoor outfitters, an abundance of eateries, a suitable variety of stores suited to a tourist town of 3600 residents, one of the bigger communities within an hour's drive of Cook. Based on the wet conditions encountered so far and, with the expectation of more to come, I had concluded I needed some rubber over my leather boots and found short rubber boots to pull over my leather ones at a shoe store in town. I ran into Nikki and Greg at the large outdoor recreation store in town, fun to see and chat with somebody I recognized, in a community so far from home. I drove to The Wolf Center on the east edge of Ely, where I had a membership and stopped in to see the impressive growth of the three wolves I had seen there in February. After my lunch of a tuna sandwich at the Fall Lake Campground I got back to the Cook trailer around 2:30 PM.

The dorm was strangely quiet when I returned, a condition I had never yet encountered there, so I was able to write a few postcards to the family, let them know how I was doing and my new mailing address. Remember this was in the days before cell phones, and only one or two pay phone booths were available in Cook. Chad joined me in my walk downtown to the post office to mail the postcards. I read a little in the trailer and packed a lot. What a pile of stuff to organize for tomorrow and fit into a large pack and a smaller personal pack, which will all be carried on my back or in a power boat. No canoes needed for our next adventure. My body furnace doesn't burn very hot so I need a lot of clothing to stay warm and dry, plus my two cameras, plus a couple books, plus my journal. You get the picture; I would be carrying some items which a number of my hardy partners could easily do without.

I didn't look forward to the packing, but it went well enough and everything I had chosen to take fit in the packs. Years of experience in camping, canoeing, kayaking, and backpacking helped immensely to sort the pertinent from the not-needed. As the crew gradually assembled in the early evening, we swapped stories of what we had done on our time off, many of us curious about the others' activities. Blaine had gone fishing for the day. I heated beef stew for supper while others barbequed outdoors. Blaine was short of tools for a repair job he was doing on a fishing reel, but the toolbox I kept in my truck supplied just the tool he needed. The music was back on and the gang was rocking the trailer with loud voices and occasional shouts while playing games of Pictionary on the living room floor and cribbage in the kitchen. I slipped away to the back bedroom for a while to read, but I was lured back to the gang because I found myself not wanting to miss out on any festivities, even though I sometimes just sat off to the side, grinning at their antics, and laughing at their zest. Already personalities were beginning to reveal themselves: Ginger was affable but a bit authoritarian, perhaps because she was a teacher; Chad emerged from a commoner's appearance, as gentle and intelligent; Nikki was friendly and had a questioning curiosity about others; Greg listened intensely and had strong opinions. Chad claimed I was even-tempered, but what did he know so soon?

The alarm at 6:00 AM felt early. I got in a quick shower and was doing my stretch exercises when Crew Chief Ginger popped into the front door and loudly announced, "Be there at 7!" I quickly responded and said we were to be there at 7:30. "Who said that!? The crew leaders decide!" To which I replied "Mike." My fellow partners quickly provided abundant corroboration and Ginger backed down and left, leaving us lowly peons to gloat a bit and question the communication chain of our leaders.

Reporting to the Ranger Station at 7:30 AM we, the volunteers, began to get a glimmer of our first major summer assignment. The first several days of introductory training, testing, and sleeping in a fixed structure were over. Now would come six days of physical labor in the outdoors, travel by boat, and sleeping in tents. Mike and the crew chiefs had organized what would be this summer's La Croix District single biggest rehabilitation project in one of their highest use areas, using all the volunteers, crew chiefs, and employees they could muster and reasonably accommodate given the work required and the available resources. The major focus was to open up the portage trail between Little Trout Lake and Gowan Lake. The trail had been subjected to a severe thunderstorm the previous summer, and a downburst of high wind had taken down numerous trees in a tangle of destruction totally obscuring portions of the trail. Other projects accessible from our camp site would also receive attention as time permitted.

By 8:30 all the equipment and supplies we would need appeared like a superfluous and exorbitant mountain. This mountain, consisting of our personal gear, canvas packs, tents, two-person saws, axes, shovels, cardboard boxes of supplies, containers of food, coolers, extra fuel, camp stoves, 2-way radios, was loaded into the trucks and into the power boats mounted on trailers behind the trucks. An hour later we arrived at Moccasin Point on Lake Vermilion and reversed the loading, heaving, and lifting, while filling our three power boats now floating at the docks with said mountains along with a dozen individuals eager to get on the open water.

Our first stop was at the south end of the truck portage which connects Vermilion Lake with Trout Lake. The truck portage literally employs internal combustion-driven trucks with large rear flat beds, which are backed into the water. The water-borne power boats are then removed from the water onto the truck bed and mechanically transported by means of driving the truck on an established, well-packed motor trail to the other end of the portage. This truck portage and a very few other mechanical portages in the Boundary Waters Canoe Area were initially created many decades ago and some still exist today as a result of complex governmental and legislative compromises, which were struck over the years during negotiations for establishment of this wilderness area, one of the most popular in the United States.

Our tools prior to loading in the canoes: shovels, bow saws, 2-man saw, sieve, wheelbarrow, axes, nippers

Tree cut with 2-man crosscut saw, nearly two feet in diameter

Although most lakes in the BWCAW are restricted to manually powered watercraft (generally canoes and kayaks) the allowance of size-restricted and power-restricted boats on Trout Lake, and a few other popular lakes like it, was also part of those negotiations and legislative actions. For our first assignment, the power boats allowed the fastest and easiest access to get our large crew and tools to the location of the blowdown on the Lake Gowan portage.

After several hours transporting all our personnel, associated equipment and boats over the truck portage and relaunching onto Trout Lake, we were able to motor across Trout Lake and arrive at our camp site at 12:30 PM. We would spend five nights on the southern edge of Sioux Pine Island, a large island in the north half of the lake. Camping supplies were disgorged from our boats and we had a quick lunch so that by 2:00 PM, Ron's crew took one power boat to the north arm of Trout Lake while the other crew chiefs and their volunteers boated east and then portaged to Little Trout Lake. This would allow the Lake Gowan portage and its obstructions to be cleared by personnel working from both ends.

At our end, the first thing we experienced was wet boots as we bushwhacked our way to higher land battling the muskeg, swampy footing, and various stages of godawfullness that can often be encountered where overland portages meet lakes. Chad and I worked with Ron, taking turns with the two-man saw and going after the biggest trees blocking the trail. Blaine, Nikki, and Greg ranged out ahead with their smaller saws, axes, and pruners, clearing the smaller brush. Chad and I were a little apprehensive about the lack of a good, powered chain saw when the three of us came to the first of several 18-inch diameter and very tall aspen trees, which had fallen across the trail. But, given that power tools are prohibited now that we were officially in the Boundary Waters, Ron gave us a slight smile, gave us the nod, and Chad and I each grabbed one end of the professionally-sharpened saw and commenced to pulling. Impressive! Taking turns as needed to give the other a breather we quickly made two kerf-widths of sawdust as we severed a chunk of tree trunk out of the middle of the fallen tree, and were proud to turn around and walk through our new pathway.

By the end of the workday, we heard reports from the rest of our crew that they had gotten to the main blowdown area obliterating the trail, and that there would be an abundance of effort required the next day. One widow-maker on our end was perplexing Ron and Chad about how to safely get it down on the ground. A widow-maker is a tree precariously hung up near vertical or at a high angle, which, with a lack of caution or just plain bad luck could make a widow out of one's spouse, if they are under that tree when it finally releases and comes crashing quickly to earth. At our own farm in Wisconsin, I had felled a goodly number of trees for firewood over several decades, so was familiar with the risks and hazards of widow-makers. I contributed my analysis and proposal to Chad and Ron's ideas and Ron gave mine his go-ahead. First, Chad and I cut an adjacent tree, and pushed it over with Ron's help. Then we made the final cut on the widow-maker and were rewarded with a safe fall of the dangerous tree. No new widows or injuries to report that day.

The temperature was hotter on this afternoon, so we generated our share of sweat which in turn attracted a few mosquitoes, sweat bees, and biting flies. A little insect repellent seemed to alleviate somewhat the repeated attacks from these flying insects. But our primary physical and mental irritant on this day was not hung-up trees, or biting insects, but army worms. Hundreds, thousands even, of ugly, disgusting, crawling army worms.

The army worms, or forest tent caterpillars, we encountered were the last instar/larval stage before the caterpillar forms its cocoon, and eventually emerges as a flying moth. Army worms wax and wane in 10 to 20-year cycles and unfortunately for us living under and with them, 1990 was a peak year. They were expected to eat the leaves off of up to five million acres of Minnesota trees that year, largely aspen trees. In mid-June army worms were at their peak population and most would be at their cocoon and moth stage by late June and early July. Prior to the cocoon stage they are about two inches long, and, viewed singly, could actually be called "pretty." Along the length of their body are broad blue stripes alternating with narrow yellow-orange stripes. White spots appear on the top of each segment of the caterpillar and the sides sport short "hairs." The aspens can stand one defoliation and will regrow new leaves once after an infestation. The following week, when I drove to Voyageurs National Park along the Canadian border north of Cook, I would see large swaths of leafless trees from the road at a time of the year when every tree would normally be fully leafed.

As we worked on the Gowan portage, army worms were everywhere in unbelievable abundance. As they chewed their way through the foliage above us their small pellet droppings (feces) on a quiet day could be heard hitting the bushes near you or at night it would sound like an intermittent rain sprinkle on the nylon tent fabric over your head. The louder, bigger "drops" were the worms themselves falling to the ground to continue their endless, crawling, gnawing search for more sustenance. Gross! If you let your mind dwell on it, it could freak you out unless you kept rationalizing and realizing this is Nature at work, in one of its myriad ways. Lay a shirt on the ground or a bush, and literally within a minute there could be ten army worms on it. Any time you would think of taking the action, you could bend over and whack off 3-10 from your lower legs or sleeves or 6-10 from the pack you had laid down. Don't try to squish or kill them, too many, too icky, just flick them off and away. As we worked the trail, we found one uprooted large tree that had left a pool of water where its root ball had been. In the pool were hundreds of floating and sinking army worms, very like a temple of doom movie scene. We didn't run away from it, but we certainly didn't linger in the area.

After several hours of good hard effort by a lot of people, the crew chiefs decided enough had been accomplished for one day and we motored back to our camp site on Sioux Pine Island, arriving there about 5:30 PM. Unlike when we six were our own crew, for this mission the Forest Service supplied all the food. Arriving back at camp, we found earlier returnees had already prepared a fine hunger-eradicating meal of burgers hot off the grill, warm beans and chips. Great! We were all famished and very thirsty. The prime freshwater source is the lake and everyone but me drank it as it was. Being older, cautious of my digestive system and, as a back-packing western mountain enthusiast who has witnessed others bearing the pain of *Giardiasis*, I had brought along my own small, high-tech water filter. Except for personally witnessing the boiling water prepared for hot tea or instant hot cereal and then consuming that, for all other drinking I pumped my water filter daily throughout my stay in the Boundary Waters.

Each of us erected or helped erect the tent we would be sleeping in while camping out. That first night eight tents went up, some of the later campers putting theirs up discovered the best sites were already occupied and were left with rough, stony, or un-level ground. Ron issued me a two-person hoop supported nylon tent with vestibule just like his, each for our individual use. With a sly grin and a wink, he issued a mocking challenge, "Here 'ya go, Mr. Engineer. All you have to do is figure out how to put it up yourself." Fortunately, although I was unacquainted with this particular tent and its convoluted shape; mechanical experience, cold engineering logic, and previous experience with broadly similar tents using flexible fiberglass poles inserted in sleeves allowed me to get my tent up in my chosen spot in short order. I was pleased to get my "atta-boy" from Ron a few minutes later as he strolled by on his way to the campfire. Chad and Blaine, as well as Nikki and Greg were each issued a four-person A-frame style tent for each pair of volunteers to share the rest of the summer.

It was a pleasant, partly-cloudy evening, the lake and pines beyond backlit by the setting sun, the campfire attracting some members of our crew and consequent conversation, while others organized their tent contents. Blaine was standing down the shore line preparing his rod and reel, I jotted a few lines in my journal before returning to the main dining area and campfire to exchange impressions of our experiences to date with my peers. The crew chiefs were nearby but had their own gathering for the evening, somewhat apart from the rest of us. Several hours of multi-hued daylight were yet available for our relaxation. The crew chiefs lived in the area, were seasonal employees, enjoyed their work and being outdoors, but their primary goal was to earn a living in an area of the state where they preferred to live. The volunteers likewise were there because they enjoyed the outdoors, but also to support an environmental cause we believed in. Most of us tended to be college-educated, and we didn't have to be working there, whereas for the crew chiefs this was their livelihood. Thus, there existed a small fault line of experience and goals, which would be our joint responsibility to bridge if we wanted to understand each other during our summer together.

There were a few light rain showers in the night and when we returned to the Gowan portage the next morning, some of those showers were persisting. All of us had our full rain gear on and I had pulled my short rubber boots on over my leather work boots to maintain dry feet while walking in the muck-bound, soggy trail with occasional rivulets of water running across or down the passage I was trying to walk on. Not as many army worms this day, but the skeeters were more abundant in the moisture and humidity of morning. We all used some bug repellent but to minimize my exposure to that man-made poison I frequently used the Bedouin Bandana I had adapted on our Wisconsin farm when dealing with similar plagues of biting insects, seemingly always attacking you on the back of the ears and neck. I took a large bandana or handkerchief from my pocket, tied two adjacent corners together, positioned it to cover the back of my neck and ears with the knot on top of my forehead, then put my cap or hat back on. It was a frequent sanity-saver throughout the summer whenever the biting insects were at their worst and was a trick Nikki quickly copied as did some of the other crew members.

Later in the morning we hit the WALL, as it was called, the thick mass of trees where the worst effects of the downburst and high winds of the 1989 storm had caused the most destruction. Downed trees were piled up three and four deep and sometimes as often as every three feet, impossible to proceed past without crawling or climbing. Nikki and I were working as a team and each had a 30-inch bow saw. A couple of the other crew members were working the two-person crosscut saw, and if you weren't sawing you would pitch in and haul the branches and tree chunks off the portage so the others could keep sawing.

Ron called for a lunch break shortly after noon and I found myself eating like a lumberjack. I was famished and found this trend continuing when we were on assignment. It takes a lot more calories to do this physical labor than it does to punch a computer at a desk inside of a corporate office, and my food consumption showed that.

Back at the WALL we continued to chew our way through, attacking it with all the gusto we could manage after a full morning of sweating and hard labor. You can tell you're working pretty hard, sweating profusely, and likely not drinking enough liquids when you don't have to pee. I was standing there watching Nikki still going at it and feeling my tiredness. The tiredness eventually accumulates, you cut for five minutes and take a break for 30 seconds, then you cut some more for three minutes and take a break for 30 seconds, then you cut vigorously for a minute and take another short break to rest your arms. But you keep going (because the others are still going at it), but you're bushed. And I was thinking to myself, most people would actually label this as excruciatingly-hard labor, and it was. We sweat buckets and swatted bugs and flicked off army worms and it was raining and thundering and we were all out there grunting, but do you know what? It was still better than sitting in my corporate office at my desk hoping the phone wouldn't ring with a service question that I couldn't answer and hoping it would soon be 4:00 PM so I could leave the company and finally drive home. At my vocational job, I admit, I am a clock watcher. Out there in the North Country I didn't even know what day it was until I looked at my journal.

The ride back to camp (my journal says "the ride home" – I think there is a message there) on the lake that day was wild. Life jackets were strapped on tight, both hands clutching the nearest gunnel or seat of the boat, as the bow pounded up and down striking the tops of two-foot waves, thundering with the aluminum hull smashing into the water below with each bounce, the strong wind whipping the tops off each wave and spraying Ron, our boat captain, with sheets of lake water. Pulling the boat into a tiny natural harbor was hair-raising, a bit treacherous for fear of crushing one's hand or arm between storm tossed boat and the boulders lining the shore. The timing of grabbing and leaping out had to be coordinated with the tossing of the boat, then multiple hands and arms heaved the boat far enough up the shoreline to get it clear of the smashing waves.

We were finally being greeted by the back side of the weather front and the sun began to appear for the first time that day. Lingering high winds helped dry out our exterior clothes. After supper we visited around the campfire of our segregated camp, volunteers on the west side of camp, crew chiefs on the east side, like gathering with like. Tom had brought along a battery-powered portable stereo player. I kept my disapproval to myself. For me, being in the wilderness was a near-sacred experience and I wanted the reverence found in a church. For the crew chiefs it was another day at work and they wanted some background man-made music. I heard the stereo playing as I sat by the lake, twilight deepening, but I focused my ears to the gentle lapping at water's edge of a quieting lake, only a remnant of its former white-capped, violent self. On the trail I had seen wolf scat, wolf tracks, and hair from a likely winter wolf-kill. I came for the Wild, found it, and went to sleep, bushed, proud, and content.

The following morning, Saturday, I helped peel potatoes for a ham-steak and fried potatoes breakfast, before a late start back at the Gowan Portage job. Instead of the anticipated eight hours work we had the portage totally cleared out before noon. Everyone was equally amazed at the rapid pace a crew of a dozen determined outdoors people can apply, as specialists leap frog over one another in quest of the next obstruction. The crew chief's boss, Mike, and his supervisor, Stewart, had left the confines of their office in Cook and came out to inspect our handiwork and join us for lunch at Gowan Lake as well as to spend the night on the island with us.

After lunch, Mike and Stewart toured the Gowan Portage project, while the rest of us piled back into the power boats and cruised up to the Norway Hiking Trail at the far end of the North Arm of Trout Lake. There had also been a blowdown on that trail. The crew chiefs were not eager to tackle this added assignment but it was Mike and Stewart's decision, so tackle it we did. We made great and rapid headway as usual for a large team and whacked our way down the trail before we came to another pile of downed trees about 1½ miles inland, which succumbed to our efforts as had the previous obstruction. About 3:30 in the afternoon I got clobbered across the bridge of my nose by a springy branch. Ouch! And at the same time, I hit my own wall, the wall of exhaustion. I struggled along for another hour hoping this day would be the low point of my energy curve and I could rebound from there.

We had a super meal for our supper. Whether the bosses brought in the meal or the crew chiefs were trying to impress the bosses, it didn't matter to the rest of us. We all chowed down on fire-roasted chicken, boiled potatoes, steamed rice, and a welcome fresh salad. Everybody was at the main kitchen site and conversing around the fire in the early evening. Nikki and I had worked as a team again this day and talked about my farm, each of our hobbies, shared music interests, her recent travels. After the effort and admitted exhaustion of the day, it felt really good to recline in camp among convivial new friends and acquaintances and marvel about our easy living, as the fire lit up the boughs of pines above us and the star-studded evening sky twinkled through the branches. Admittedly, there were always army worms to flick off and they seemed thicker than the previous night. Before dark, many of us made special note of the fact that hundreds of worms were floating in the lake adjacent to where most campers had (emphasis on "had") been collecting their drinking water.

It was most likely due to two more levels of management being in camp last night that we arose from our slumber the following morning a little earlier than usual, the lake water slapping shoreside rocks gently as the day promised to be a good one, the early sun illuminating the treetops above us. With the addition of Mike and Stewart's two tents we had a total of ten tents on site during the night. If a crew member was old enough, like me, or if at least crew chief level or upper management, the forest service issued tents, like my corporation used motel rooms during company business trips; one tent or room per person, each to their own.

After a wholesome and filling breakfast of pancakes and fried ham we sent Mike and Stewart on their way, out of our hair and self-consciousness, and went back to work on the Norway Trail coming at it from the Trout Lake side. We were soon through the parts of the blowdown that required manual effort with our hand tools, retrieved from our hidden cache of the previous day, and had made it to the northern boundary of the BWCAW. From that point on to the nearest access road, the Forest Service would use chain saws to clear the rest of the downed forest trees and brush still remaining and obstructing usage of the full length of the trail. Derek and Sandy had stayed at the Trout Lake camp to install a new latrine there and were jealous upon hearing some of the crew had seen a bull moose with velvet antlers near the wilderness boundary.

Ron boated his crew to a camp site on Trout Lake and gave us instructions on how to perform routine cleaning maintenance: tidying the fire ring, raking out trash from the ashes, collecting surplus ashes and unburned residue and trash inside plastic refuse bags we carried for that purpose, disposing of unseemly brush piles, dispersing rocks or stumps used for seating and attempting to bring the overall campsite to a neat setting appropriate to the wilderness versus that of an over-used city or county park. We would do a lot of that type of campsite maintenance work at many more sites in the coming weeks. The goal was to allow visitors the illusion they were camping in an old camp site, seldom used, instead of a site used dozens or hundreds of times in the recent past. While we were gathered, Ron also took a few moments to explain how we were to comport ourselves if we accompanied him in a "Contact" with a wilderness visitor. Part of Ron's obligations as crew chief was to act as a "compliance officer" and periodically confirm that BWCAW visitors were complying with Forest Service regulations. If any one of us were with him at such a contact, whether just in passing another canoeist on the portage trail or whether Ron had purposely taken one of us to visit campers on their camp site, we were to be quiet, but polite, and defer to him for all face-to-face communication with the other party.

Ron then dropped Chad, Blaine, Greg, and Nikki at the Pine Lake portage. While the four of them brushed out and cleared that portage, Ron and I quickly cleaned up three additional near-by camp sites and then shot back up the lake at great speed now that only two of us were on the boat. We met Tom, Dan, and Elaine at the Norway Trail where they were crafting and installing a hand-hewn cedar log bridge across a small creek and shallow defile. After admiring their fine work and helping them clean up and put the wraps on their project, Ron boated himself and me back down lake, stopping to pick up a half bottle of Windsor Canadian Whiskey from a hidden cache of the previous Fall. "Wow, where in the world did that come from? We just as well take it back to camp with us." Then we collected the other four crew members and headed back to camp for a grilled steak, roasted potatoes, and green salad supper.

Although I did not arrive as a "Be Prepared" Boy Scout, apparently my time as an engineer and my previous experience back-packing and camping allowed me to be a valuable asset and team partner.

My tent with vestibule at our camp on the north shore of Lake Agnes

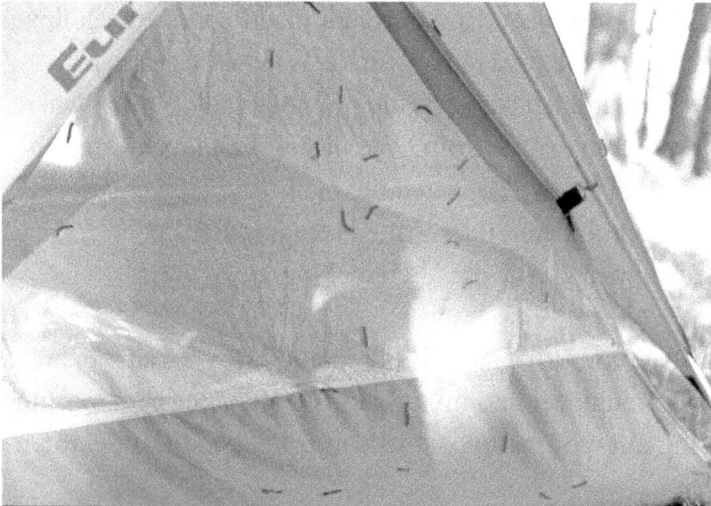

Army worms crawling on the screen of one of our tents, they were everywhere on our first work tour

From the Journal: Nikki is impressed with my organization. This morning I shared our upcoming schedule with her by pulling it from my billfold while we were cruising up the lake. This noon I gave her a Band-Aid from my billfold after Ron could not find any in his Forest Service-issue first aid kit. Tonight, I pulled Q-tips and cotton from my tiny personal first aid kit for Dan after he cut his hand. The Forest Service didn't have any of these items in their kit. Dan borrowed my Gerber lite knife to cut his steak. The Forest Service didn't have any matches so I donated mine. Same thing with the can opener on my belt. The forest Service needed it to feed the rest of us.

It was early in this particular trip. It was early in all of us getting to know one another and sharing thoughts, and the conversation around the fire and amongst the groups of two or three chatting was still rich and meaningful. Later in the summer we would discover after five or six days of being together hour after hour, it was enough. It would be time then for some time apart. Chad, perhaps because he was the youngest of our group, said some of the deep conversations he was a part of were new in his experience. Yet, even I as the oldest could understand what he was saying, when I remembered how it was to be fresh out of high school and discovering new people carrying new thinking. I told him how pleased and surprised I was at how similar the philosophies were between him and me and the other individuals who signed up for this experience. No half dozen people at my company in La Crosse would have such similar views. But a great weeding took place when we volunteered—those who didn't share similar views of the wilderness, canoeing, volunteering, economics, the environment, purposely did not join us. Greg and I commented on how it felt good to be "doing our part" there in the Boundary Waters, and how we could not understand those who left behind the trash we were picking up each day. Nikki said she and Greg would like to see our farm someday.

Near dusk, after a few folks had drifted off to a personal spot, as the sun was setting, I grabbed my life jacket, laid it on the rocks for padding and reclined in the comfortable sofa of earth, wind, sky, and man-made flotation in my own personal spot. I had my book along, *The Aquarian Conspiracy*, but that particular evening was made for pondering. The day had been a pleasant, easy work day, a real treat from the past several days of heavy exertion. I concluded I liked it all: the people, the work, the outdoors, the lake, the fresh air. I thought I was doing okay, feeling okay physically, feeling comfortable on the social interaction level, both of which I had worried about. I wondered if I would stay with the company. I wondered what I would do with my life after this. I wondered if I would stay in contact with any of my new acquaintances. As the sun dipped below the horizon and the last rays licked a few clouds in the west, as the breeze died down and the waves three feet from my feet shortened to little swells, and a small fish flopped on the water, I surprised myself by saying out loud, "Gawdammit, this is nice! This is Sweet!" I lifted my upper torso and looked around quickly to confirm who said that? And was relieved no one else was nearby.

As I awoke the next morning to large waves crashing against shoreside rocks I remembered the date, June 11, was my and Jean's 25th wedding anniversary. Surely, a momentous day for the average married couple, which we did in fact, celebrate with family before leaving home for our summer adventures. But we were not average, and on this day, we were not together. I could not discern any camp noises from the nearby fire ring and camp kitchen area, and rolled over for another hour's worth of shut eye. Prior to exiting the tent for breakfast, I dug out the special candy bar Jean and I had been buying for our yearly anniversary celebration. I knew she and I would consume each of our treats on our anniversary day, together in thoughts and action if not in physical presence.

High winds approaching 30 miles per hour were whipping branches and tree tops vigorously back and forth, the sky was thickly layered in dark bands of clouds, lake waves were two to three feet high with abundant whitecaps, the entire shoreline was wetted inland a dozen feet from shore edge because the wave-top droplets were being blown off of the endless cascade of crashing peaks. No rain falling yet but it was nasty. The crew chiefs had access to two-way communication with Forest Service radios, had determined thunder storms were forecast to come rolling over us, and so declared the day to be a camp day. No work, it was too dangerous to leave camp. After Dan and I washed breakfast dishes I walked over to the west point of the island near our camp as the rain drops began to come down.

From the journal: As I watch the waves pounding the shore one can't help but be impressed at the power of nature. And we are in such slight shelters but they will probably be okay. Man is always making better shelters to control his personal environment. Nature always retains the power to destroy even the strongest shelter. Looking into the eye of this storm I am not particularly fearful. I probably would be if I were in a bouncing boat with water crashing in. But I certainly feel, ... , feel, ... what? Like I am more part of the ecosystem, living in the moment, living in common with all around me, instead of apart and separated from it, like we are when we are in the shopping mall or dwelling in the separated shell of our company or the vocational jobs we have and living in fancy houses built not only for shelter or as being in alignment with the earth's needs but built to impress others. Some of our crew, like the crew chiefs or easy-going Chad, may have trouble with passing the time of this day. Not I.

Late in the morning, with many of us tucked in our tents avoiding the rain, the call, "Time for Apple Melba!" rang throughout the camp. As the rain intensity lessened, we gathered under the camp kitchen tarp to discover the crew chiefs and several crew members were busy peeling and cutting up apples and tossing them in a large stew pot over the camp stove. Tom, Jack, and Ron cooked them down to a pleasant consistency, then Jack added a bottle of his home-made maple syrup to the kettle. After the syrup had been heated the pleasant two-ingredient concoction was ladled out for everyone to enjoy. Each with cup and spoon in hand, we all labeled it "Delicious!"

Another passing shower dispersed many of the campers back to their tents, me included. When I headed up to the latrine in the early afternoon, I was surprised to find not a soul around the fire ring or kitchen area. With such a large group in camp I hadn't ever seen it that way. Returning to my tent I concluded a vestibule on a tent is a very good thing in these conditions.

From the Journal: The vestibule allows one more level of storage, dirtiness, shelter from the rain, a place to shed the filthy boots, and is excellent for wind shedding. It's like a porch on a house – seems now well worth the price and weight in exchange for the convenience it delivers.

Although still cloudy, by 2:30 PM the winds had died down considerably, and the rain seemed to be past and headed east. The crew chiefs started up one of the motor boats and took off down lake. I was visiting with Blaine and Derek when we heard it come back some time later and we wondered what that was about.

As the oldest guy in camp, I figured the crew chiefs wouldn't toss me out of their territory so I moseyed over to their side of the camp to strike up some conversation and learn a little about these leaders of the rest of us. As an introvert I did not take this step lightly, but I was determined to have the whole of this Northwoods adventure and not to skirt shyly around the perimeter. It turned out the boat run was for some additional whiskey, cleverly hidden and cached for just such an emergency as a storm-bound camp. A little whiskey, with a splash of lake water added, on a non-work day provided the lubrication and relaxation these Ranger Chiefs needed to properly assess their roles in life and what exactly it was that Life meant anyway. At least that is what I got from it as Ron freely shared some of the golden liquid rations with me as we four explored answers to troubling philosophical questions. I got more light-headed and tipsier than I had been in years, probably not since those teen-age years on the remote country roads of Iowa on several dark nights, and I wound up being inducted, so to speak, an official "Big Dog," a "North Country Woodsman." (More on these designations later.)

A late supper of tasty mouth-warming chili was prepared by Dan and Derek and they came to get us "drunks," as they crudely labeled us, to come and eat it. While cleaning up the last of the chili the crew chiefs, led primarily by Jack, told us what a good job we had been doing, to keep up the good work, and gave us some tips about how we will break up camp tomorrow morning, our last day on this assignment, as we take most of the day to get our big work crew and all the equipment back to the Ranger Station in Cook. It was a bit odd listening to such a sober, well-meaning lecture from someone who was still glassy-eyed and likely legally drunk. But, given my own condition at that point, who was I to judge?

The following morning, we awoke to small waves gently lapping the shore of our camp, calm winds, and fair to partly-cloudy skies. The Big Blow was gone, gentle breezes throughout the night had dried out the moisture on the tents and tarps and left our crew chiefs elated. That meant we wouldn't have to hang up everything in the storage sheds back at Cook in order to repack. What we packed and rolled up now, would be ready for immediate use on the next assignment. After a short, quick breakfast, by 8:00 AM our tent city with main dining hall, auxiliary tarps, folding table, two propane cook stoves, gas canisters, over a dozen canvas packs, numerous coolers and boxes, plus ourselves were ready to be loaded into our three power boats.

We crossed the truck portage again and three Forest Service vehicles and boat trailers met us at Moccasin Point on the south side of Vermillion Lake. By noon we were back at the Ranger Station in Cook, had unloaded, and were a little surprised to learn we were to be back at the Station for more work at 1:00 PM.

We headed to the trailer and discovered Lila, an educator hired by the District for the summer, had moved in, literally. She had moved a lot of everyone else's stuff around, took over Elaine's bed, and was occupying turf once occupied by others. These are serious moves in a crowded dormitory, not to be undertaken lightly. But my bed was left as my bed, thankfully, it's just that I now had a new bedroom partner as Elaine was completing her stint of work for the District. Frankly, I was feeling rather heady and bold and ripe with accomplishment and glory. I could sense the same feelings in everyone else. We had all been baptized, got rave reviews from our bosses, were feeling part of a well-oiled team, and assumed we had earned the right to be certified working components of the Cook District of the U.S. Forest Service. No longer were we untested novices.

Over noon lunch break I read my letter from Jean which Ron had given me from the Ranger Station office. The crew quickly finished our latest assignment, washing the boats and trucks and we were dismissed until seven days later, free to do what we wanted with our own time. Any of us could have stayed in the trailer and hung around Cook if we wanted. Nobody did.

Before departing the Ranger Station, Ron came to each of us to collect cash for our share of the food for the next trip. The first trip's food and consequent cost had been supplied by the La Croix Ranger District. For our future work tours Ron would select and buy all the food necessary, but we would each pay him an equal share. That arrangement was perfectly acceptable to the rest of us, was easier and more convenient for all involved, and Ron, having developed this technique over several summers, turned out to be a very good supply officer. He was not the world's finest chef, but he kept us supplied with a variety of foodstuffs and the necessary abundance of calories.

My first stop was to go to one of the two phone booths in town and call Jean. We talked for over an hour, me blabbing on about my excitement over the adventures of the last nine days, she reviewing activities at our farm and home, news of our daughters, a few business issues. Jean said she could sense the joy and accomplishment in my voice and the self-satisfaction with what I was doing. And, I could tell she was more fired up and excited with knowing what she wants than I had ever seen her. Soon she would leave for her two-month assignment hacking Peregrine Falcons in Idaho, overlooking Hells Canyon. She and I had pride in what the partner was doing and a sincere desire for the partner to achieve their own happiness. Not a bad point to be at after 25 years of marriage.

Per agreement with my company in La Crosse I next called my boss there and we reviewed several corporate matters. But not until after he had asked for a report on my activities and satisfaction with the BWCAW. It was great to have a boss like that. Then a quick stop at the local liquor emporium to buy two half pints of Jim Beam™. Such cute little indestructible plastic bottles (no glass allowed in the Boundary Waters), easy to tuck into recesses in my pack. Now I could supply my own whiskey and meet the recently exposed attributes of a North Country Woodsman.

I also stopped in at the local quick stop gas station and junk food dispensary to buy one of those low-cost plastic, insulated coffee mugs then coming into popular usage. One carried in their own cheap plastic mug, richly adorned with advertising for wherever you had purchased it, and filled your own mug from the coffee machine available at those establishments. I was not a coffee drinker but I had observed the utility of such a mug from watching Greg and Nikki use theirs while we were camping on Sioux Pine Island. As the summer wore on, I used mine as they had, and my mug, combined with my back-packing indestructible nylon teaspoon became my light-weight personal portable cook kit: pour hot water in and make my morning tea, mix hot water with dry instant oatmeal for a hot breakfast, ladle soup or stew or macaroni in it for lunch, stir in hot chocolate mix in the evenings, and rinse out with hot water after each use, dry, and repeat the next day. When our cups and spoons were only lightly soiled, we referred to this level of quick sanitation as "The Boundary Waters Wash."

I spent the rest of the day cleaning up, taking a shower (hoo-boy, did that feel good!), unpacking, repacking, organizing, cycling a couple loads through the local laundromat, fixing my supper. Somewhere in there, Lila called us together at the trailer and gave us a lecture on how to share the kitchen and how to deal with her things – it was amazing – I really had to bite my tongue and just nod politely. Not everyone adhered to my example. Some sarcasm and biting looks were tossed in her direction, to no avail. Later in the evening the stereo was cranked and the crew was rocking to rock and roll, love torn country tunes, and other pop music when Lila put some weird Iowa dude on the tape player and asked if we couldn't have something more soothing on the stereo. I tried to explain to her how we just came off of a big trip and most of us were feeling still pretty pumped up with accomplishment. Verbal explanations don't always do a very good job of defining emotions and response to emotions. The sad truth was Lila was outnumbered; individual rights don't always trump the will of the majority.

Compromises were made, expressed emotions tapered off and those of us still at the trailer for another night were all able to relax and "Oooh" in wonder at an immense display of Northern Lights, which one of the group had discovered at 11:00 PM. There were few street lights or house lights in that outlying part of Cook and we stepped out the back door and gazed upwards. Derek went back in to their bedroom and got Blaine out of bed to join in with Sandy, Lila, and myself as we watched silent beams of green, yellow, lavender streaks of light, dancing, flowing, gliding east and west and back again, shooting south and receding north, and repeating, and shining in our beauty-feasting eyes. The lights covered the entire east-west horizon, 180 degrees of our view to the north to our right and to our left, and in a north south perspective reached to 120 degrees from the horizon to 30 degrees beyond vertical behind us. One had to physically move and turn from side to side to see it all. Truly, none of us had seen anything like it before. Most impressive was a center of radiance directly overhead which was thrusting out rays of light in all directions around it. We called the fantastic display our gift for coming to the North Country.

Our camp kitchen area, Ron claimed the table for our use after we found it thrown away near shore by others

Taking a restful lunch break on an island in Lac La Croix while gazing at Warrior Hill

Time Off 1, Days 11 through 16

Elaine came back the following morning to pick up the last of her things. The four women were having a good discussion, saying their last good-byes, and I joined in bidding Elaine a fond Adieu. I already knew I would prefer my first roommate over my second. Derek had engaged Lila earlier in the morning in a sound battle as she turned up the volume on an NPR Radio broadcast and Derek fired back with a George Strait recording bellowing from his bedroom. I left the war zone and put on my backpack filled with clothes needing supplemental drying and hiked to the laundromat to finish the job. Derek and Blaine drove there and joined me a few minutes later. We finished our laundry while I told them what I was up to for the next five days.

After loading my truck and topping off my gas and grocery supplies, I drove north to Voyageurs Park stopping along the highway where appropriate to photo document the voracious leaf eating consumption of the forests by the army worms. Huge swaths of trees were totally denuded of their leaves. Being directly under them while the worms were munching overhead us at Trout Lake, I was dismayed to see the impact of their numbers as I viewed their work from a panoramic distance. At Voyageurs I found the visitor center closed, and camped out one night at Ash River Minnesota State Campground instead, pleasant, quiet, with only one other camper.

By then, I had already decided the Voyageurs area was not for me: too many extravagant houseboats, too few canoes and then only heavy, clunky, aluminum ones, too much development, too many people for a silent sports enthusiast like myself. But I decided to tour a few back roads before supper in camp, the goal being to see any large fauna. As I drove on a slight uphill curve overlooking a swamp, I stopped to pull out my binoculars and rolled the truck back a bit to peer through some intervening branches. Oops! There isn't any shoulder, just a little six-inch-deep ditch cut for drainage, a soggy bottom holding a tiny rivulet of water bleeding out of the hillside. The right rear wheel had dropped in and was spinning. Oh-oh! Won't go forward, won't go back, damn Minnesota soup just inches from a solid road bed.

I hopped out of the truck and gathered some tree limbs and foliage to put under the wheel, but that didn't help a bit. I immediately put on my jeans instead of shorts, so I could appear like a normal country boy instead of an amateur city dude, and dug out and mounted my tow cable on the front of the truck, stretched out near the road bed. It was not a highly traveled road, I had already decided I could sleep in the back if I had to, but after some wait time a small Nissan pickup truck came by pulling a boat, and I thumbed the driver over. He wasn't eager to try but both of us were nice enough and cordial so he gave pulling my truck out with my cable a brief try but he just spun his rear wheels on the gravel.

The driver and the woman accompanying him kindly offered to take me to the nearest resort or phone to arrange for a tow truck, but that would cost me serious money. A brief consideration by the formerly risk-averse family man, me, versus the middle-aged bum searching for adventure, also me, landed me firmly on the side of being cheap and whimsical in emulation of my new young friends. I sent the Nissan on its way gambling something better could result from my predicament.

From my journal: Standing there in the middle of the road watching my sure bet depart I again examined my rear wheels only to discover the truck is sinking deeper. Oh-oh. Maybe I should dig out the jack and jack it up. Nope. The axle is touching the roadbed. No space to get a jack under there. So, then I'm thinking I could pull the truck out by winching it to a tree and using my come-along ratchet winch. Oh-oh. I carefully supplied Jean with a winch and packed it in her truck but I neglected to pack a winch in my truck. But wait! – I hear another truck coming. A big one. Pulling nothing at all. The driver stops, seems friendly, smiles, and with a shit-eating grin that says I'm a dummy says, 'Looks like you could use a little help.' And I say, smiling in return, 'You know, I sure like the looks of a big four-wheeler with wide tires.' I explain I have a cable already laid out in front. My new savior whips his truck around, backs into position, I hook up the cable, and he pulls me right out with hardly any effort or time consumed. Wow! I unhooked my cable and went to his window after he turned back to his original direction, thanked him profusely, and offered him cash for his help. He grinned at me, waved my offer away, and he was off.

Before going to Ely, Minnesota, 130 miles away, my new goal for this first period of time off, I spent the next day and night touring a part of Minnesota I had not seen before and to which I was unlikely to return. I drove some roads in Ash river forest, hiked a bit, went to the Katebegoma Visitor Center on the lake of the same name, checked out Wooden Frog State Campground, walked around in downtown International Falls, Minnesota, and then camped at Pfeiffer Lake U.S. Forest Service Campground.

During that interval I had ample time for some reflection and getting my journal up to date. As the days of the previous two weeks had ticked by, I discovered how important communicating with myself via the journal was to being fully aware of the changes in my life perspective which this summer was bringing. During the call to Jean, I learned her Uncle John had just died at age 71, and her Aunt Donnie had a heart attack at age 70. It is inconsiderate to the memories their survivors cherish, but the news about these two individuals we had regarded as "still young," was giving us impetus and rationalization to seek our own life of meaning in our middle 40's, unwilling to wait until after "normal" retirement age. One of Life's reminders: the future is uncertain.

I also recorded how freeing my currently unstructured days were compared to my life at home engaged in the weekly requirements of working at my company. I was deciding when to wake in the morning, what to eat, what to do each day, when to do it without clearing that with anyone else or bearing responsibility to anyone else's priorities. Jean was noticing the same thing at home; we were still in love and full of concern for one another, but there was no spouse to consider in one's plans for the day. Neither of us knew enough about what could happen during a separation, and in our tentative sharing of our feelings of "freedom" with one another, we were relieved to hear the other understood.

On day three of my time off, I drove into Ely and rented a sleek, light-weight, solo Kevlar canoe for the next three days and two nights, from one of the outfitters in town. I strapped it on top of my canoe-ready truck, picked up a few food items from the local grocer, organized my gear using the picnic tables at the city park, and drove to the parking area, and canoe launch of Fenske Lake about seven miles north of Ely. There, I unloaded the truck for a solo canoe journey.

After 3¼ hours, I had paddled on four lakes, portaged 248 rods (about ¾ mile) and was setting up camp on a lovely site on Grassy Lake, about four miles from the truck. I had chosen this location and route for its lack of the need to secure official permits and risk the queue requirements of the BWCAW. I had selected a known canoe route devoid of power boats that received infrequent use by travelers. This route and these lakes were not part of the BWCAW, but they were included within the Superior National Forest. My choice of route gave me all the solitude I could desire, likely more solitude than many popular access points and routes within the true BWCAW.

My campsite was on a rocky point of land on the north side of Grassy lake and provided all the features I was hoping for: a gradual inclination of ancient bedrock extending into the lake to easily disembark from the canoe, adjoining boulders to sit on, a backdrop of pine and aspen trees, level shallow soil to place my tent nearby, an expansive view of the lake and entry portage. After setting up camp, pulling up and securing the canoe, I took my small, folding camp chair with backrest to my preferred viewpoint and just sat there for an hour, resting and admiring the scene; no book, no music, just sat there and took it all in, and once in a while, thought.

That early in the season the bugs ruled the world up there in the North Country. There were still millions of army worms lurking about: I sat and read my book outdoors, flicked ten worms off, read a bit more, flicked five more worms off. And the insects' timing and trading off of specialty conditions was exquisite. They shared the natural world and portioned it out. By bright day, the large black flies were in control, same shape and size as a house fly but much more aggressive. They almost darkened my life jacket and wet shoes set out to dry and, if ignored, were capable of a harsh bite of one's flesh. In the evening and at twilight when the sun set and it got cooler, the mosquitoes and gnats took over. Other moisture or wind or vegetative conditions may favor the sweat bees, their bite is painful and the resulting itch persists a long time. The bugs there were in great proliferation and mere humans needed to take guard, whether in seeking a breeze to keep the insects in abeyance, applying bug dope, or use of the Bedouin Bandana.

Our crew chiefs and many of the local citizens seemed to take the world about them for granted. I'm sure this is a human characteristic that we all fall victim to at one time or another. It is contrast that allows us to perceive the range of human response. Residents of Northern Minnesota are used to or immured to conditions around them, which we newcomers may view with distaste. For example, living in the presence of Common Loons, the locals seem ambivalent to the needs of loons and may drive their power boats at what to us seems much too close for the loons' safety. Loons are very special to newcomers who do not live daily with these unique creatures.

On this sojourn I found again, just like the crew did on stormy Trout Lake, the weather ruled my world just as much as the calendar. Time has less meaning than the weather as it impacts your world when you live outdoors. I was relieved when checking out my canoe from the outfitter to confirm that the date I assumed it to be, was the day it was supposed to be. I had lacked reference and I did not want to miss the next trip into the BWCAW. As I sat resting at lake's edge, I saw impacts of rain drops dappling the lake and coming closer and knew the weather was again deciding my actions and I would be eating my supper inside the tent to escape this latest shower. Earlier in the day I noted the American Robins near camp were acting just like they had at our home in Wisconsin, but a month separated each observation. The robins were acting with much joyous singing and vocal disputes and establishment of territory. Even the seasons affect what a person engages in much more than the clock or the calendar. It would be grand to travel northward with the seasons in the Spring, southward with the seasons in the Fall, and thereby cause those glorious and best of seasons to last longer for the individual traveling within them.

In the night I awoke to the sound of leaves rustling, a twig moving, a shuffle-snuffle, a sense that my space was being invaded by a moving mystery. In bear country, suddenly awake and aware, the first thought at that point tends to be, "Bear?" The sounds gradually decreased and the creature went away. Much more likely to have been deer or racoon. I resumed my slumber.

The following morning the moisture laden clouds dictated breakfast and lunch in the tent with plenty of time to read my book in between, head and back comfortably supported by my pack as I reclined on my sleeping pad and bag. At noon I packed the canoe for a day paddle to the east end of Grassy Lake with the intent to make it to Low Lake. The calm water and meandering water pathway made for interesting exploring in spite of having to don my rain gear in the canoe for a passing shower. At the end of the lake, I paddled to the right, portaged over a beaver dam, and floated right into a dead end. By this point I had developed "Ruhser's Axiom – If it doesn't look like a portage, it probably isn't." I extricated myself and continued paddling my way to Low Lake along a lovely, winding, waterlily-covered, narrow waterway. It was twisty, intimate, fun, and slow, easy going, until at last the water widened and I entered Low Lake and began to see distant power boats and cabins lining the shore of this motor-accessible lake. Having found again signs of what my favorite author, Edward Abbey, described as "Syphilization," I quickly reverted from my exploratory self to my reclusive self, and after stepping out to stretch my back, turned around and returned "home" to my solitary camp.

On the last morning of this sojourn, I awoke to the dictates of the clouds and, after breakfast, was able to finish the book I brought to the sounds of rain drops pattering the tent above me and dimpling the surface of Grassy Lake. As the dark clouds shifted east, I rolled up my wet camp in plastic sheets, loaded the canoe, and paddled back to my truck, making it out in only 2 ½ hours. It helps when you know where all the portages are and needn't discover them anew. At the last portage I granted passage priority to six husky, excited, young Germans lugging full packs and two 80-pound aluminum canoes. They were a raucous bunch, exhibiting an excess of frivolity, wearing what appeared to be brand new leather boots and hiking shorts and plunging into thigh high water before climbing back into their canoes. They were friendly, eager, and had their faces painted with thick black mud streaks emulating what they imagined early native Americans might have looked like. I had to smile watching their antics, but was very relieved I did not have to share Grassy Lake with them.

At the local A&W™ and Dairy Queen™ in Ely I treated myself to a hot fast-food meal of burger, fries, and a malt. After a week of my own easy-prep camping and canoeing meals I had gotten hungry for some good old American fast food. At the trailer, being without a full-time engineering job, I had copied my young friends and discovered one could buy a lot of day-old bread and cheap jelly for what the price of donuts or restaurant meals cost. But it was time to splurge. While waiting for my meal I watched another couple toss chunks of hamburger to their dog and then set a malt on the sidewalk outside, which the dog promptly licked up. Lucky dog. I was not so lucky though when I discovered my order had been way-laid in the system and I waited and waited until I complained and my order had to be prepared again. Some fast food joint! I asked myself, "Why me??" Eventually I rationalized it wasn't the world against me. It was the world giving the new, young, waitress a lesson in customer satisfaction. I was just collateral damage.

After returning the canoe to the rental facility, I drove back to Cook and parked in front of the dormitory trailer, and found myself looking forward to seeing my summer compadres again. With just Derek and Blaine "home," I tossed my gear on my bed in the back bedroom, and we three just had the best yarn-swapping, bubbling conversation, exchanging with genuine interest what each had done during their six days off. Derek went back to the Dovre Lake trail to hike and backpack camp, claiming he had a fun time tossing blowflies to the fish and pulling off dozens of ticks. Blaine, our piscatorial aficionado, went to the Ely area for several days of fishing. Nikki and Greg came back from their time off and had just enjoyed the sauna (yes, if one is in Northern Minnesota, it is not hard to find a sauna) down at the Corner Store off Main Street in Cook.

After my shower, supper, and hanging up a few things to dry, we continued the talk fest. Derek and Blaine were sharing a few horror stories of their interactions with Lila, when Lila returned to the trailer. A three-minute demonstration of personality conflict quickly took place between Lila and Derek, and Derek went off in a huff to the front bedroom while Lila retreated to the bedroom she and I shared. After the smoke cleared and Lila had gone to bed the talk fest resumed for the five of us until midnight as we exchanged opinions on China, over-population, Japan, dictators, and a few other topics of shared interests. The difficulties Lila experienced in living with the rest of us were prime examples of what I had worried about as applied to me before coming here, and what I wanted to avoid. It was clear to me then that my concerns as applied to myself were unfounded and I was able to get along well with all of these good, young adults, even my new roommate, Lila. At one point in the summer Chad told me, "Aw, Gary, you don't have a mean bone in your body." I knew things about me which Chad didn't, but at that point, it was still nice to hear.

I spent the following day catching up on all that needed doing: drying out my gear from the solo trip to Grassy Lake, doing my laundry, organizing the chaos of my truck so that I would be ready to drive back home to Wisconsin immediately after our next assignment, prepping and packing for our crew's next trip into the

BWCAW. I picked up a letter from Daughter Gayle at the Ranger Station, its kindness and understanding left me a little teary-eyed, and I called her that evening from the payphone with my thanks and appreciation.

Ginger and Sandy came back from their trip, and Chad returned also. It would be another full night in the dormitory. Folding army cots accommodated two people in the living room, but the floor was still needed for others. The more, the merrier, and a contented rowdiness took over in the trailer, laughter, joshing, teasing, conversing, all perhaps made somewhat easier by Lila's absence as she rode her bike around town and went to visit her parents at a nearby resort. Nikki and Greg went out on the front deck to smoke Nikki's pipe. She looked quite cool so I asked to photograph her and then we discussed my cameras and lens choices. She and I brought Greg up to date on the farm Jean and I own, and the fact we just paid off the mortgage. Harboring similar dreams, Greg was pleased to learn how Jean and I had done that and what we wanted in the future.

The "tunes were jamming" in the trailer, as Derek said, and the living room floor became littered with a half dozen laying, sitting, kneeling bodies yelling their way through another game of Pictionary, which along with card games, were well beloved pursuits of many of the part-time inhabitants. I got a kick out of watching the games but neither Greg nor I were game players. If not engaged in conversation, he and I were more likely to be reading a book or writing in our journals. Listening to the tunes enjoyed by the gang I took a gamble and put on the tape Daughter Gayle and I had created from the music she and I listened to, groups like Van Halen, Mike and the Mechanics, INXS, Chicago, Aerosmith, Bon Jovi, and was rewarded with approbation and head banging from the crew. Nanci Griffith was new to most, but Nikki and Greg were already fond of her music. At 9:30 PM Blaine wondered if the local Dairy Bar might still be open and offered a ride to anyone else interested. Blaine was a big lad and needed his nourishment. Chad and I joined him and all were pleased to find it still open. We came right back to trade more stories but by 11:00 PM, it was time to hit the sack and rest up for our BIG DAY!

Work Tour 2, Days 17 through 24

Going to Lake Agnes today! Ron had made our next work tour, that of going to Lake Agnes, sound very special and it would become an honor to be there, so we were all anxious to join him and see what the attraction was. By 7:45 AM we had all helped Ron pack the trucks, load all the gear and three canoes, and were pulling out of the Ranger Station. We stopped to buy some leeches, bait for the fisherman to use on Walleyes, south of Orr and by 9:30 AM had driven 60 miles and were unloading at the Moose River parking lot. Our trip in to Lake Agnes required five portages and started with the first portage being about one-half mile in length to get from the Moose River parking area to the river itself. Arriving at the water we found a lovely little stream, just barely wide enough for a canoe, but with depth and volume sufficient to carry us downstream. Four additional, shorter portages take the canoeist around rock laden obstacles and steep inclines until one reaches the final portage and a lovely waterfall is revealed, best photographed from the surface of Nina-Moose Lake. Ron and Chad were in the lead, Nikki and Greg in another canoe, Blaine and myself in the third. With all our gear and three canoes there was plenty to be carried on each portage, but many hands made short work of each. Worrying about my back, I gave preference to carrying packs and other gear and purposely avoided carrying a canoe. Among this hearty group someone was always willing to hoist a 75-pound canoe onto their shoulders first, including Nikki. She was one tough little lady, built thin and short, barley five feet tall.

It had been cloudy all that day but at the last portage it started to rain and some of us pulled on a light jacket or rain coat. By 2:30 PM we had canoed and portaged nine miles and reached Ron's favorite campsite at the north end of Lake Agnes, featuring large rock slabs at lake's edge, an open expansive view of the lake, flat sites for our four tents, and scattered White Pines forming the back drop to the forest beyond. Fortunately, it was open and available. Unfortunately, the rain picked up in intensity and after setting up the camp kitchen tarp to cover our eating area and squaring away our possessions in our tents, we all dispersed to our shelters, some to grab a nap, me to read. The rain was puddling on the ground and beginning to weep under tent floors so I trimmed out the piece of plastic I had brought for this purpose and shaped it to form a waterproof bathtub under all my gear and bedding to keep it dry and comfy. Worked great. Around 6:00 PM we took a break from the confines of our tents to have a quick supper of spaghetti and canned sauce while huddling under the tarp at 53 degrees, in the wind, and continuing rain, before retreating again to our tents for the night. A tough and soaking start to our week.

The following morning, our first full day at Lake Agnes, Ron was banging pans and getting water from the lake by 6:00 AM. He was anxious to paddle over to "ticket island" and "pinch" two campers who were on a nearby island that did not have an official campsite, hence were camped illegally. "Ticket island" was a bit like that speed limit sign hidden by dense foliage in a small town which the local police use as a speed trap. All the crew chiefs and District Rangers knew this island was a temptation to those canoeists less rigorous about following regulations, and so it was the "speed trap" of Lake Agnes. Ron had talked tough about bringing the hammer down on them and tossing them off before he and I shoved off to confront the campers. Upon landing at their site Ron immediately announced, "United States Forest Service, I'm Ron Davison and this is my partner, Gary. Please show us your

Boundary Waters Permit." Per previous instructions I stood beside Ron, but remained silent. Inwardly I suspect I tried to look official and authoritarian while simultaneously feeling sorry for these two young men. I had to admit theirs looked like a nice place to camp. The two campers explained they had come in late in the day, it was raining, and all they desperately wanted as first-time visitors was a place to set up their tent and go to sleep. Having flexed his vested power and explaining they could be subject to a fifty-dollar fine, Ron quickly switched to being lenient and understanding, voided the fine, but with the proviso they pack up soon and proceed to a legal campsite. It was a good "pinch," nicely done with professionalism and empathy.

Back at camp we all piled into our canoes and Ron led us to the Boulder River exit at the end of the north arm of Lake Agnes and thence to Boulder Bay of Lac La Croix, a large and beautiful lake encompassing 29,600 acres bounded on the north side by Canada. On the bay, we paddled circuitously east to a short portage, which led to the La Croix District Ranger Cabin located on a peninsula at the east end of Lac La Croix. This cabin would be manned for the summer by Jack and Derek, an idyllic setting with a boat house on the lake, a large lawn area, tall White Pine trees for shade, and two separate frontages each with docks on the lake. Jack and Derek would patrol the local waters and work on various District assignments maintaining the cabin, local campsites, and portages. Power boats are legal on the Canadian side of the United States/Canada border passing through the middle of Lac La Croix, but are illegal south of that border, those portions of the Lake south of the border being part of the BWCAW. Jack and Derek came to the cabin on the Canadian side of Lac La Croix via power boat from Crane Lake and then through Little Vermillion Lake, Loon River, and Loon Lake, and down the length of Lac La Croix. They had brought in additional supplies and equipment we were unable to bring, and we met them at the cabin to transfer those items with our canoes back to our camp on Lake Agnes.

The cabin was small but sweet, two rooms, about 20 feet by 30 feet in size, built of logs around 1930. We were all impressed, jealous of their accommodations, and declared we would be happy to live right there forever. And this was actually only the smaller bunk house of what used to be on site. Some horrible, dreadful, careless skiers had "accidentally" burned down the main lodge around 1984. After our early paddle, we were all starved and some of us helped Ron cook us a fine big breakfast of fried ham, served with multiple slices of bread, while we visited with Jack and Derek.

After breakfast everyone made repeated trips down the portage and loaded our canoes with food boxes and packs to get us through the end of our current assignment, axes, shovels, rakes, saws, pickaxe, 20-pound tank of propane, 300 White Pine tree seedlings, 25 pounds of grass seed, 4-foot by 4-foot roll of one-quarter inch galvanized wire mesh, 2" by 4" wood pieces to build a sieve, a cooler, AND a full-size, heavy-duty contractor's wheelbarrow. Technically wheels were also illegal in the BWCAW along with power tools but our wheel was given an exception and it was silent. Our canoes were full but now we had all the resources to do our work and keep us fed. Blaine and I were not pleased to be assigned to transport the wheelbarrow, as it would not fit into our canoe but had to be transported on the gunnels, thus raising the center of gravity and making the canoe "tippier." Unfortunately, due to simple precedence, my canoe and partner became the wheelbarrow carrier for the duration of the summer. It made for quite an eye-catcher when we met other visitors on the lake or portage.

Ron and Chad led us back to camp via the far southeast arm of Lac La Croix, an extremity of Boulder Bay, past large boulders in the midst of clear calm waters, and I was enchanted by the route and peaceful scene. I felt I was a voyageur and *coureur des bois*. But then we came to what all of us fondly referred to as the "Mud Dog Miserable Portage From Hell." It had begun raining again and we could only get the canoes to within 30 feet of firm footing on the portage, which meant we were wading and carrying everything, gear and canoes, through standing water and silty, shifting mud. The west end, near our camp on Lake Agnes, wasn't much better. The 1200-foot-long portage had standing water and running rivulets of water in numerous portions of the route and an abundance of mosquitoes. It took each of us three separate trips across the portage to get everything to the Lake Agnes side. On our applications we had been warned of "Strenuous Work in Primitive and Arduous Conditions." Here we found it.

Back at camp, Dlaine and Chad were assigned to fetch some new latrines from a cache on an island where they had been deposited by the District earlier in the year, and then install a new latrine at our camp and close off the old one. Greg and Nikki planted 55 of the new trees around the camp site while Ron and I assembled one new latrine and used the wire mesh and 2" by 4's" to build a four-foot by four-foot sieve that would be used to sift gravel down to packing sand at some of the campsites and portages we would be working on. The sieve had extended wooden handles on two sides so that two people could grasp the sieve and shake and roll it vigorously while others would man the shovels and toss gravel into the sieve.

Late in the afternoon Ron announced our work day was complete with a rousing "The Bar is open!" and a fifth of vodka miraculously appeared. While a few of the crew fished from shore others of us partook in Ron's offering. Gatorade™ highballs were tipped up to thirsty lips. Feeling I should be providing my own refreshments I switched to my Jim Beam and Orange Tang™ as the stories began to be woven. Ron started supper of stir-fry chicken and vegetables, but as Ron became more and more wound up and the laughter increased, Chad took over supper duties.

As we ate, Ron waxed philosophic and pondered: what were the mysterious forces that brought us all together on a point of land of Lake Agnes in the North Country, is there a meaning to it, is there something behind it? He explained the crew chiefs participate in the selection of personnel along with their boss, Mike. Then after the selections are made the crew chief's tease each other and punch each other in the ribs about who got who. "Eh, this refrigeration engineer, the oldest person ever to apply in the La Croix District, what brings him here?" and "Eh, this young couple who applied, I wonder if they'll be all lovey-dovey and blowing kisses to one another over the campfire? I better get them a four-person tent."

After our philosophizing, Ron entertained us with some songs, wishing he could perform them with a band, such as the "Decoys without Heads" band, or the "Cabinet Makers Without Drawers" band. Some songs he knew, other tunes and songs he made up extemporaneously. Quite the entertainer. He at one point worked for a resort and was a hunting guide, and demonstrated his prowess at moose calling (no instrument used, just his mouth and hands) as he emitted "Love Whimpers of the Moose." "That really gets 'em," he added. Even though none of us were moose, we were very impressed.

We were all gathered in the kitchen area when another passing shower floated over. Greg couldn't withstand it any longer and yelled out, "Fucking Rain!!" Up to that point, still feeling out each other's boundaries, any cursing had been somewhat restrained. But Greg's emotional outburst released our pent-up frustration over all the rain and wetness we had endured for nearly all of the past two days. Ron agreed, screamed out a "Fucking Rain!" and it became a rallying call for all of us. It felt much better to tell it like it was, and verified that all of us were equally frustrated with the weather and yearned for better days ahead.

The rest of us leveled off to a state of sober-enough joy while Ron continued to drink, talk, swap stories, and sing a few songs. He ordered his crew to join him in the chorus of, "In the blue Canadian Rockies where the sun seldom shines." There was much merriment in the camp and we had to do multiple takes mixed with laughter at our studio in the woods before Ron agreed the last one was worth recording.

A fishing expedition was next on the crew's ambitious agenda. Ron tried to get me to go fishing, but I am not a fisherman and hadn't even purchased a license. We finally convinced Ron that he, Chad, Greg, and Blaine were the fishermen and would nicely fill two canoes. But Ron kept standing there, drink in hand, pronouncing to all, "The canoes will launch in 30 minutes!" Then, "We will only stay in one spot 10 minutes." Then, new drink in hand, "We launch in 20 minutes." Then, "We launch in 24 minutes!" At that point I teased him about his modern math. He grinned at me and took another swallow. Eventually, Ron said, "We launch when we hear the first loon!" One called. And they were off. I helped launch Ron and Chad. Ron was too drunk to hook his leech and declared, "I'm really plowed." But the fishermen were on the water at last, high-hearted, with a strong urge to hook into a bunch of Walleyes.

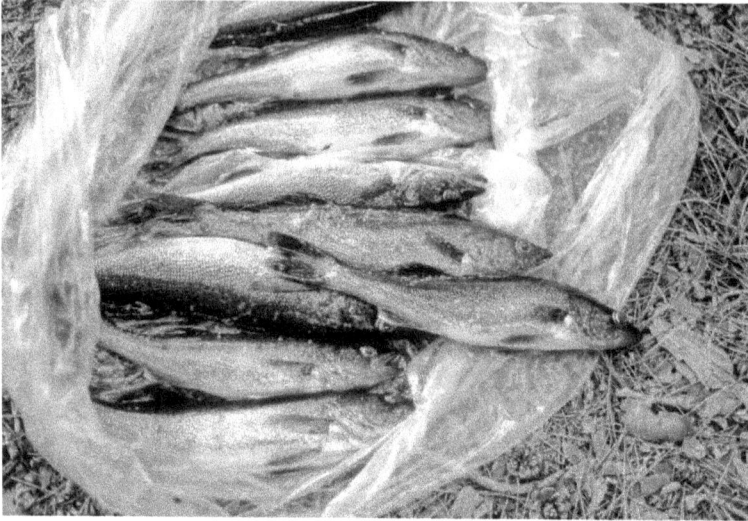

When free time and good weather permitted, the fishermen of our group enjoyed adding walleyes to our menu

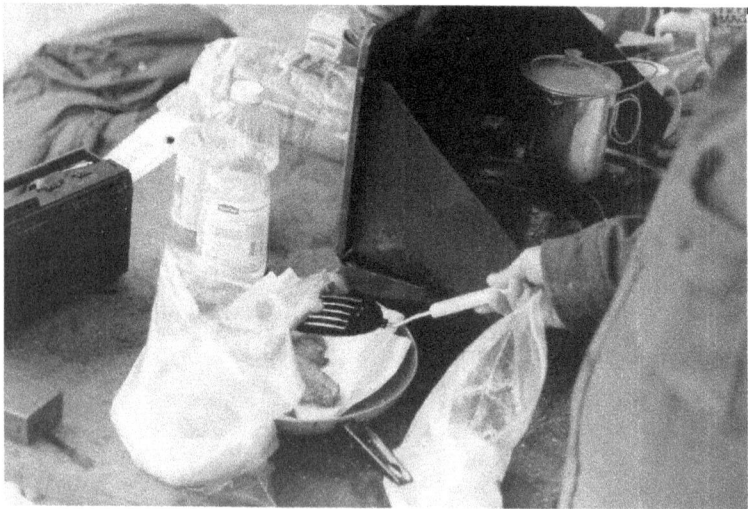

Ron used his own recipe to bread and fry delicious walleye filets for several breakfasts

In a much quieter camp, Nikki and I huddled near the fire and under the tarp and traded events from our lives and how relationships among the young are more varied and diverse than the confines of relationships Jean and I observed around us when we were Nikki and Greg's age. Near dark the fishermen came splashing back, wet from the rain, disappointed, and yelling "Fucking Rain!" We visited around the fire, calmed everyone down, Ron had a nightcap and shared a couple more stories. Lake Agnes was known for its bear population so before bed we attempted to hoist our food in our bear bags up a tree, per recommendations of the Forest Service. There was a lot of weight and food in the bags at this point of the trip and with most of us laughing too much to do any coordinated good, we only got the bag about six feet off the ground, too low to prevent a mature bear from ripping it down, but said "To Hell with it!" and gave up getting it any higher. With a final chuckle Ron said, "I hope no tourist sees that thing in the morning. Gary, take a picture of that mess when it's daylight." The bag was suspended near my tent and I told the crew I would come and get them if a bold bear happened by. Ron offered some pepper spray and an air horn, but I turned him down.

The following morning, we paddled to a campsite on the north arm of Lake Agnes and were flabbergasted to discover previous BWCAW visitors had built a large structure of logs and fresh cut fir boughs on the southside of the campsite, between lake and camp, to act as a windbreak. It was huge, appalling, and totally not in character with USFS goals of providing a "natural experience." There were about 30 trees, logs, and large branches thrust together, interwoven with recently cut fir boughs, many components illegally cut, and this structure spanned 20 feet and was six feet high. By now Ron was used to me photographing our sites and experiences and requested me to thoroughly document this travesty. Blaine and I spent several long hard hours tearing it all down to restore the appearance of a wilderness experience to the camp area. Large logs were tossed into the lake or hauled to the woods in back of camp. We hauled three canoe trips worth of boughs to a small bay west of camp and tossed them into the water. Whatever we placed in the water was positioned to absorb water, sink, and then become a sanctuary for fish.

While my partner and I worked on the windbreak, the rest of the crew was busily engaged in those acts that would form the core work requirements of the rehabilitation we would apply to all the campsites we worked on that summer. A tent site, which was obviously overused, was deemed by Ron as being inappropriately located and a danger to both visitors and forest health. Several large rocks and boulders, too heavy for one person to lift were moved from nearby rock deposits and "planted" (buried with part of the rock exposed) in the midst of the tent site to discourage users from erecting a tent at that spot. Two "hazard trees" (in danger of toppling onto camp visitors in high wind) were cut down and dispersed in the woods. A number of new white pine seedlings were planted around the site, their location selected for the best chance of growing and maturing. Grass seed was spread in thin areas and where we had planted the rocks, and raked in. The fire pit was raked through to pull out unburnable garbage (illegal in the first place) and to remove excess ash which was scattered in the forest. Any garbage found was collected for eventual transportation to the Ranger Cabin and removal from the BWCAW. If two or more rock fire rings were present on any one site, all fire rings except one would be destroyed, raked out, brought back to normal forest floor appearance. Excess rocks or an abundance of logs gathered for seating would be redistributed to the forest to minimize the non-natural impact for future visitors. The old latrine built of wood and now beginning to rot was smashed apart with our tools, its pieces scattered about in the forest far in back of the campsite. The hole underneath, usually nearly full to once in a while in danger of overflowing at the sites we worked on, was filled with soil, rocks, brush and topped off. A new hole, about two feet in diameter, and as deep as we could dig with our hand tools, usually around three feet, was dug nearby so that the semi-obvious trail from camp would still lead to the approximate location of the campsite latrine. Sometimes intervening rocks discovered below our digging start point would need to be removed, sometimes with our pickaxe, so we could attain our desired depth. Occasionally an abundance of rocks would defeat us totally and we would have to select a new site nearby to dig and hope there were no rocks there. Back at camp one or two people would be pounding together the new latrine. The latrines we installed had all been transported by Will Steger, and cached on an island in Lac La Croix during an earlier winter. Steger provided this service while training his dog teams for the crossing of the continent of Antarctica he was planning for 1989-90. The new latrines were uniformly formed of fiberglass and came with a pre-cut set of four wood structural members which we had to nail in a defined arrangement on the bottom side of the latrine. Two of those wooden parts would extend beyond the perimeter of the latrine and thus hold it above the pit beneath. Grayish-green in color, the fiberglass structures were unobtrusive in the woods, blending into the forest background. After installation, flat rocks were positioned around the latrine for a foot step or to bridge any gaps between latrine and the edge of the hole. Digging latrine holes in rocky soil ranked high on the list of rehabilitation jobs to avoid, but the entire crew was very good about rotating through the various jobs. We tried to be fair about taking turns on the tasks required at each site.

We had cause to revisit one of the sites where we had carefully scattered the old boards of the former latrine far into the woods, appropriate care always taken to toss them in thick brush or ravines and out of sight from the new latrine, which itself was normally out of sight of the campsite. In other words, we threw the old boards a long way away. But upon stepping into the camp area of this site we were appalled to discover some camper had located several of the boards, taken them back to camp, and there we found fruity table jelly spilled on them, apparently from their being used in sandwich preparation in that camp by unknown campers. Yuck! Be very careful, campers, what you choose to use as a table! After that rude discovery we henceforth referred to the old latrine boards by the inappropriate and crude moniker, "jelly boards."

At some sites a new level tent pad was needed or a portage trail would have to be built up over swampy conditions. Then the wheelbarrow, sieve, and shovels would come out of the canoes. A "borrow pit" would be located nearby with an abundance of easily dug sand, soil, gravel, some rocks. Two people manned the sieve while others would shovel the local soil structure into the sieve with wheelbarrow underneath, until the wheelbarrow was full of uniform fine sand and soil that had passed through the ¼ inch screen openings. One of the crew would next wheel it to the new tent pad or portage location and dump the contents. Other crew members would level the dumped contents with shovels and rakes, then pack the area, and seed it down, if applicable.

We built two new tent pads as directed by Ron, had lunch, and paddled to another campsite. Our second site didn't need nearly as much work as the "windbreak site," and after its rehabilitation we went back to our own site for an early supper and quiet night.

I awoke the next morning at 5:00 AM but was able to roll over and get back to sleep. I was awake at 6:45 AM and doing my normal morning stretch exercises in my tent, when I heard Ron trying to clear his scratchy, sleepy throat to answer his radio. The office was calling him to warn him of possible storms and high winds later in the day. By the time Ron was up, I had started heating water on the camp stove and making preparations for a quick breakfast before we packed up to go to some sites on the east side of the lake.

In our food supplies, Ron always provided 10-packs of individually-packaged Quaker Instant Oatmeal™, which have a variety of flavors included. Each of us went for our favorite flavor and fortunately most of us did not tend to duplicate one another, mine being Maple and Brown sugar. None of us cared for the Regular Flavor so it was always the last one or two available. One morning Chad was eating the Regular Flavor but upon rummaging deeper in the large food pack he discovered a whole unopened 10-pack of instant cereal. He couldn't stop himself from disgustedly and loudly blurting out, "You mean I'm eating this gosh-awful Regular flavor for NOTHING!" Since then, Chad and Regular Flavor became the brunt of much fun-poking and teasing. After Rich joined the crew halfway through the summer, we tried to get him, as the new guy, to eat all the regular flavor.

Blaine and I had forgotten the sieve at the last site yesterday so while we retrieved that, Ron took the rest of the crew to the next site. With my small binoculars, which I carried in my daypack each day, I was able to spot Ron's red shirt and we paddled to join the rest of the crew. We completed two sites that morning, but then encountered a broken-off tree stump needing extricating, which we just couldn't budge with the tools we had. Ron said we'd bring a stout hand winch along on our next trip and get it out then. After lunch, we weaved our way through a series of small islands on our way to the third site of the day, as the clouds increased and the winds gradually picked up.

Chad, Blaine, and I quickly sifted four wheelbarrows of tent pad fill for Ron from underneath a huge root ball of a tree that had come down revealing a handy gravel deposit. Nikki and Greg took care of new and old latrine duties. One of the access points to this site was overused and subject to severe erosion. To control that problem, Ron had us deposit large rocks and old logs in it in a bold and random fashion which would encourage sprained ankles and thereby force visitors to use the access we wanted them to use. By that time of the afternoon, it had started to look bad in the northwest, and Ron warned us we might have to run for home and to start packing the tools away and leaving them on site. Blaine and I proceeded to do so, but the next time we looked up, Ron and Chad were already 50 yards away paddling hard for camp. We ditched our tools and followed everyone else through 20-30 mile per hour winds, one to two-foot waves, and with the bow smacking the lake surface, spray came into our canoe about every tenth wave. Near our own campsite the danger lessened considerably. Ron suggested we could do a few jobs in our own camp, but we reminded him all our tools were left behind and he announced our day's work as being complete.

I relaxed with a mixed drink of Tang and whiskey in my tent, read, and brought my journal up to date. Chad took a nap. Everyone was hot and bushed from the invigorating paddle home. After an early supper of burgers, macaroni, and bread, Ron and Blaine went fishing, while Chad, Nikki, and I discussed religion, death, and reincarnation. With Chad being our youngest member, he admitted that some of these fireside, and shoreside, conversations we have, kind of make his head swim. Chad asked me if I would like to go for a short evening paddle, so I asked him if he had previous experience in a canoe apart from being Ron's forward propulsion partner here in the Boundary Waters. He replied in the negative, so I put Chad in the rear and gave him some paddle-handling and steerage tips. After rather a curvy first circumnavigation of ticket island, he improved rapidly and by our second trip around the island Chad was doing nicely and managed all the fundamentals well.

Blaine and Ron came back to camp with seven nice walleyes before dark, but Blaine got a short lecture from Ron about not leaving any fish gut remnants near camp to attract bears. Greg and Nikki made popcorn to share around the fire as we wrapped up the day and hoisted the bear bag once again. This time, higher.

The next morning, I joined with the others and ate three fresh pan-fried Walleyed Pike fillets with a couple pieces of bread. Best tasting fish in the world, especially after a few days hard labor in the Boundary Waters! We faced three more days of work before we paddled back to our entry point and ceased our initial efforts at Lake Agnes.

One camp site on the west shore was apparently highly coveted and well-used. It was located on a ridge above the lake, open and grassy, and nearly the whole lake was visible from one end to the other, an expanse of green trees and blue water. Unfortunately, the winds were calm during our lunch there, and although the army worm intensity was going down, the big, black, blow flies took their turn at a population explosion. I have pictures of over 100 of them landed on and darkening my life jacket, another of 15 of them covering my watch band and the exposed flesh of my wrist. If you swatted too hard and they were female flies, their white eggs burst out. Very Obnoxious! We ate lunch quickly and went back to work just to be able to ignore them. Ron and Greg patrolled three sites of visitors and checked their permits, while the rest of us continued site work and then canoed to the rocky point west of our camp. During sundown, the sky and thin clouds pleasantly painted in reds, golds, orange, I had a little whiskey and Tang and visited with Chad. He was reading Eric Sevareid's Book, *Canoeing with the Cree*, and thought I would really like it.

On Sunday, we had cut down two hazard trees but the third one got hung up in the trees above and wouldn't come down. Blaine was called over and due to his impressive size and strength was able to lend the power to push the tree over and down in the opposite direction. The engineer of the group, me, had said it wasn't possible. The Minnesota lad, Blaine, built strong as an ox, six feet plus tall, 200 pounds plus of muscle, with an appetite that could down six hamburgers and three hearty helpings of macaroni at one meal (the rest of us were counting), proved the engineer wrong.

Then Ron received an emergency message on his radio. The Cook District Office was requesting assistance in searching for two young men reported as missing and long overdue, traveling in a green We-no-nah™ canoe. A broadly encompassing airplane search had started, but we were to specifically search the area of Lake Agnes. Ron and Greg inspected and visited all the sites south of us and on the west side of the lake. Nikki and I paddled over to the "Mud Dog Miserable Portage From Hell," walked the length of it and checked nearby sites. None of us found the canoeists, but it made for a good change of pace in our routine. Several days later we heard the missing canoeists had made it out of the Boundary Waters and reported in, but they had exited miles from where they had been expected.

Toward late afternoon, Ron had weak radio contact with his boss, Mike. As anticipated Mike was coming out to spend the night camping with the crew and wanted to review some of the work we had done. With my binoculars I soon spotted Mike at mid-lake paddling a nice solo canoe similar to the one I had rented in Ely. Joining with Ron, the two of them paddled off to tour three sites we had worked on, all of us hoping for the seal of approval. The camp was a little more subdued that evening. Perhaps it was due to the presence of the boss. Or the quiet pensive mood of a tranquil evening. A beautiful otter had crossed my path to the latrine at a distance of 15 feet. But an equally likely cause, based on my own interpretation, was that our crew was tiring of one another after days and nights spent solely with each other, and it was just plain time for a break, some different people to talk to, some different pursuits to engage in. Supplies were running out, no Gatorade, no Tang, lunchmeat was looking a little "ripe," no powdered lemonade, bread was running low, and worst yet, our favorite cookies, Keebler Pecan Sandies™, were all gone. Members of the crew were speaking dreamily of their favorite foods and first meal back in civilization.

Our final full day in the wilderness, before some time off, was spent finishing work at the rocky point site west of camp. There Ron had us scheduled for Aqua-Ninja Training, his term. This site also had several entry paths, one of them overused and eroded. The plan was to close it off with large rocks and boulders (ankle twisters), which littered the nearby shallow lake floor and entryway of the site. With no suitable rocks nearby above water or in the surrounding trees this meant several strong crew members would have to get in the water and lift said rocks into the canoe for several trips to shore and deposition of the rocks in the eroded path. Hence, Aqua-Ninja work, promptly and efficiently performed by volunteer Ninjas. In addition, Greg spotted a nearby huge boulder that he felt would be better located and utilized to re-direct future visitors and proposed working together to move it. There was no way that I felt its movement would be an appropriate use of my back but Ron, after reviewing its potential, bought into the idea. With me acting as spotter and safety officer, the rest of the crew, grunting, straining, trying to be careful, we succeeded in the audacious plan and rolled it to the perfect location. Everyone, pleased with the success, breathed a sigh of relief, no crushed bones or torn ligaments requiring medical assistance. Had the movement not been fully under control at all times, it was that big of a risk, that big of a boulder.

Cooling down by swimming in the lake after one
particularly warm work day

For several weeks, flies were abundant and troublesome

We oiled our tools and took them to a cache near the Mud Dog Portage where we could hide them from visitors and collect them at our next trip in. It had reached 87 degrees that day, was hot and sunny and with our work done everyone relaxed with a little swim and frivolity in the lake. Near enough to shore the waters were just tolerable for my body thermostat and it felt good to splash around a bit and get some grime off. Ron appreciated my photography and once in a while would ask me to document some aspect of our work. He requested me to work up an arrangement whereby he could purchase a set of slides for his or the office's future review and possible use in training. Passing thunderstorms shortened our evening at the fire. With my tent being mounted on top of the shallow tree roots common on these well used BWCAW sites, and the thunderous strikes of lightening getting closer, I moved my small aluminum framed easy chair onto the foam insulation of my sleeping pad and sat there on the assumption it would reduce the charge of electricity coursing along the roots of any strike on a nearby tree and thereby save me from immediate electrocution. I was relieved to note the storm passing to the east and instead of sitting in the chair on the pad, I put it away and replaced it with my slumbering body on the mattress pad.

Tuesday, June 26, our last day in the wilderness on this trip. We have totally rehabilitated nine sites on Lake Agnes, six more to go on the lake next trip in. It took until 9:00 AM to get everybody through breakfast, to burn our burnable garbage, pack the remaining camp gear and cooking utensils into a duffel bag, to clean up the camp, grab the remaining canister of propane and load the canoes. We paddled to the cache established yesterday, added the final items to it, and hung the cooking duffel bag in a tree. Blaine was in the rear of the canoe and I was just stepping in when my front foot reached too far and my back foot slipped on a wet rock just off shore and I tipped over the canoe. Dammit! Blaine and I were in the water up to our beltlines, soaking wet, but we were able to quickly dump the water out of the canoe, reload, get back in and rejoin the rest of the crew. Chad said we were funny-looking and he wanted to laugh, but not in front of Ron. Ron took a moment to confirm we were all right. We were, just bruised egos. Nikki and Greg were just arriving to join the rest of us and she asked where we went in. I replied, still grumpy and embarrassed, "The water!" which brought a chuckle from Ron.

The paddle out was pleasant enough, calm water, warm temperature, sun, good discussion between Blaine and me, our wet pants drying down nicely. By the time we made it upstream against the flow of the waters of the Moose River and covered the portages back to the parking lot, we were a bushed bunch of wilderness workers. Someone from the office had kindly left cold Gatorade at our vehicle, which was relished and appreciated by all! After depositing the trailer and canoes at the District's nearby storage lot, we drove back to Cook, but stopped at the first possible store for some decadent, high calorie junk food, chocolate, and ice cream.

This was Blaine's last tour with us as he was returning to college-related obligations for the duration of the summer, but another volunteer would fill his place at the next work tour.

Back at the Ranger Station at 3:45 PM, we hung up our wet tents to dry, washed out the coolers, and got paid $204, in cash! By 4:30 PM I had said goodbye to Blaine, and the rest of the crew, and was headed back to our farm in Southwest Wisconsin. After I had driven 300 miles, stopped for a burger supper, called home, and bought some groceries it was 11:00 PM when I was finally meeting Wahoo, more often referred to as Kitty, our cat, at the back door to our house. She greeted me affectionately, it's nice to be loved, and I read Jean's anniversary card waiting for me on the kitchen table, it's nice to be loved. I was freshly showered and in bed a little after midnight.

Time Off 2, Days 25 through 30

I got up at 5:00 AM having slept poorly, perhaps due to the opossum on the back deck rattling Kitty's dish, but perhaps also due to sleeping in our bed inside of the bedroom of our home. I recognize few readers can relate to that last statement but both Jean and I, probably Greg and Nikki, and a small number of other wilderness tent campers "miss" being close to the ground and feeling the outdoors intimately encompassing you, and affecting your spirit. Lacking any other term, we might say we feel the emotional absence of "living in the Wild."

I was back at my corporate desk by 7:00 AM Wednesday morning, ready to answer the phone calls and service questions, and put in my agreed 40 hours of work effort for the company before returning to the BWCAW on the following Monday. I had a fun start with friendly visits from my work cohorts, Rita, Charlie, Ron, Jerry, Dave, Frank, Bruce, all of them filled with questions and support for my summer adventure. Being a non-standard employee at that point, I took advantage of my position and engaged in non-standard hours for those days I was at the "office," working late, starting early, taking time off at midday to go to the credit union or to my favorite camera shop in downtown La Crosse to develop my pictures and buy additional rolls of film. I visited our daughters and shared a pizza with them when they were available, not when the company would normally allow me.

My main job task on this "time off" was to meet the representative of our company-labeled, product supplier at a job site in Milwaukee and replace the control mechanisms of a large fan located in a four-foot diameter duct, about 15 feet above the floor of the work space being temperature controlled by my company's equipment. At the end of my second work day back at the company, I drove 20 miles to our farm and home to put things in order there and re-packed my clothes. Then drove back to the airport where I picked up a rental car and drove 225 miles to my motel in Milwaukee where I arrived at 10:30 PM that evening. The next morning, I drove to the airport at 7:15 AM to meet Ed, the supplier representative. Guess what? – No Ed, his connecting flight from southern Illinois was delayed by bad weather. I called Ed, I called our secretary, we made arrangements, Ed drove the rest of the way and we finally met at noon. We went to where the fan was located, but our contact there was out for lunch. Finally got into the job site, finally crawled down the duct and completed our task and I delivered Ed back to the airport late in the day. After driving back to La Crosse and turning in the rental car, I arrived home around 10:00 PM and let Kitty back in the rear door. I had to question if this cushy office job as an engineer was any less strenuous than working in the Boundary Waters.

In between a couple more days over the weekend at my company office, I mowed our acre-sized lawn, visited with the daughters, Jean's sister and her parents, washed clothes, mailed off a package of camp supplies to Jean in Idaho, made my meals and washed the dishes, aired out and repackaged my BWCAW packs and gear, changed the filter and oil in my truck, went through the accumulated mail and paid the necessary bills, bought groceries, and kept up my exercise regimen of stretches and walking, and once in a while I watched a television show in the evening and put my brain in neutral. Whew!

From my journal: A note I wanted to record – I am embarrassed and ashamed of today's societal excesses, a 40- foot-tall blasting volcano inside of a Las Vegas casino, a jousting match inside of a 4000-room hotel cooled by the company I work for, a $400 million *sports stadium in Toronto, a ball picker-upper at a golf course picking up hundreds of golf balls, my gawd, we can't even pick up our own golf balls anymore, we hire someone and a machine to do it for us! And then it seems chic to go to one of these joints and then tell your friends you've been there, my gawd you're supporting this idiocy! Oh, well, it's back to the boonies tomorrow and simple clean living for this kid.*

The drive back to Cook on Monday was fundamentally relaxing compared to the pace of the previous days. In Cook I stopped at the Ranger Station to drop off pictures of the illegal windbreak on Lake Agnes for Mike, and saw Ginger and Sandy there. Derek, Greg, Nikki, and Rich were already at the trailer when I arrived. Rich was Blaine's replacement as the two of them were both putting in a half session of the summer volunteer season to bolster their environmental resume. Chad walked in shortly afterward. It was easy talking, everyone just gathered around the latest arrival and questioned how they've been, what they did on their "time off." There is a mutual curiosity and interested friendship and sharing. Rich was a senior at college, already had canoeing experience and would be my new canoeing partner. He was tall and lean and affable. During the next few weeks, he and I would learn we had a shared interest in the author, Edward Abbey, and that we were both monitoring the "Earth First!" environmental organization.

Rich had grabbed the bed I had been on so I set up a camp cot in the living room for sleeping and put my truck camping pad on it as a mattress. Six of us walked up to the Northwoods Dairy Bar on that hot night for some cooling and refreshing ice cream. Dan and Lila came to the trailer later, just in time for the evening's uptick in laughter, noise, "jamming" tunes, and a rousing session of cribbage in the kitchen. Good sleep came hard though, when it did come, inside a hot, stuffy, and crowded trailer. The window fan didn't really so much find any cool air to pull in as it found hot air to blow over us. The following morning everyone was complaining about the poor sleeping conditions and the endless trains traveling on the nearby tracks. Or, perhaps like me, some of them were excited to be getting back to Lake Agnes and the forthcoming assignments.

Work Tour 3, Days 31 through 38

Drove to the Ranger Station at 7:00 AM and, by afternoon, had retraced our previous transit, driving, portaging, paddling, to a campsite at the north end of Lake Agnes. I enjoyed being in the last of our three canoes, and being able to look forward, watching the other canoes wend and wind, as they passed through swift river waters, glided over smooth lake water, paddled through grassy beds in shallow, wide swamps. The path in these grassy beds were revealed by deeper, clear waters and the absence of reeds and stems. We paused to rest on an open expanse in the midst of water lilies. Greg and Nikki are fast-paced paddlers, a strong, well-matched, experienced team of canoeists. As a result, they sometimes get far ahead of Ron on the lake and Greg caught a little Hell from our leader, Ron, for Greg's assertive actions that day, "It frustrates the shit out of me!" yelled Ron.

The temperature kept climbing during our paddle in to the north end of Lake Agnes, and we were glad to finally stop and set up our new camp on a site opposite the one we had used on our previous trip. Greg and Nikki set up the kitchen area while the other four of us paddled to our cache and retrieved the rest of our equipment and gear. Some of the crew went swimming in an attempt to cool down while I washed up our supper dishes. It was still 83 degrees at 9:00 PM, very hot for this country, and it was difficult to sleep while we lay there sweating, until after the temperature dropped a few more degrees.

96

We left camp early the next morning, paddled and portaged to the Ranger Cabin to get the rest of our supplies. Jack offered to take two of us with him and Derek up the lake in the District's 115 horse power in-board, boat to pick up six more latrines from Will Steger's cache. Chad and I jumped at the opportunity. Jack took us past Warrior Hill, a granite monolith up which young Native Americans used to run races to ascend to its top ridge. Then we boated to the famous pictograph site on a vertical cliff edge of Lac La Croix. By the time we had returned and pulled into the boathouse at the Ranger Cabin, Ron had sorted through our food, repacked it, and we hauled it, the latrines, a heavy-duty pry bar, and a 2-ton come-along, and a large natural chunk of Lac La Croix ice, back to our camp on Lake Agnes. This ice had been harvested the previous winter from the lake, purchased and brought to the cabin by Jack and Derek.

It was July 4. We wrapped up work on two more sites and pulled the troublesome stump out of the ground with our new come-along (ratchet winch), after which Ron declared quitting time in honor of Independence Day. To celebrate both it and our vigorous efforts here in the North Woods, we chipped ice from the carefully preserved Lac La Croix ice chunk, kept cool in the soil and deep shade in back of camp, and added it to our drinks. Ah, nothing like last winter's lake ice in my Jim Beam to round out a productive day and add to our nation's history. Forced to choose between the chance the lake ice might harbor Giardia versus the ambience of cooling my drink in this time-proven local tradition, I went with the magic of the ice. Maintaining my polite social buzz, I helped Chad write up his summer course-required journal. Chad had rather ignored the requirement till now so was very impressed and pleased with the detail in my journal as he briefly recapitulated our experiences in his own journal.

After an hour we were nearly done with Chad's journal, when we looked up to observe activity across the bay at our former camp site and began to pay attention, deep and studious attention, significantly enhanced by means of my small pair of binoculars. The binoculars were being passed from one to another of the four of us males gathered there at shore's edge in what passed for a fair rotation of use for my now-precious observational tool. An attractive young lady, long brunette hair caressed by the breezes, wearing a long loosely draped turquoise shirt, was engaged in an exercise routine and various yoga poses. One of those positions included standing on her head for a time. It was then we observed the shirt was now loosely draped around only her shoulders and head, thankfully, by the natural pull of gravity, and made note of the bare fact the shirt was her only item of clothing. She then assumed a new Lotus position and, for an hour, sat facing the setting sun. Very impressive. Quite the wildlife sighting. Ron concluded she had great Karma and was locked into a deep communication with Mother Earth. We all agreed. Definitely Karma in the air.

From the Journal: I feel good being back out here, it will also feel good to go home again. Out here, there is physical danger, but it is good and exhilarating to be here, what a different life, what different people, so freshening to be doing this. Time is as it should be, a function of living life and enjoying it, the whole day is a continuum of time, instead of increments mandated by the schedule of the clock on the company wall. Out here, I don't even know what day it is without consulting my journal. And another thing, I'm out here doing things that matter to me, with people who share those ideals, in a lovely outdoor setting that matters to me.

The following day was highly productive for the crew. We completed the rehabilitation of five of the remaining six sites on Lake Agnes and started on the sixth. When we got back to camp some of us were disappointed to discover Karma Lady had moved on and a new group occupied the site across from us. I took my Buck Knife, excellent chipper, to the ice store in the woods to chip ice for the crew to put in our late afternoon drinks, and finished off my first 250 milliliter bottle of whiskey. Our propane ran out today, so Chad baked our potatoes and grilled our steaks over the wood coals, doing a wonderful job of it. As dusk turned to night, Ron and I reviewed possibilities for a slide show with my photos and talked of bears, what is valuable in life, and how we should live life. Ron and I have very different backgrounds, our economic status is very different, our goals are different. But that doesn't mean we still can't learn from one another and that summer I did learn from Ron, as well as from each of my crewmates. As we prepared to go to our respective tents on that quiet, calm night, darkness descending in a peaceful cloak, the lake waves having declined to ripples, and the moon piercing a yellow path across the lake, we heard a group singing Amazing Grace from some camp site on the lake. Comparing impressions, Ron and I discovered we share Judy Collins rendition of the same song as a special favorite. Who could have guessed he and I might have that in common?

From the Journal: Some days and evenings I want to read my book or write more in my journal. But I am reluctant to leave the group gathered by the fire or at the kitchen area and thereby miss out on any interesting exchanges. I seek maximum variety and difference from this experience. I can always read and write, I can't always have this opportunity, this moment to be with these people, and to share with them the celebration and work of an ideal day or to share with them the vision of three mergansers swimming across a smooth silent lake. The canoeists and fishermen have at last left the waters of the lake and returned to camp, and the lake is once more the sole domain of the wildlife living here, not us temporary visitors.

On our fourth day of this trip, as the fog slowly rose and turned translucent above the glassine sheet that was Lake Agnes, we finished work on the last campsite, and returned to our camp to tear it down and make the eagerly awaited move to Lac La Croix, Canadian water, Big Water, extending 34 miles in length along our country's northern border, its blue enhanced by waters as deep as 168 feet. Before venturing too far on Agnes from our old camp, we all checked each other's freeboard, the distance from water to gunnel, (just barely adequate assuming the wind would not pick up) to make sure we wouldn't swamp the canoes, as we were very heavily laden. At the mucky Mud Dog Portage, we made multiple trips each to get everything from Agnes to Boulder Bay of Lac La Croix, moving about 1000 pounds of people, 1000 pounds of gear and equipment, and 230 pounds of canoes across the portage. Fortunately for weary voyageurs, the first site we encountered was a real beauty and was available, had a good, rock landing, multiple flat areas for our tents, nice fire pit, huge rocks on which to sit and admire the sunsets. The rest of us set up camp, erected the kitchen, and staked out the tarp cover while Ron and Chad made a quick short run to the Ranger Cabin to fetch more propane and food supplies, which Jack and Derek had brought to the cabin with the power boat.

Jack and Derek paddled over for a visit in the early evening which allowed Jack and Ron the opportunity to finalize arrangements for our work on and near Lac La Croix. Like good, hospitable guests they brought some alcohol-laden refreshments to sweeten the negotiations. A good time was had by all as the stories, conversations, and laughter flowed as readily as the whiskey and beer. Our crew chiefs here, Jack and Ron, never endangered the crew members safety and never drank "on the job," but they were often very concerned with what the rest of us might think of their actions. When they observed Greg or me writing in our journals, they were sometimes suspicious or would teasingly implore us not to publish a book. (Oops!) More than once over the summer, as they slapped us on the back in passing, each of us tonight with drinks in hand, one of them would remind any listeners of the Code of the Wilderness Rangers, "What goes on in the woods, stays in the woods." And of our obligations to them, "When you run with the Big Dogs, you gotta learn to pee in the tall grass."

In the end, our crew chiefs couldn't help but be what they fundamentally were. The same could likely be said for any of us. Our leaders adapted as best they could to a seasonal job, and every winter had to evaluate if they would be re-hired the following year, and if they wanted to continue in this vocation. Any judgements I might have made before I became a volunteer in the BWCAW, became moot and had to be re-aligned as I lived and worked with all those skilled and well-intentioned people.

Near midnight, in the dark, his orientation and mental abilities impaired, as they were disembarking, Jack miscalculated and nearly tipped their canoe. With some difficulty and frustration, Derek took charge and managed to re-position the canoe and get Jack safely into the bow seat. Paddling from the rear seat, on calm smooth waters, Derek commenced a dark paddle back to the cabin, the pathway enhanced by the glow of a full moon.

The rest of the crew was in pretty good shape the following morning, having carefully monitored our consumption, but Ron, not so much. He arose late, but it was of no significance to our start time as it had begun to rain and thunder, as we cowered in our tents and tried to deduce our location within the moving storm. The thunder sounded so different there on La Croix, perhaps the taller rock-encrusted ridges and density or height of tall trees affects it, or how far the storm has traveled over these big waters along the border. Or perhaps it is the impact on our spirits of being fortunate to live in Big Wilderness under only a thin sheet of nylon, and ponder the realness of living in the elements.

From the Journal: The thunder is quick, and then it sneaks up on you. It smacks you across the ears and sounds as though there is a lid over everything, yet it is hollow and reverberating, like thunder in a rain barrel, close to you, deep and sharp.

After the rain passed, Ron gave us the word to pack up and roll. The negotiated plan was for us to work two days on the Iron Lake Portage, a physical area technically under Jack's responsibility, hence the need for negotiation. But the coolness factor was, we all got to sleep in the Ranger Cabin that night, and there was promise of a meaty barbeque and a big party involving the building of International Relations. We grabbed our day packs, a change of clothes, our sleeping bags, and our Therm-a-rest™ mattress pads and hit the water. Ron was eager for breakfast and did not even wait for Nikki and Greg to complete their packing.

When we eight were gathered at the cabin, Jack and Derek fried up a large delicious breakfast of potatoes and pancakes smothered under Jack's homemade maple syrup. The uniqueness of cooking and eating indoors and sitting at table and chairs amazed all of us on Ron's crew, it just seemed highly irregular and unusually comfortable. While we were trying to contribute to the largess of Jack and Derek's efforts, we discovered chipmunks had gotten into one bread loaf, and, horror of horrors, also into our bag of M&M's™. After breakfast, Derek, Nikki, and I washed up the dishes before we left for the day's effort.

The Iron Lake Portage was a mess! It had seen little maintenance the past few years, only the continual passage of determined canoeists carrying canoes and gear from Lac La Croix to Iron Lake or vice versa. Standing, even running, water appeared in several lengths of the trail along with deep muck and mud. Limbs and trees had fallen across the trail, others threatened to do so. And woody brush was creeping in on both sides. Numerous mosquitoes hung in the air like mist and the Bedouin Bandanas and insect repellent came out of our daypacks again to thwart the little devils.

Chad and I helped Ron fell, limb, and strip the bark off four eight-inch diameter spruce trees. Spruce lasts in water and the weather much longer than pine. The main trunks would be used as stringers and fill support for the trail through the muck. Other crew members cut fallen trees, tossing manageable-sized pieces off the trail to clear it. Those with shovels worked the muck and mud out of the trail, and dug drainage channels to move the water out of standing ponds obstructing the portage. Jack cut down a ten-inch diameter tree, limbed and debarked it, and then sawed off the bottom and stoutest ten feet of length. He and I then cut saw kerfs down to about 3/8 the diameter every two inches in a consistent series. After that was complete, I held an axe parallel to the log and perpendicular to the saw kerfs at the halfway point of the diameter while Jack swung his axe against mine and we quickly hewed off numerous two-inch-wide half circles of wood thereby making a half-round, ten-foot long "beam." The beam was then cut into two five-foot-long pieces to form a bridge over a small rivulet of running water. The 5-foot linear beams were nailed on top of two notched cross pieces, which formed the supports of our five-foot bridge. Great progress was made by an eight-person, experienced team working well together. We cached all our tools near the trail to take up the challenge again the next day.

Shoveling fill sand into the wheelbarrow to build up the
portage trail we were repairing

A small bridge we built to allow water to flow under it,
fill sand would be added at each end of the bridge

We returned to the cabin late in the afternoon. Our crew chiefs, Ron and Jack, changed out of their grubby, trail-mucking clothes, and back into their official uniforms. They advised us where all the food was, not to wait up for them, hinted at visiting Canada, and went roaring up the lake in the District's power boat. We all shrugged our shoulders, cleaned up ourselves, and enjoyed some earned lounging time in this peaceful remote setting.

From the Journal: We six have been lounging around, exploring the cabin contents, visiting lightly, me writing this, passing the time of another wilderness day, thrown into this life by forces unknown to do things we can't predict, not of our own choice, and making the best of circumstances as they are.

In casual conversation with Derek, I explained how I had developed back problems some years ago and after diagnosis at my health clinic I did a prescribed regimen of stretch exercises each morning to keep the pains at bay. Derek was a physical fitness enthusiast and lifted weights to stay in shape at his home in Illinois. He explained his routine and how weight lifting might benefit me and urged me to review its possible advantage for me. Now, after 30 years of weight lifting, I look back in time and give Derek full credit for my current capabilities.

As hunger returned late in the day, Derek started the grill and we all enjoyed barbequed hamburgers again, and another big helping of fried potatoes. With all this outdoor living and hard daily labor, I found myself eating twice my normal quantity, be it breakfast, lunch, or supper. Quite amazing! As we were finishing supper, we heard the sound of power boats and our intrepid leaders returned with two dozen eggs (Boundary Waters code for two cases of beer), accompanied by two Canadian Wilderness Rangers, one a volunteer like us, the other his supervisor, from their Quetico Provincial Park, a large Canadian wilderness area of 1838 square miles adjoining our own BWCAW. Quetico and BWCAW work closely together on any search missions needed or law enforcement issues, which arise in their respective areas of jurisdiction, so the agents of both wilderness areas know one another, and these relationships are fostered by periodic social gestures, such as tonight's visit. Such get togethers are endorsed by Mike and Stewart back at the office and enhance International cooperation of these unique, adjacent wilderness areas.

It was fun to learn more about the Quetico Rangers, and both were pleasant conversationalists. Quetico rangers travel extensively in two-person teams in a lightweight canoe, with no qualms about some teams consisting of one male and one female. Further, the Canadian teams could use powered chain saws as needed. Each volunteer was paid per day about what we were paid, but the Canadian Government would issue that individual a grant of $6000 if he pursues any higher education following their summer volunteer position. During their off days, they have access to a large dorm, each having their own room, with maid service, and their meals at the dorms were cooked for them. It all sounded very pleasant and enticing compared to our utterly plebian Cook Trailer.

Jack and I had a good chat about marriage and child-rearing. Jack was the only other parent amongst us eight and we shared the complexities, challenges, and joys of family life. Again, I found it revealing and interesting to relate to this crew chief and wound up revising my judgment of his playful, flirtatious actions earlier in the summer with Elaine. It was borne in on me that people are all more meaningful and complex than first impressions might suggest.

The beer had added to the joviality of the event as we all commonly experienced the rapport of lives shared in the North Country. By the time the Canadians left and returned to their base in Quetico, the rest of us had held our consumption to a pleasant level of conviviality, but Ron and Jack continued to pull and quaff "eggs" from the carton. The two of them were out on the lawn near the cabin, when the rest of us heard loud vocalizations, accusations, and anger as they started to argue, call the other names, and loudly debate continuance of the Iron Lake Portage work. In retrospect, we conjectured the project was not approved by Mike, and the issue was who would get the credit for its completion. But this explanation came later, all that we observed at the time were two very angry and boisterous men.

The anger quickly devolved to physical wrestling for dominance over the other. Throws were initiated, bodies hit the ground, harsh restraints and twisting were applied, grunts and yelps and verbal abuse came out of their panting mouths. This was a genuine fight, the likes of which I had never personally witnessed, only heard or read about. Those of us gathered around the fighters jumped back to stay out of their way as the wrestlers vied for dominance, and to provide them clearance for their next moves. It was a REAL scrap.

As the next two oldest individuals apart from these two crew chiefs, Derek and I went into a huddle near the edge of the activity, and briefly debated if we should try to break up this fight between two individuals who were not only our bosses, but whose character we had come to know and respect. We quickly decided, based on the earnestness of what we saw, and the strength of the contestants, that we had better let this activity play out, for better or worse. We cautioned Nikki to stop making any comments from the window where she was observing, which might make the situation worse. I was thinking, "Gawd, this Bull Moose mentality!" as they fought, slammed into the cabin, and rolled in the grass. In spite of Ron easily outweighing Jack, it was a pretty even match because both had been experienced wrestlers in high school.

And then, just as suddenly as it had started, both called a truce, started laughing, shook hands, and arms thrown casually over each other's shoulders as they stood side by side, Ron loudly declared, "Boy! That was a GOOD fight!" Most of us were dumbfounded. My mouth hung open in dismay and wonderment as I tried to make sense out of senselessness and I thought, "Cheeze! Is this all really weird or what?!"

We all went back into the cabin, my mind still swirling. Ron and Jack had more beer. Chad joined in. The chiefs harassed Greg and Nikki about going to sleep too early and warned them not to clutter up the living room floor because there was to be major wrestling again tonight. And there was. Ron and Jack cleared the floor and went at it again (!?!?), announcing, "This time, for the pleasure of it!" Furniture was knocked about from their impacts, audience members having to jump out of their way, and the floor was being thumped soundly when either or both landed on it. Each really went at it to win, a real joust for supremacy. Then at the end, Ron went white as a sheet and Derek and I wondered if he was a goner. But no, each came out of it laughing. and the crowd had impartially cheered for neither side, only for the good moves.

Chad had over-extended himself into the dwindling supply of beer and, responding to its cumulative effects, like some others in such a situation, changed a bit from his soft-spoken, quiet self, and became louder, boisterous, rowdy. With Ron side-lined, Chad challenged Jack to a wrestle, and without further ado or clarification of any rules, both went at it. Chad had learned his moves "on the street," and did really well against an older, stronger opponent, but then had his head knocked soundly on the floor and then both he and Jack bashed into the solid steel wood-burning stove. It was a much shorter match. Northwoods Rowdies! Fortunately, by now, all manner of drink had run out, party participants were getting tired, and bed assignments were being negotiated.

After midnight Ron kicked Derek out of his normal bed in the two-bed cabin that Derek shared with Jack, and Ron became the bed's one-night occupant. Derek was relegated to the kitchen floor with Greg and Nikki, Rich and Chad were on the living room floor, I found my semi-protected area under a large heavy-duty wood table whose legs nicely encompassed my mattress and sleeping bag located adjacent to Jack's normal bed, and Jack fell into his own bed.

The battery-powered tape player had cranked out songs all night long. Tracy Chapman was new on the music scene and everyone liked her singing and likewise enjoyed any of the songs of The Traveling Wilburys. Whenever I hear "End of the Line" by The Wilburys or "Crossroads" by Tracy my thoughts go racing back to my time in the BWCAW when I ran with the "Big Dogs." One last tape was put in, Ron blew out the lights, and as more and more individuals fell asleep, the drunks sang along with Paul McCartney, until the player turned off, and all was quiet. Except for me, that is. I was at full wakefulness, my brain was in overdrive, over stimulated by experiences not in my staid life's repertoire, just so many unbelievable events this day. Like a kid at Christmas, I was busy lapping up Life. I was awake another one to two hours, laying there in the dark trying to brain-file it all. Sometime in the wee hours of the morning Jack fell out of his bed and his arm landed on my head. In my dozing, I couldn't figure that out for a while but about an hour later he stumbled out of the cabin to pee and then again fell properly back into his own bed. What a day! What a night!

Predictably, our next morning started late, but bodies arose from lethargy, wise-cracks were traded, we made our own breakfasts, and by late morning were back working on the Iron Lake Portage. I installed a wood culvert by cutting a six-foot spruce log in half, peeling its bark, then positioning the two 3-foot sections a couple inches apart, perpendicular to the portage, to allow water from a beaver pond to pass between the logs and "under" the portage. The borrow pits were in heavy use: two crew members shoveled fill into the sieve over the wheelbarrow, two crew members ran the sieve then moved the wheelbarrow to our retaining walls and fill area, two members dumped, leveled, and packed the sand fill to create a dry elevated portage trail. Many wheelbarrows of sieved sand were moved and I took numerous pictures of everyone's activities that day, attempting to document our work. And in the end, we felt we had created an interstate super-highway across the swamps and muck. We could only be pleased and proud of the transition from a dreaded, mucky nightmare the day before, to the impressive result of our hard day's work. Our teamwork triumphed again, a good deed was accomplished, a sound structure resulted. Nicely done!

In the afternoon Ron took our crew back to our campsite on Boulder Bay where we completed the rehabilitation of that site. Nikki and Greg planted trees, Rich and I assembled two latrines, installed one there, and destroyed the old one. I filtered my water, aired out the sleeping bag, rinsed some clothing, and washed up, felt good!

The evening was spent similarly to other, most-fondly remembered days and evenings: winding down, resting, admiring your surroundings, possible casual visiting, reading or journal-writing if not. The waters were calm, reflecting the rays of the sun as it slowly set in the northwest, and the sun-warmed rocks we sat on counterbalanced the cooling effect of evening, before us a long wide bay of blue water and wilderness, with no permanent habitations. On my trip to our farm and home in Wisconsin, after our second work tour, I had purchased some Swisher Sweet™ small cigars on the broadly-accepted theory that mosquitoes would harass you less while you are smoking a cigar and liberally distributing its smoke about your person. Chad and I had established a periodic, shared ritual of each smoking a Swisher Sweet™ late in the day, as we sat on the rocks philosophizing and admiring the scene before us. A sixteen-inch snapping turtle swam past, varying its depth as it maneuvered in the clear waters of Lac La Croix and Boulder Bay, and we were surprised how far down we could still observe the turtle. Later, near dark, we had been quiet and motionless a few minutes, and a beautiful large otter swam past us. Chad and I felt richly rewarded for our "smoke" that evening.

From the Journal: I have come to the Northwoods knowing not what to expect. I have learned to play the brash role of the Northwoods Bull Moose as we roll into town triumphant from eight days of living and working. I have lived the life of the "locals" – drinking my whiskey, smoking my cigar, eating the hot spicy pepper jack cheese, and marveling with the "It just can't get any better than this" attitude. And yet sentimental tears and throat constrictions of emotions and thoughts and memories come easier each year to this 46-year-old. I read a chapter about a dying cat from "Just Beyond the Firelight" and tears well up in my eyes – here in this beautiful sunlit camp with the waves lapping the shore and the wind singing in the Red Pines. I no longer fight these emotions. Preferring to feel them in their simple rawness – perhaps to atone and make up for those times I fought those feelings, those tears back. And to feel that total realm and wonderment of life – so precious. And so, although it may appear an anomaly – this whiskey-drinking man of the woods sitting here crying at the words written by another man about his dying cat – I see it as both ends of the same circle – the circle of Life and Living and Loving.

I found the easiest way to carry a fiberglass latrine by oneself is to put it over your head and hold it by the base

Greg and Nikki admiring the pictographs on the cliff of Lac La Croix from their canoe

On the final full day of this third trip into the BWCAW, we spent the bulk of the hours rehabilitating another three campsites on Lac La Croix. As usual, my partner and I got stuck with hauling that damned wheelbarrow around balanced on top of the gunnels of our canoe, but precedence rules and I had had the duty of transporting that beast since the first day we saw it. We paddled two miles to get to this series of sites, planted the last of our trees, cut down two large hazard trees, performed the usual clean-up at each site, plus we seeded grass, "planted" rocks, used the sieve and wheelbarrow to provide fill where needed, busted up the old latrines, filled in old latrine holes, dug new ones, installed new latrines that one or two of us had assembled on site. We took a lunch break at the farthest-north extremity of our paddles that day and had Warrior Hill in Canada across the water from us as our lovely frontispiece. Chad and I dug what we called a "ten-year shitter" at that site, digging the hole deeper and wider at its base than need be, in an effort to avoid the other camp jobs.

Because Ron had heard an earlier forecast on his radio, by mid-afternoon he had been observing the wave action on the lake, knew the wind was increasing, and he declared a weather emergency. Unless we wanted to spend the night on the island we were working on without our tents, he directed us to head home for our base camp before it got worse. We quickly packed our tools and cached them in a corner rock formation, grabbed our daypacks and paddles, put on our life jackets—nobody was gambling with those white-caps—and hopped into the canoes. Travel was good until we got to the main channel where the breadth of the lake caught the full impact of the wind and the waves had longer to build in height. Then it got scary.

Rich and I went to the kneeling position to lower our center of gravity. Although it made the transit a little longer, we quartered into the waves for stability instead of paddling parallel to the waves and risking getting rocked out of our canoe. White-caps, one- to two-foot-tall waves, 30 miles per hour winds do not make for pleasant canoe paddling. All our bow paddlers, including Rich, got soaked on their right sides from waves splashing over the right front quarter of the canoes. Greg and Nikki were such well-matched, experienced paddlers they were able to outpace the rest of us and lead us home. But I remember being torn between wishing I was nearly to safety like they were versus wishing they were closer to the rest of us so they could provide assistance if any of the rest of us flipped over in those winds and waves.

Putting all our effort into surviving and paddling smart and hard, all canoes finally made it to the lee of another island and then turned left down a channel of Boulder Bay that led to our home camp. The white-caps didn't follow us into those narrower and tree-sheltered waters, but with the strong wind perfectly aligned to our backs we rapidly scooted down the remaining channel and breathed a sigh of relief and accomplishment when we got to camp.

We had supper early and by late in the day the weather front had passed over us, the strong winds had died down, the clouds diminished, and near sundown it was still over 70 degrees. I invited Chad over to the sitting rocks overlooking our bay for our evening smoke of Swisher Sweets™ and resultant chat. The rest of the crew gradually assembled to join us and we partook in hot tea or cocoa, Greg and Nikki provided fresh-popped popcorn, day turned to night, as the flames of the fire dwindled, on our last evening of this work tour on the big waters of Lac La Croix.

After a quick round of exercises and some gear packing, I got out of my tent at 5:30 AM the next morning and put water on to heat for our breakfasts. Ron was already up and tearing down his tent. We hauled our large heavy packs over to the Ranger Cabin for

Jack and Derek to deliver to Cook via their powerboat. We stored our cooking gear in a locked compartment of the boat house. Taking only our small personal packs, unburdened by heavy gear or double trips across the portages, blessed by good weather and no wind, we made rapid time and were back at the Moose River Portage parking lot before noon. We stopped at the first possible junk food store near Buyck and had our traditional "welcome back to civilization" snack, ice cream bar and soda for me.

We made such good time we beat our packs back to the Ranger Station. While waiting for Jack and Derek's delivery, I had ample time to give Rich and Chad a ride to the trailer, have lunch, read my mail, collect my dirty clothes, arrange the rear truck bed, write a post card to Jean. In addition, I had the opportunity to take a shower, which would save me valuable time in the evening when I made it home to our farm. Leaving Cook by 4:00 PM, I arrived home before 11:00 PM, our faithful cat greeting me at the back door.

Time Off 3, Days 39 through 44

From the Journal: Went to sleep last night in the comfortable, clean, bug-free bed and bedroom of our house, but noted I rather miss the sounds, coolth, freshness of the night, and odors of the tent, the feel of being in the outdoors, moonlight flooding the tent, mixing shadows in the woods, the lake lapping at the shore.

I was back at my company job by 7:00 AM the following morning, answering service questions from the field when my boss, Charlie, came in and shook my free hand in passing. I worked late each day and put in a day's work on Saturday in order to get in my obligatory 40 hours of work serving corporate needs over the next four days. Charlie and I were having a meeting in a break area off the hallway later on my first day back, when the Vice-President who had reluctantly granted my final request for Leave of Absence happened by. "How's that tree planting going, Gary?" to which I replied, "Going good!" He added, "How do you like it?" I answered, "Great!" and ZOOM, he was gone. Charlie had seen him coming and in a clever sleight of hand had put the map in a stack of company papers we had on the table. After the VP left Charlie brought the BWCAW map of the La Croix Ranger District back out and we resumed our "meeting."

From the Journal: I'm comfortable in the Northwoods with my long hair and shaggy growth of beard and mustache, but note I feel self-conscious at my company. It is teasingly commented on ("You look like a wolf." And "Wow, you're rough-looking!") because it is non-standard to the corporate culture. My crew partners don't have those comments in the woods. There I am accepted as I am, as I come to be with them, not as I am "supposed" to be.

Thinking over my experiences in the BWCAW, I dreamt up a little memento I wanted to share with my fellow crew partners. I visited a trophy shop while I was in La Crosse and ordered six medallions, each suspended on a colorful ribbon adequate to hang around one's neck, and had each engraved on the back with the names of our major accomplishments of the summer including the year:1990, Dovre, Trout, Gowan, Norway, Agnes, La Croix. I planned to present them to my crew on our final Work Tour and was able to pick up the completed medallions before returning to Cook.

Being at the farm a few days allowed me to schedule a phone call with Jean as neither of us, when working our jobs that summer, had ready access to a phone. I could hear her grinning ear to ear as she described her work, the falcons, and mountain-top, river valley splendor of the area, even though it was 102 degrees in the small community where her pay phone was located. I likely responded in very much the same way. It was neat to hear the glee in her voice, and we briefly explored how we could continue these types of adventures in the following summer.

I was able to get in several warm visits with our daughters, very refreshing to see them doing well and to have their blessing for what Jean and I were doing. While in town I picked up my developed photos at the camera shop, replenished my small mobile supply of whiskey for the next Work Tour, and purchased two packs of Swisher Sweets™ for Chad and me. At the farm, I caught up on farm tasks, mowed the lawn, did the laundry, repacked, and, coping with Time's rapidity of passage, by noon on a Monday I was on my last drive to the North Country, to Cook, and headed back to Lac La Croix.

I pulled in and parked at the trailer dormitory at 7:00 PM and met Lila at the door. She was just leaving to escape the raucous reunion gathering of crew members and warned me of a water fight inside the trailer. Sure enough, a resounding water fight had just been concluded between Ginger, Derek, Rich, Sandy, and Chad and they were busy mopping up the kitchen floor. Upon my entry they teased about wetting me down too, but they took it easy on the old man and let me pass to the west bedroom where I tossed my stuff. I think Rich had gotten the word from the rest of the crew to give the old man back his bed (which Rich occupied the first night he came to join us), but he couched it in terms of saying, "It was too soft and sway backed for me."

We all gathered in the living room and lounged around excitedly trading stories on what each had done during the latest "Time Off." About an hour later, Greg and Nikki drifted in and joined the reconvening of the crew and reunion meeting. Nikki showed up in a dress, all fresh and clean, sporting a ponytail hairdo. Wow! She was very attractive and smart-looking, in such sharp contrast to the grubby clothes, long pants, headgear, boots, and dirt we all normally use for attire during our work on portages and campsites. She and Greg had camped and canoed for five days in the Sioux Hustler Trail area, and on to Fat Lake. The rest of us were a little jealous of their journey.

Ginger bought a birthday cake for Sandy, and served it with ice cream to all of us, because it was the last trip for three of us. After our treat, the Pictionary game took over the floor of the living room and participants shouted, argued, entreated, laughed, and teased with glee. I didn't play, but I always enjoyed watching how happy and enthused everyone was while playing. Nikki and I gravitated to the kitchen to reduce the sound intensity and were able to carry on a conversation there. As the night ended, Ginger hugged the three of us who would be leaving and bid us fond words acknowledging the friendship we had developed and she went to her trailer. I was touched.

Work Tour 4, Days 45 through 52

Rain, peals of thunder, and the intense, searing flashes of lightning delayed our loading in the early morn. After the storm passed, we gave our heavy packs and new food supplies to Jack and Derek to haul to the Ranger Cabin with the powerboat for us, and we paddled/portaged five hours and ten miles in, to Lac La Croix along our by-now normal route with just our day packs. Sure makes for a fast, easy glide down the river, onto the lakes, and over the portages. We stopped at three eagle nests on the way in for a quick biological survey: one active with adults, one empty, and on the third we spotted a chick. Ron sent Greg and Nikki to Professor Island with instructions to grab and occupy one of the sites there while the rest of us went to the Ranger Cabin.

Unfortunately, like last time, we had again beaten Jack and Derek's powerboat transit to the cabin with our hand-paddled canoes. Granted, their route is long and complex, involving miles of open water and a rail-line portage which hauls their powerboat overland to the next lake. But, just as Jack and Derek were cruising by Warrior Hill, Ron made radio contact with them and they delivered our packs and food directly to our new campsite on Professor Island.

No sooner had we dragged the boat to our landing, than Ron and Jack declared it was bar time and began to partake of the spirits. The rest of us weren't ready for that yet and kept busy setting up camp and finding level sites for our tents. With Ron being preoccupied, shall we say, I eventually set up his tent for him. When he finally noticed what I had done, he thanked me personally and sincerely, and promised I had earned some "comp time."

Six drinkers tackled two bottles of hard liquor as the sun sank lower and went behind the screen of trees across the lake. We each had an ample intake to reach the individual buzz level sought by the particular drinker, but the crew chiefs chose the option of "more than ample" and then bared their souls about their jobs. They love their USFS positions and all they want is to have their seasonal jobs guaranteed from year to year, but USFS budget and politics make that impossible. They receive poor renumeration and no insurance or vacation benefits. Each vowed not to wrestle again after the cabin experience of the last trip, ("Getting too old for this! It hurts. Could be dangerous!"). But after a few more drinks and depressing conversation about their work, Jack couldn't handle it any longer and went after Ron in the trees. The match was blessedly short-lived and congenial after Ron hurt his wrist on a broken branch. Talking, laughing, consuming our beverages, and listening to meaningless negotiations between Ron and Jack, over what work our combined crews could accomplish, continued until Derek could stand it no longer and prepared to take Jack back to the cabin. The party broke up and most of us shuffled off to our tents. The next day we learned the push-off of a powerboat from shore in the dark did not go smoothly and Ron and Derek wound up waist deep in the lake.

From the Journal: I kept thinking today – Well, this is the last this, or the last that, but it all still feels too good to feel bad or to dwell on the negative. One of Life's lessons – to live for the moment and get what I can out of it. Because tonight I walked around the camp admiring the set-up and location, saw the tree silhouettes of sundown, heard the wind, thought of Canada next door, stared at the waves coursing across the lake and, like Jean, I thought and felt how lucky I am to be here, to be here at all, to be here now – and loving the feeling, loving the thought, loving just being here, living this life to the hilt, 350 miles north of home, on beautiful Lac La Croix.

It was another lovely morning in the Northwoods. Understandably, based on last night, it was a late start, but by noon we had completed rehabbing two sites near camp. Midway through the morning Ron directed Chad and I to go to the cabin and bring back the last of the seedling white pine trees and grass seed. We jumped at the opportunity, paddling to the cabin was way better than digging a new latrine hole. Later in the afternoon we encountered big waves as we were paddling at the north end of our island and Ron declared the rest of the day to be "wind-bound," so we went straight to our camp.

After we had our canoes beached and gear put into our tents, we discovered there was still some ice left from the Lac La Croix chunk which Jack had left at our camp, so Happy Hour was declared and the ice distributed. Ah, the cool refreshing taste of last winter! I was pretty sure I had consumed more hard liquor here in the last month than I had the previous two decades. It must have been the pleasurable company and the ambience/décor of the outdoor bars we inhabited. Chef Ron surprised us with the epicurean delight of roast turkey breast, stuffing, potatoes, and gravy for our supper. Magnifico! Afterwards, the wind had died down and Chad handed me an after-dinner cigar and four of us sank back against the properly inclined boulder luxuriating in the majesty of it all and our good fortune. What contentment! What a setting!

In the early evening some of the crew went fishing for walleyes, and Jack and Derek brought two new Canadian Rangers, Joe and Vera, to our camp to meet us and visit. This was done in continuation of Mike's official policy of good International Relations with compatriots from the country across the border working the same types of jobs we were engaged in. The Canadians brought two dozen "eggs" in a gesture of friendship. Being the sole individual from La Crosse, Wisconsin, the home and corporate headquarters of G. Heileman Brewing Company, I made special note the eggs this time were not Molson™ but were instead Old Style™ beer, made in the city where I worked as an engineer.

During the story swapping over the beers, our faces shimmering with the dancing flames of the fire, Jack told us of the California Yuppie he and Derek met while on boat patrol. Jack and Derek were flagged down by a man and his wife in their canoe as they were laboriously paddling across Lac La Croix. The husband had quit paddling and two small children were also in the canoe. The man told Jack there was too much wind, he wanted out NOW, and money was no object. Jack said he would have left them sit right where they were except for the children. The California family had been flown in by a portage aircraft outfitter company several days

121

ago, the man was sick of it, so Jack contacted the same company with his radio and had the pontoon-equipped plane come in and pick up the family and canoe. Our jaws dropped, and we could only shake our heads in disbelief.

As we sat there visiting, a little large-eared gray deer mouse was watching us from a rock and one had been by the table earlier. Rich said he has seen several around camp. Perhaps it was these mice, and not frogs as I had earlier conjectured, which had tried to climb the slick walls of my tent occasionally in the middle of the night, and then wound up sliding down the smooth nylon, their little claws making a slight zipping sound, as they attempted to regain traction.

Over the next three days we completed work on nine campsites scattered in the near vicinity. Each site was picturesque in its own way and located in the recesses of magical bays, with names like Tiger Bay, Never Fail Bay, Lady Boot Bay. Thanks to the persistence and skill of our fisherman we breakfasted on full servings of walleye fillets each day, served on one or two pieces of bread and a slice of onion, my favorite breakfasts of the summer. Near dark, we had instructions from Ron to light a generous fire to have as a beacon home in those twisted waters and bays for any night when our fishermen had not yet arrived. One night the fisherman arrived late so I helped illuminate their fish-cleaning work by rigging two of my small flashlights over the cleaning area to help speed them past the mosquitoes. It always amazed me that I seemed to be the only member of the crew armed with a flashlight.

Everyone had worked together well that summer, trading off the jobs in order for each of us to experience and learn the task, but Nikki had not assembled a latrine yet, known amongst our group colloquially as a "shitter." The two main components, again as referred to by our crew, were the "Jam Jar" (main fiberglass latrine supporting one's rear end), and the "Runner boards" (treated-wood 2x4's, which held the latrine over the dug hole). I coached Nikki through the process and she banged several together. The latrines, with or without runner boards attached, when we had them in our campsite prior to installation, were often used as comfortable seats of a convenient height, as we gathered in the kitchen area for our meals. My pictures of us dining in that manner always invoke a chuckle. Two people can carry one assembled latrine by each grasping the ends of the runner boards with the latrine suspended between them. The easiest way to carry one by oneself is to lift the assembly over your head and thrust your head through the seat opening, your shoulders wedged into the wider base portion of the latrine, and a hand grabbing a rail on each side to balance it evenly. I knew Chad was waiting for a completed assembly up the hill at his freshly dig hole and volunteered to carry it by myself up to him. As I neared Chad, he couldn't resist saying, "Why, Gary, you look like a real shithead!"

Paddling to a site on Never Fail Bay, Ron took us all past the pictographs north of Warrior Hill. Fascinating to see them up close, to recognize they have been there hundreds of years, painted by native Americans of the region sitting in some type of watercraft at the same lake level and location we now were, a journey back into time. Before we left, Ron wedged a cigarette into a small crevice as a traditional offering of tobacco to the mystical god, Mishipeshu, The Great Lynx, who lived underwater, and whose thrashing tail could cause storms of wind and water. This was to assure we would not be victimized by the capricious ways of this god while on these big waters. Seeing this action, we felt humbled and none of us objected. We had canoed and paddled seven miles over Lac La Croix that day. If this would help protect us, we were all for it.

This campsite view from my tent is one of the reasons I came here

The last portage out, going back to the Moose River parking lot

From the Journal: The black feather, raven or crow, I care not which, either is a black bird, and both are accorded a certain religious respect by earlier peoples, appeared one day on my path. I noticed it and let it lie. On the next day the feather moved to one side of the tent. I noticed that and let it lie. On the third day the same feather appears on the other side of the tent. I notice that and marvel briefly at its tenacity for this site. I sense its call and pick it up. I place it in my tent. It is hanging in the loft of my tent, next to my flashlight, waiting to go home to the farm with me. I seek now messages in things once ignored, but magic is all around us if we but listen, look, notice. The Muse is there. Be it in the Cardinal flitting over the birdbath at the farm, or the black feather lying on the ground, or the Peregrine practicing its majestic powers of flight while my wife watches near Hells Canyon in Idaho. The Muse is hard to notice in our modern, fast paced, technological life. But we know now, Jean and I, the Muse is still there. Listen. Look. Notice.

One day, after we had completed the scheduled work, Nikki accompanied Ron as they went to make three "public contacts" of campers, checking their permits, and ensuring compliance with BWCAW requirements. Each site's occupants were gracious and welcomed the visit of our Rangers. While they were gone, the rest of the crew continued work on the current site. Greg had the misfortune to "hang up" three hazard trees. Not easy to calculate and make a considered cut to drop the trees where one wants to in a crowded forest. Working together we got them all down to the ground.

At several of our campsites here at Lac La Croix, whether at our base camp or on one of the sites we were rehabbing, the local Herring Gulls would often make an appearance during our meals, sensing there might be free food available. One gull was particularly adept at gobbling pieces of bread tossed in its direction. We fondly named it "Blaine" in honor of our past work crew compatriot, Blaine, a voracious eater. Ron would look up at the occasional gulls following us and begging at camp and say, "Hello again, Blaine!" and "Are you hungry, Blaine?"

Ron had elected to bring a boombox radio on our last trip in. Personally, I hated that damned boombox. To me, my time in the wilderness here was almost a religious experience and I wanted all the ambience the natural world had to offer, and I did not want anything coming into my time there from the outside world. I recognized, however, that to Ron this time here is his job. He, and some of my crew, enjoyed a little touch of the outside world, primarily the music, and getting a daily temperature or weather forecast. So, I kept my personal opinion of the radio to myself. And, we had a little fun with the radio. The station, which Ron often played and that offered the best reception in that remote corner of our world, had an often-repeated slogan for the music it chose to play, "Not too soft, not too hard." To which we fondly added, "And not too good."

The weather on most days allowed us to continue our, by now, traditional cocktail hour-or-more, as I rationed my dwindling supply of Jim Beam. Chad and I would have our smoke, several others might join us at dusk. Green needles of the red pines in back of us were intensely colored against the brilliant blue sky when the sunlight yet struck them, the vivid green in back of us in sharp contrast to the black silhouettes of the far distant trees in front of us. The myriad shades of sunset changed almost imperceptibly until the sun went behind the horizon, and the color and rapidity of change slowed and transitioned to bland scenes of black and gray. Lac La Croix had an abundance of Common Loons. Their calls were frequent, of long duration, and came at all hours of the evening. Their evocative notes seemed to speak to us best in the dim, waning light of sunset. Once in the night I awoke and strained to hear if the distant sound was possibly a wolf, but quickly discerned it was a loon, a wonderful sound with which to roll over and drift back to sleep.

No walleyes in the cooler, so Sunday morning we awoke and had our more normal Boundary Waters breakfast, coffee or tea, bread, jam, an instant oatmeal packet or two. We tore down our campsite and moved to the lawn of the cabin. We planned to be there two nights, our last camp of this trip, allowing everyone their own normal sleeping accommodations while joining the two crews together for a bit more portage work and reclamation.

That afternoon found us putting in some hard labor on the east end of the Boulder Bay-Lac La Croix portage opposite the Ranger cabin, shoveling, moving, dumping, leveling, compacting 20 wheelbarrow loads of sand fill to build the portage up and raise it above water level. After the sweat and mud of the portage work and back at the cabin, Derek jumped off the boat dock and took a quick cold swim, while others likewise cleaned up and changed out of their grubby clothes. A gentle late afternoon commenced with Derek, Ron, Jack, and Chad enjoying a cribbage game and mixed drinks at the cabin table. I joined the literary group in the cabin and read with them. When I noticed the late-day sun was nicely illuminating the cabin lawn I organized a photo shoot and pictures were taken of our rehabilitation crew, including Derek on one of the photos, to memorialize our summer together.

After a delicious supper of veal parmesan and home-made noodles, some of the group went fishing, some of us visited and jammed on music from the boombox, others had a card game going. By 10:00 PM the fishermen had returned, the card game was winding down, and Nikki announced she was going to her tent for bed. With everyone sober, or close enough, I said, "Wait! I've got a speech to make and things to give away!" That got their attention, and their mouths were agape as I herded them into the kitchen. They wondered what this could possibly be about as I began to speak, "As the oldest fucker ever to apply to be a volunteer in the La Croix Ranger District, I've earned the right to give a speech. When I signed up, I knew what I wanted to get out of this adventure: wilderness experience, beautiful new sights, lots of paddling, remote camping on historical pathways, the opportunity to contribute to our natural world, and I received all of those in abundance. But what I didn't expect, and yet have definitely gotten, is camaraderie and your friendship. We accept each other for who and what we are. So, in appreciation of that and in thanks I have this gift. Also, because I knew the Forest Service couldn't afford a souvenir for us. Hell, the Forest Service can't even give our crew chiefs a decent wage. I wanted people to have a physical commemorative of what we accomplished in our time together, so I got us our own souvenir. With my thanks to you all, here …." And with that I gave the first one to Ron, said his name, and shook his hand, and repeated that process with each individual. They each looked at and read their own medallion which I had purchased and had engraved in La Crosse two weeks prior to this last trip. On the back of each: 1990, Dovre, Trout, Gowan, Norway, Agnes, La Croix.

They were all a little stunned and blown away. It was quiet for a moment. And then Ron hung his over his head, suspended below his neck, and the others followed suit. Ron came into the momentary silence and told us, "You were the best damn crew I ever had in my eight years' experience of doing this job. Everyone worked hard together without any upsetting arguments. Just a great crew." Jack jumped in then and vouched for the truth of Ron's comments as witnessed by himself. People stopped by later for a one on one with me and added personal thanks for the gesture and for the friendship we had established. Derek came to shake my hand, add his positive comments and said he was sure Ginger and

Sandy would say the same. Done with my speech and the ceremony I had imposed on my fellows; I finally was calming down my brief embarrassment and went to bed feeling all warm and fuzzy. After Ron's crew was in their tents and drifting off to sleep done with our unique day in the Northwoods, Jack stepped out of the cabin and gave a loud, "Hooaahh!" mimicking the call of a Barred Owl on that quiet night. Jack had taught Ron to make the call and so Ron worked up a rousing "Hooaahh!" from his tent in return. The two of them exchanged a few more of the calls of the Barred Owl. Greg initially thought it was real (Jack and Ron are that good!) until Nikki straightened him out.

Awaking the next morning in my tent I gradually came to the awareness this was to be my last full day as a member of a rehabilitation crew in the La Croix District of the BWCAW. Replaying the events of the previous night as I did my stretches and pulled on my clothes, I was quite content with what was said, what was unsaid, but perceived nonetheless. Walking into the cabin we discovered Jack and Derek making a whoppingly large and delicious breakfast of fried potatoes, bacon, pancakes, and, of course, Jack's flavorful homemade maple syrup. We each grabbed our selection, piled it on our plates, and walked outdoors to the picnic table to dine. Everything looked enticing and tasted great! The bugs were few and it was an attractive setting on a pleasant day as the sun crept up over the pines.

We loaded the canoes, paddled across the bay, and then hiked to the east end of the Iron Lake Portage to complete that project. It was the typical mucky portage work that we were all, by now, quite familiar and experienced with: cut spruce trees, debark them, install stringer beams to hold our fill in place, establish borrow pit, shovel and sieve into wheelbarrow, dump, level, pack, clear the rest of the trail, in addition to the building of a canoe rest at the midpoint. It was a huge accomplishment and it felt good to have the whole thing completed, one mile of, for a portage, easy walking. Near the end of the project Chad and I snuck away from the crew to get a look at Iron Lake. It would have been weird to complete the mucky part of the portage work without seeing where the end of the portage led. We found a few bear tracks. And, typical of the area, Iron Lake was lovely. We wished we could linger a while.

Back at the cabin, most of the crew jumped off the dock and took a swim to clean up. I was almost too tired to untie my shoelaces. But after some rest and cleaning up, began to feel normal again and think of my good fortune in being there. I had made more good friends, all of them two decades younger than myself, than I could possibly have done at my company in the same amount of time, largely because of what we shared philosophically.

Greg and Nikki were pleased and impressed with the support extended by my partner of 25 years and our two daughters. I had the feeling they were hoping for the same 25 years down their road through life. I had leveled with all the crew and classified myself as an old rebel. They all had called me "old" and made "old" jokes but I believe I was genuinely accepted and respected by these good, young people. Chad was the youngest and called me "old man" and "Grandpa" but with affection and a grin. He backed off a little after I responded by calling him "my son" and "grandkid." It was neat.

We had a gentle afternoon and evening, with a mixture of warm visiting and privacy enough that Greg and I could get our journals up to date as we sat on the dock. Chad and I shared one more, the last, Swisher Sweet™ cigar smoke together, as night descended and the bats began to circle overhead, gathering their "breakfast," having just awakened from a long day's snooze. Frogs were gaining momentum in the bay, croaking the strange resonance of

130

the evening. I remember the overriding impression of a calm, quiet and gentle closing of a curtain on this chapter in my life.

The next morning, Day 52, the sun was shining brightly and helped to dry off a heavy load of dew on our tents. We had breakfast, prepared a sandwich lunch to eat partway out, and then left the cabin at 8:45 AM. Arriving at the end of Boulder Bay, the "Mud Dog Miserable Portage From Hell" proved its name again. The water was lower and we grounded out 30 feet from any firm ground. Rich, my canoe partner, got his boots sopping wet when he slipped and went jogging off through the shallow, arms waving for balance, to find a solid shore. We had a quick, floating lunch in our canoes as we pulled off into a patch of reeds before we reached the Moose River. The river was dramatically lower, by 9-12 inches, easily justifying Ron's vow to come back to the following week's Lac La Croix work via transit through Crane Lake, The portages were quite busy. Ron broke up one large group for a little lecture on separating out in small groups to make passage easier on other groups traveling in the opposite direction. Also, Ron chewed out a different group for moving someone else's 100-pound food pack down river and turning it in to Ron for his handling. Ron, in his official Forest Service regalia, briefly exploded, "Don't EVER move someone else's' packs, canoes, or equipment! You have no idea what the other individual's plans are and now the item is lost to the original party." Ron hauled it to where the miscreants had picked it up and left a note for the original owner.

We saw a bear cross the road near Buyck, had our traditional quick junk-food stop, and arrived back in Cook at the Ranger Station at 3:00 PM. Those three of us who were leaving got our final paychecks, a free Superior National Forest T-shirt, a Certificate of Appreciation, and a handshake from the top boss, Stewart. Then I made my rounds, saying goodbye and shaking their hand (or hopefully, can't remember now, giving Nikki a hug), to Ron,

Chad, Greg, Nikki. I gave Rich a ride to the trailer and bid the same to him. Derek saw me from inside and came storming out with a big eager grin to grasp my hand and say his piece. Nice bunch of people. As I said at the beginning, "It was to be a summer of life-altering experiences," and, at that point, was the grandest adventure of my life. I hit the road home.

Day 53, The following day, I was back at my company as a Corporate Engineer.

No vacation was now available to me until I put in another year of employment.

Postscript

When I made my arrangements with the company for time off and a leave of absence for my BWCAW Volunteer work, I was told by upper management to NEVER ask for such a favor again. After a long, slow year passed, I asked again. They denied my request. Having prepared for such a possibility, within two weeks I resigned from the company to join my wife in Idaho to tend to the needs of captive-bred young Peregrine Falcons being reintroduced in the wild at a remote site overlooking Hells Canyon. The next adventure had started.

Part 2 - Jean

Bald Eagle Nestwatch

Arizona

1993

PREVIEW

After a 10-day solo trip, driving from my Wisconsin home to Phoenix where I had been directed to check in at the Arizona Game and Fish Department, plus two nights camping during training with the Department, I and the other 20 Nestwatchers submitted to a "schoolyard pick" process to each find a partner. Avoided by the half dozen other women trainees, I ended up partnering with the other unchosen person, whereupon he and I were given a small camper parked in a government lot as our shelter. However, my Nestwatch partner and I soon found our first assigned nest had been abandoned by the eagles, and then the nest tree was pushed over by a flood.

Reassigned after only two weeks as a Nestwatcher, I awoke on the first morning after a rainy night at the new location, to find I was camped, in the back of my small Toyota pickup, on the emergency spillway of a dam behind which the water had risen eight feet overnight. I would be working for the next four months with three men, all at least a decade younger than me, a 49-year-old woman with two grown daughters and a currently-unemployed husband. Along with other members of my team of Nestwatchers, I would be camping and hiking February through mid-June with wild burros and rattlesnakes as neighbors, enduring dawn-to-dusk observation duties, copious note-taking, and detailed report-writing, on a schedule of 10 days on duty/4 days off, 1800 miles from my home and family.

INTRODUCTION

If you are at all familiar with Bald Eagles, you probably correctly associate them with water and fish. The basic term "eagle" refers to the larger hawks. The ten species of eagles in genus *Haliaeetus* form a subgroup that are known as sea eagles and fish eagles for the dominance of fish in their diets. Our national bird, the Bald Eagle, *Haliaeetus leucocephalus,* is one of the sea eagles, although Bald Eagles are not dependent on salt water habitats as the term sea eagle might suggest. The diet of all ten species is composed largely of fish, especially in the breeding season, but may also include small mammals, birds and, in winter, carrion.

The Bald Eagle, with a range from Alaska and Canada south through the continental United States and into northern Mexico, was adopted as the U.S. national symbol in 1782, at which time there may have been as many as 50,000 nesting pairs. By the late 1800s, declines in the eagles' prey species and habitats, plus shooting, had greatly reduced the population of Bald Eagles in the continental U.S. In 1940, realizing that the species was threatened with extinction, Congress passed The Bald Eagle Protection Act. Precipitous declines continued with the additional causes of lead-poisoning through consumption of waterfowl with lead shot in their tissues, and reproductive decline due to DDT. By 1963 there were only 487 nesting pairs.

As early as 1967, the Bald Eagle received protection in the U.S. from a pre-cursor to the Endangered Species Act (ESA). The ESA was passed in 1973, with the Bald Eagle included as one of the original species to be protected by this historic legislation. In 1978 Bald Eagles were listed as Endangered in 43 of the lower 48 states, and as Threatened in the other five states. Severe reduction in the use of DDT, along with other conservation measures, resulted in a comeback for Bald Eagles, and their status was downgraded to

Threatened in 1995. By 2006, surveys provided an estimate of 9,789 nesting pairs in the lower 48 states and delisting occurred in 2007. The 2021 Bald Eagle population in the lower 48 U.S. states is estimated at well over 316,000. However, this success was not as evident in the small population of the smaller, desert-nesting, non-migrating Bald Eagles in Arizona.

What does a person visualize, when the state of Arizona is mentioned? Deserts, mountains, the Grand Canyon? Since Arizona is 42% desert, it does not automatically seem suitable as Bald Eagle habitat. In fact, the state hosts most of the small United States population of desert-nesting Bald Eagles, sometimes considered a subspecies because of their smaller size and lack of the migratory habit. Their size is an adaptation to high temperatures; smaller size means a higher proportion of surface area to body mass, which increases heat loss and better adapts the eagles to their desert living conditions.

For Bald Eagles in Arizona, life is about water—water with a good supply of fish—and they choose to live along Arizona's rivers, lakes and reservoirs. Suitable Bald Eagle habitat also requires large trees or cliff sites where they can build their nests.

Bodies of water are not common in this big state—sixth largest in the United States—and by their very rarity, they are also valued by humans as places to live, and as destinations for recreational activities such as fishing, boating, swimming, off-roading, horseback-riding, hiking, and camping. The problem is that human activities near Bald Eagle nest sites can disrupt their reproduction by disturbing the eagles during incubation of eggs and care of the young, as well as by interfering with the eagles' ability to successfully catch fish and to hunt for other food for themselves and their young.

To address this problem, the Arizona Game and Fish Department (AZGFD) devised a program to both study and protect nesting Bald Eagles. This program involves establishing "closed areas" around those nests at risk of human disturbance, and hiring pairs of Nestwatchers for the at-risk nests during the eagle breeding season each year. Nestwatchers are tasked to inform the public about the closed areas, and to gather data about the eagles, their reproduction, behavior and food-gathering, and about threats to their nesting efforts.

The Arizona Bald Eagle Nestwatch Program began in a small way as early as 1978, first as a volunteer weekend activity. At that time only 11 breeding pairs were known. Less than 30 nesting pairs were found in Arizona in 1988, but this number had increased to 47 pairs by 2014, according to the project website (and other related sites). By 2021 the Arizona Bald Eagle population had been estimated as high as 74 breeding pairs by one non-AZGFD website.

In 1997, the Southwest Bald Eagle Management Committee included members representing the AZGFD, six federal agencies, a public utility, four Native American Tribes, and Arizona State Parks. The Nestwatch Program continues to the 2021 publication of this book, however, since the 2007 delisting of the Bald Eagle, funding has been more difficult for this very successful conservation program. In the period 1983-2004, Nestwatchers were responsible for the rescue of 46 nestlings, which represent ten percent of all the eaglets that fledged in the period. As plans for delisting developed, the Center for Biological Diversity, Maricopa Audubon, and others continued to press the case that the desert-nesting eagles in Arizona, with their non-migratory habit, smaller size, and earlier nesting season, were "isolated behaviorally, biologically, and ecologically" and that these factors should qualify them for continued listing, continued protection. [2005]

Jean, illustrating the terrain and hiking effort involved in her experiences as an Arizona Bald Eagle Nestwatcher, spring, 1993. (photo taken during the climb out of the "big wash" en route to the Hilltop Observation Point for the Ive's Wash Nest)

NATURE OF THE BALD EAGLE NESTWATCH JOB

Finding the Arizona Bald Eagle Nestwatch Job

If you have read my husband's and my first book of fieldwork adventures, *Seven Summers with Peregrines: Finding Midlife Adventures*, you already know that I love to do biology as well as teach it, especially to do ornithological fieldwork. You also know from that earlier book that, while my career had mainly been teaching lectures and labs for various biology courses at the University of Wisconsin-La Crosse, including the lectures and labs of the Ornithology course there, 1995-2002, my job was not tenured or very secure. In fact, my teaching contracts usually varied semester by semester and were often part-time, ranging the gamut from 25%, through 33%, 36%, 38%, 50%, 67%, 75%, and 88%, to scattered semesters of 100%. Before retirement, however, my last six years (12 continuous semesters) were full time, and by the end of my career, my salary had slowly risen to almost equal that of a high school teacher with similar years of experience and a master's degree. Scattered among my years as an instructor (Academic Staff Lecturer) at UW-La Crosse, however, were four spring semesters, 1979, 1986, 1993 and 1994, when I was without teaching contracts. In the first instance, I found a teaching job for spring quarter at Winona State University (then Winona State College). During spring semester, 1986, I was unemployed. By 1990, however, I had discovered fieldwork and was doing Peregrine reintroduction work each summer (1990-1996). For the spring semesters of 1993 and 1994, I was able to obtain other interesting fieldwork jobs to fill the gaps in my teaching career, and two of these are described in this book. The Arizona Bald Eagle Nestwatch job was the first of my "spring semester" field jobs.

Having originally found the Peregrine Falcon hack site attendant jobs by means of an advertisement in an issue of the "Ornithological Newsletter" loaned to me by a colleague, I returned to that publication in fall 1992 upon being told I would not be teaching in the UW-L Biology Department the following spring. This newsletter contained news, various announcements, requests for assistance, and listings of positions available, and was published by the American Ornithologists' Union for the members of this and the other three organizations of professional ornithologists. The advertisement for Bald Eagle Nestwatchers in the December 1992 issue stated in part:

> "ARIZONA BALD EAGLE Nestwatch Program. Arizona supports a small population of Desert-nesting Bald Eagles. Approximately 20 Nestwatchers will work in teams of two collecting information on nesting and foraging activities and habitat use, and monitoring disturbances near nests. Nestwatchers will be camping in the field, ... maintaining a ten-days on, four-days off schedule beginning the first week of February, and continuing into June. Nestwatchers must provide their own camping equipment and transportation (high clearance vehicle desired) to and from the field. If you are interested in contributing to the protection and recovery of this endangered species and gaining valuable field experience in the process, call or write,..."

I contacted AZ Game and Fish Department by mail and received a packet of information detailing the application process, which included submission of a lengthy (18 pages plus cover letter) grant application. At first, my husband, Gary, also expressed interest in this Arizona eagle job, but he was able to obtain a good, five-month contract for a consulting engineering job with his former employer that would cover almost the same period, so I sent in my application alone.

Getting to Arizona

Once I was accepted to the Nestwatch Program, I began organizing my gear, purchasing and preparing food supplies, making plans to be away from home for four and half months, and for traveling across country in winter. Since Gary would be staying home, one big concern was taken care of—keeping the home fires burning literally and figuratively—including responding to family needs. Our younger daughter was in college, the older one had graduated and married, but she and her husband were looking for work. An additional relevant circumstance affecting my plans was that, after eleven good years since diagnosis and treatment, my dad's cancer had returned. Considering Dad's condition at Christmas, I made a worry-fraught judgment that he would be "okay" while I was gone and that my mom would be able to manage whatever help he needed, an erroneous judgment as it turned out.

In 1990, our first year of fieldwork, Gary and I had separate jobs in widely-separated geographic locations. I was in Idaho for my first Peregrine release that summer, while he was in Minnesota working in the Boundary Waters Canoe Area Wilderness as described in the first section of this book. After 25 years of marriage, during which we had rarely been apart more than a day or two at a time, we found the 82-day separation in summer 1990 very challenging. Still, two and a half years later in late January 1993, we were about to separate again, for almost twice as long. To try to ease the actual good-bye, we decided to spend the night before the separation visiting good friends Sandy and Mike. Accordingly, we drove separate vehicles to their Iowa home, my small pickup with topper fully packed with all my gear and supplies for the Arizona eagle job. We had a good visit with our friends and they made us very welcome in their home, but the time was imbued with sadness for Gary and me at our impending good-bye. After a good breakfast, we said our thanks to Sandy and Mike and drove off, one behind the other. A few miles from their home, at the stop-signed intersection where our routes diverged, we engaged in one last hug and kiss and I admit to turning south in tears, while Gary turned north toward home and drove out of my rear-view-mirror sight.

From my Journal: Sunday, 24 January 1993
I am glad for the intensity of feeling to know how much Gary
means to me and how alive I am, but this goodbye was almost too
much for me. I think I had too long to think about it in advance.

Leaving our Midwest home on 23 January posed special travel problems. I packed a separate "visiting suitcase" and also sorted all supplies that might be damaged by freezing into containers that could ride up in the pickup cab with me, and be carried into the homes where I planned to stay the first several nights.

From my Journal: Sunday, 24 January 1993
While loading my truck, I fell on the ice, striking my knee on the
ground and my right cheekbone on the side of my truck.

After parting from Gary, my next planned stop, also in Iowa but several hours away, was at the home of my parents. As my sister, Patti, had arrived ahead of me on a visit to provide help and support to Mom and Dad, I also got to spend time with her.

From my Journal: Monday, 25 January 1993
I tried to talk to Dad about personal business, to find out if there's
anything he wanted help with, or anything I should do. I learned
more about where his banking is done, asked about his lawyer, and

he showed me where his will is kept. He brought out a tax credit form he wanted filled out and I helped him finish that.

Patti and I went along for Dad's bone scan, blood tests and checkup with the Oncologist. I saw the prescribed bone scan as bad news, but did not say that to Mom. I did not receive the results of Dad's tests until after a letter reached me in Arizona; they were not good results.

After three nights at the home of my parents, I drove next to visit our daughter and son-in-law, also in Iowa, where they were temporarily trapped in minimum-wage jobs while seeking jobs that would use their hard-earned college degrees (her bachelors, his masters). I stayed with them one night.

From my Journal: Thursday, 28 January 1993
Gayle helped me carry stuff down to my truck and I said yet another sad good-bye. Strange to have one's daughter comfort one: "It's only temporary, Mom."

After a long day of driving due south, I stopped in the southwest corner of Missouri, first for an afternoon visit with Gary's aunt, uncle, and one cousin, then to spend that night in the home of another of Gary's cousins and her husband. I was served wonderful home cooking, taken for a walk along their quiet back-country road, and given good directions for getting around Joplin MO and onto the Oklahoma Turnpike.

After these six nights in the homes of friends and family, I had finally gotten far enough south to try camping. In preparation for this, I had researched places to camp, paying special attention to whether the campgrounds I hoped to visit were open year-round. After leaving Missouri, I stayed one night in a state park in Oklahoma, one night at Palo Duro Canyon in the Texas panhandle, one night in New Mexico south of Albuquerque, and one night in northern Arizona before finally reaching Phoenix. These four nights of camping were cold, and the back of my small pickup was very full of gear and supplies. We had fashioned a narrow shelf above some of the gear, just under the topper roof with about 18-inches of clearance, and with some difficulty I crawled in each night to sleep on that shelf. At Foss State Park in Oklahoma on the night of 29 January, I was the only camper so the park ranger allowed me to park near the heated restroom building and I cooked and ate my supper and breakfast therein. That night I heard coyotes and Great Horned Owls and, in the morning found frost on the pickup's windshield, a testimony to the ranger's prediction of an overnight low temperature of about 18°F. After preparing my truck for departure, I spent a long while in the warm restroom building to prepare and eat my breakfast of instant cream-of-wheat cereal and green tea, and to catch up on my journal entries. I walked about the campground a bit that morning too, and added Carolina Chickadees to my trip bird list.

I found Palo Duro Canyon to be an expensive place to visit and camp, but beautiful, and I took a two-hour hike the afternoon I arrived there (30 January), finding Cedar Waxwings and American Robins, and seeing a coyote. The robins sang up the next morning's dawn, and I heard Wild Turkeys gobbling while I took an early walk to get some exercise before beginning another long day of driving.

In New Mexico, I visited Bosque del Apache National Wildlife Refuge, which I found to be a magical place. I talked to the rangers in the Visitor Center and saw Gambel's Quail just outside the building, then paid $2.00 to drive the 15-mile loop. I spent two hours on the loop, stopping often to observe birds and other wildlife.

From my Journal: Sunday, 31 January 1993
At the recommended spot near the exit, I stopped to watch and
listen to flocks of Snow Geese and Sandhill Cranes returning from
their daytime foraging in nearby fields to the refuge marshes for
the night. It was lovely in the fading evening light to hear their
wild calling and to see the flocks in flight against the darkening
sky. Somehow these sights and sounds evoked in my mind an
earlier time, when the effect of humans on the earth and its other
creatures was less.

As darkness fell, I drove north to camp in Senator William Chanez
State Park, chosen merely for its convenient location. The next
morning, there was frost on the truck again. After heating water to
both fill my thermos, and to make a cup of soup, I set off driving
again. The soup, along with a can of mandarin oranges served as
my breakfast that day, the day I would finally reach Arizona.

It was the first of February when I arrived in northern Arizona and
found several inches of fresh snow in Flagstaff, causing me to
worry about my plan to camp that evening. Fortunately, the snow
disappeared as I descended the 3000 feet from Flagstaff to
Cottonwood, but there I found Dead Horse Ranch State Park, a
place where we had camped on a family vacation several years
earlier, closed due to flooding. I stayed instead at Turquoise
Triangle RV Park in Cottonwood, where I enjoyed a hot shower
and read in the heated lounge in the evening.

From my Journal: Tuesday, 2 February 1993
I was awakened at 5:30 AM by roosters that apparently live free-
range in this private campground, crowing in the pines by the
restroom building—I saw them go to roost there last evening and I,
farm girl and woman that I was and am, thought nothing of it! The
roosters were joined in this well-before-sunrise chorus for a long
time by a pair of Great Horned Owls.

148

<u>Job Training</u>

Upon arrival in Phoenix the next day, I checked in at a formerly-KOA campground, again a place where we had stayed during our family vacation in 1982. In the intervening years it had deteriorated to apartment-alternative housing for families. Its location was convenient, but it was an expensive and noisy place to camp. I called home to report my arrival in Phoenix, read another chapter in a book I had brought along, *Eagles of the World*, studied again the materials mailed to me about the Nestwatch job, and prepared a day-pack for the next day.

Through my previous birding experiences, four Peregrine Falcon Hack Site Attendant jobs, the Nestwatch informational materials provided by ASGFD, and my other readings about eagles, I was well aware that Bald Eagle males, as is the case in many other species of raptors including Peregrines, are significantly smaller than the females. There are a number of theories about why this sexual size dimorphism developed in raptors: having the female larger facilitates her ability to hunt while developing eggs during the reproductive season; since she is larger, she is less likely to suffer aggression from the male; different-sized adults can specialize in different-sized prey, reducing competition between them and increasing prey possibilities. In any case, the significant size difference made it relatively easy for us, as Nestwatchers, to identify the sex of any eagle we were observing.

Training began Wednesday, 3 February, with meeting the man to whom we would direct our questions and turn in our data sheets and reports; his title was Bald Eagle Management Coordinator, but we referred to him as our Nestwatch boss. Next, a cap and notebook were issued to each newly-arrived Nestwatcher, and we were asked to each briefly introduce ourselves. I said I had been teaching for some years and wanted to go beyond teaching the subject, and <u>do</u> some biology. We then were sorted into cars and drove out to visit a nest site where the eagles had begun nesting early and Nestwatchers had already been on duty for a month. We were given a briefing about enforcement of nest-closure areas and about all the forms on which we would be required to record our observations. We were also given special photo-ID cards with which to identify ourselves to the public, when enforcing nest-closure areas or explaining about the Nestwatch project and our duties. These looked very official with a photo, the name, weight, height, and Social Security number of the individual Nestwatcher. During a break, we ate the food we had each brought along and tried to get acquainted. Some of the group made plans to camp together, but Kathy, one of the few other female Nestwatchers, elected to come back to the RV park and share a site with me.

On 4 February we attended an all-day classroom presentation at the Bureau of Reclamation offices, about the job and the information that had been learned about desert-nesting Bald Eagles during previous Nestwatch Program years. We were shown slides and given information about the nest sites that needed watchers, so we could choose a site to work. During all these training processes, Nestwatchers began to pair up, and Kathy and the other females, all much younger than me, made sure they did not get me for a partner. I had assumed I would be able to find a partner among the other women, but they were all young, and most of them seemed to be hoping to find a young man for a partner. The process of choosing a partner reminded me uncomfortably of the schoolyard-pick system, used for example to choose softball teams in junior high gym class—if you were not a good ball player, you would among the last to be chosen. In this case too, one young man and I were overlooked by everyone else, and eventually Peter and I turned to each other and asked if we were each willing to work with the other.

From my Journal: Thursday, 4 February 1993
This partner selection process was unpleasant; I hope to learn
from it and not do it again. It remains to be seen how Peter and I
will work together. Site selection was just as difficult. It was a case
of being chosen almost last for a softball game, and trying not to
get stuck with the worst-sounding site.

In the late afternoon we were given a break and dispersed to run errands and get groceries before reconvening at the program director's home for supper. I found it a long evening to endure. One woman, trying to be kind, I suppose, to the obviously-older woman present, asked me what grade I taught. I have encountered that thoughtless assumption on other occasions and take a kind of perverse pleasure in setting people back with, "I teach biology at the University of Wisconsin-La Crosse." Not that this helped anyone there relate to me. After the "social," Kathy and I followed Peter out Carefree Hwy to a spot he knew, where we could camp free in the desert, each sleeping out on the ground.

In the 1993 season, twenty-one Nestwatchers were teamed up to cover twelve nests, albeit one nest, Camp Verde, where Peter and I were first assigned, was under observation only ten days. There were four of us (3 males, 1 female) working the Alamo Cliff and Ive's Wash Nests after Peter and I were taken off the eagle-less Camp Verde nest, and a team of three (all males) watching the Ft. McDowell and Orme nests. Two Nestwatchers were assigned each at the Bartlett, Cliff, Ladders, Pleasant, 76, Sheep and Tonto nests; of these, two teams were made up of men, one team was composed of two women, and the remaining four pairs of Nestwatchers were mixed teams. According to a Nestwatch newsletter dated 22 Feb 1993 and my journal notes, the 1993 totals thus were: seven female and 14 male Nestwatchers. A modicum of uncertainty, however, arises from two given names that do not clearly reveal gender.

TIMELINE OVERVIEW

Journey from home to Phoenix: 23 January – 2 February

Nestwatch Training: 3-5 February

Camp Verde Nest assignment & eagle surveys: 5-14 February
Off duty: 15-18 February, I stayed at the Camp Verde trailer

Phoenix Meeting and reassignment to Ive's Wash and Alamo
nests: 19 February
[Scott & GC had already been on Nestwatch duty from 5 January.
The Alamo eagles started nesting in a tree on the southeast side of
the lake, but heavy rains threatened that nest; two eggs had been
rescued by AZGFD and taken to the Phoenix Zoo 8 January and all
three tree nests previously used by the pair were under water by 16
January. The Alamo eagles had begun a new nest on a cliff located
on the northwest side of the lake by 17 January.]

Ive's Wash Nest Observations: 22 February – 10 May

Alamo Cliff Nest Observations: 20 February – 14 June

My off-duty dates and activities:
1-4 March, at Alamo Lake area
15-22 March, to AZGFD in Phoenix, visited friends in Tucson,
        flew "home" to Iowa to visit my dad in hospital
29 March – 4 April, visited Hassayampa River Preserve (Nature
        Conservancy), flew to Iowa for my dad's funeral

Gary's April visit: 8-20 April

Off duty dates and activities continued:
12-15 April, Gary and I toured southeast Arizona

26-30 April, I drove to L.A. to visit cousin Janis

10-13 May, but I stayed on duty to observe Ive's Wash fledgling eaglets below Ive's Wash Nest 10-11 May, then

12-13 May, to Wenden, Wickenburg, and Hassayampa, and

13-14 May, to Coconino Forest near Camp Verde for Willow Flycatcher survey training

24-27 May, worked on report in camp, to AZGFD office in Phoenix, volunteered at Hassayampa

7-10 June, but observed eagles 7-8 June, then

9-10 June, to Hassayampa & Phoenix, met Gary's plane

Willow Flycatcher Surveys: 2-3 and 8 June

Trip home:

14-20 June, including visit with Scott in Flagstaff, my mom in Iowa

Alamo Cliff Nest eaglet, the day it was banded by AZGFD biologists

LOCATION OVERVIEW

Phoenix AZ is the location of the Arizona Game and Fish Department (AZGFD) office, where Nestwatchers met for training, and returned on days off to turn in interim data sheets and rough drafts of reports, and to pick up paychecks.

The Camp Verde Nest was beside the Verde River just outside the town of Camp Verde in Yavapai County, Arizona. Camp Verde is located about 90 road miles north of Phoenix.

Alamo Lake is on the border between two Arizona counties, Mohave County to the north and La Paz County to the south. Alamo Dam is at the southwest end of the lake; Alamo Lake State Park is along the south side of the lake. Alamo Lake is about 136 miles northwest of Phoenix by the most direct route.

The Alamo Eagles began the 1993 nesting season with a nest in a tree on the south side of Alamo Lake. After rising waters destroyed that nest, they built a new nest on a cliff on the north side of the lake, referred to herein as the Alamo Cliff Nest. This pair of eagles claimed as their territory about 2/3 of the upper end of Alamo Lake and the land bordering that portion of the lake, and along the lower Big Sandy and Santa Maria Rivers at the upstream end of the lake.

The Ive's Wash Eagles nested on a cliff on the south side of the Bill Williams River canyon below Alamo Dam. This pair of eagles hunted and fished the lower portion of Alamo Lake and the Bill Williams River below Alamo Dam, as well as adjacent lands bordering these waters.

From Alamo Lake State Park to Wenden, Arizona, (the nearest post office) was about 38 miles (plus a couple extra miles from our spillway campsite). Alamo Lake to Wickenburg was about 85 miles (about 47 miles beyond Wenden), and Phoenix was a further 66 miles beyond Wickenburg (153 miles from our spillway camp below Alamo Lake by that route). It was shorter (about 136 miles) to go more directly, but I often did laundry and shopping in Wickenburg, and visited and volunteered at the Hassayampa Nature Preserve on my days off. If it was my turn to go on to Phoenix to the AZGFD offices to turn in data summaries and report drafts, make copies, and pick up our mail and paychecks, it meant driving the longer route in at least one direction.

Hassayampa Nature Preserve is about four miles south of Wickenburg, Arizona, just off the road from Wickenburg to Phoenix.

Part of Camp Verde Ranger Station, showing shop
building and the small trailer assigned to Peter and me

Verde River in flood and Bald Eagle nest—not very large
as it was new—which was about to be swept away

CAMP VERDE NEST – U.S. FOREST SERVICE, PRESCOTT NATIONAL FOREST DISTRICT

The First Assignment

From my Journal: Friday, 5 February 1993
Woke in the desert just after 7 AM, took a private moment in the bushes. Stuffed our bedrolls into our vehicles, then Kathy, Peter and I started up the road in caravan, with one stop for gas/coffee/restrooms. Arrived quite early at the Camp Verde exit MacDonald's where we read, wrote letters, etc. as we waited for John, who didn't arrive until after 10 AM. We all went to the Post Office to set up "General Delivery" to receive our mail while working in this area, deciding against renting a mailbox. We then went to the USFS Verde District Office, to be introduced to staff there and showed around. Spent <u>five hours</u> there when it could have been accomplished in one (my opinion), were issued keys radios, a truck (for Kathy and John), a camper-trailer (for Peter and me), address cards, maps, and volunteer forms we had to sign. Finally, we took our trucks across the road to the shop side of the Verde District compound, and Peter and I talked to Mark, the District soils guy, while John and Kathy selected and loaded gear to set up their camp.

There were two Bald Eagle nests in the Camp Verde vicinity; Kathy and John were assigned to the "Ladders" nest, south of town. Peter and I were assigned to the new nest that had been discovered beside the river near town the year before, with an unbanded pair of Bald Eagles and two eggs. Those 1992 eggs failed to hatch and the eagles abandoned the nest. One eagle was seen near the nest later in the summer of 1992, and a pair was observed in the area that September, so the nest was included on the 1993 pre-nesting season aerial survey. It is characteristic of Bald Eagles to add more sticks to their nests each year; eventually, a nest may become so large and heavy, that the tree branches holding it finally break. During the 1993 pre-nesting survey, new sticks were noticed on the nest, hence our assignment to monitor it. During a January storm, however, the river level had risen, toppled several trees in the vicinity, and water surrounded the nest tree, undermining its roots.

The offices of Camp Verde Ranger District consisted of two fenced compounds across a road from each other. Several buildings and two office trailers on one side contained most of the offices, a compound for USFS vehicles, and a parking area. The main building had a lobby and receptionist, restrooms, a copy machine, and refrigerator, as well as several offices. The District had quite a few employees, including specialists in biology, archaeology, grazing, recreation, enforcement, and fire-fighting, for example, plus a variety of support staff.

In our compound on the other side of the roadway were a small building that included an office for the soils guy, a large maintenance building with a desk for the maintenance man, a wood-burning stove, and a bathroom. Next to the maintenance building was a small camper trailer for temporary workers like us.

After our orientation to the Camp Verde District of the U. S. Forest Service (USFS), the jurisdiction in which both the Ladders and Verde River nests were located, Forest Service personnel took the four of us Nestwatchers on a tour of the active nest site in the district where Kathy and her partner would be working. Known as the Ladders nest, it was on a cliff overlooking the Verde River several miles south of town; when we arrived on 5 February, the Nestwatchers' campsite was partially ready. The camp included a large, old, wall tent, which was already set up, a full-sized, gas-powered refrigerator, and a fiberglass outhouse. The latter was laying on its side beside a barely-started latrine pit. Kathy and John faced a great deal of work to develop this site into a decent camp.

The small camper trailer assigned to Peter and me was parked in one of the fenced District compounds in the town of Camp Verde, with a gate that was closed and locked at night and on weekends; we were given keys to the gate and the trailer. Late that afternoon, Peter and I were shown our nest site a few miles from town, but saw no eagles there, so we returned to town and moved into our trailer to make supper and write out notes about our first, brief observation period. We had to use the bathroom in the District shop building beside which the trailer was parked, and carry in our water supply, since the trailer's plumbing was not connected. We were allowed to take showers in the main building across the road. The trailer consisted of a single room that included a tiny kitchen/dining area and two narrow bunks. Initially, I felt a bit awkward to be sharing this space with a 29-year-old man I had just met, but Peter was very matter-of-fact about it and made it easy.

Our first "dawn-to-dusk" period of duty, 6 February, was spent working out a record-keeping system and dutifully watching all day for eagles, but seeing none. We began our site bird list and also started to develop a dislike of this site, with boats going by on the river before us, vehicles on the road behind us, and a bulldozer, backhoe, and chainsaw each noisily in use to repair an irrigation ditch, as close to the nest as 150 meters. Boaters stopped along the bank for picnics, as close as 20 meters from the nest tree. It seemed to us a very inauspicious site for a Bald Eagle nest, or for Nestwatchers. We could hear roosters, donkeys, horses, dogs, even peacocks, and guineafowl, from our Observation Point (O.P.), not at all the kind of habitat in which we had hoped to work There was frost at dawn, sun to combat the mid-day breeze, and a chilly evening that first day, frost again the next morning, and several rainy days during this first 10-day work period.

Our Nestwatch instructions stated that we would be required to be on-site 24-hours a day for the ten-day periods, and that five of those days would require dawn-to-dusk observations. To serve that end, we got up early and brought along foods to be able to eat our breakfasts and lunches while on duty. On that first full day of work, we discovered how very <u>long</u> a dawn-to-dusk duty would seem, even in early February when the days were not actually very long yet. With no eagles to watch, sitting still in small camp chairs out in the field during the cold days was tedious, to say the least. Not thrilled with "camping" in a trailer in town, Peter thought he would look for a spot to set up a tent near our O.P. and camp out at least some nights. However, the unattractiveness of the nest vicinity, and the lack of eagles, caused him to give up this idea.

The only breaks in those first long days of observation at the Camp Verde nest (6-7 February) were short walks taken separately by Peter and me, but these walks helped us with the additional required task of observing and listing birds (33 species in the ten days we were on watch here) and mammals (only beavers and desert cottontails) for the nest site area. I had brought along a shovel and used it to dig a small, several-day latrine for myself in the vicinity of our Observation Point. Having developed the technique of reading or writing in very short stints, interrupted frequently to look for our charges, while serving as a Peregrine Falcon Hack Site Attendant, I had brought along a book and writing materials. This helped me pass the time, and allowed me to get letters and postcards written to send home.

From my Journal: Sunday, 7 February 1993
Peter confesses to some restlessness, and to not realizing how sedentary this job would be. (As an experienced Hack Site Attendant for Peregrines, I had expected this aspect of Nestwatching.) We had a Ferruginous Hawk to identify and to watch as it circled above the city, and we determined from our books and Nestwatch materials, that this is a threatened species in Arizona, and must be reported on our data sheets.

160

The only other available tasks were note-taking about being on-site and observing no eagles, about our methods, characteristics of the site, and the extensive human activity nearby, which on the river included boating, fishing and picnicking. These and other details would be needed when we wrote up the required report at the end of our ten days of duty at this site.

No Eagles – the Nest Is Abandoned

On Monday, 8 February, Peter called our boss at AZGFD in Phoenix to report our lack of eagles, the road construction going on near the nest site, and other disturbances that may have caused the eagles to abandon this nest, as well as the flood-caused loss of other trees adjacent to the nest tree, and erosion of soil around the nest tree's roots. He told us to keep checking the site for eagles, but let us off the dawn to dusk intensity. He also okayed the eagle survey work the Forest Service wanted us to do. For this work we were given information about previous surveys, maps of the survey locations we were to cover, and were able to check out a Forest Service green truck.

From my Journal: Monday, 8 February 1993
To the Branding Iron Café for pie and report-writing. Rain continues, three inches and a flooding forecast. Back to the Forest Service compound about 5 PM to build up the fire in the shop stove and sit by its heat to read and write.

The weather during this period was often rainy. During the wettest days, we spent an hour or two sitting in one of our vehicles, parked along the road as close to our O.P. as possible, to check for eagles at the nest, and worked on our data forms and reports in the city library. The USFS shop had a wood-burning stove, and sometimes Del, the man who worked therein, lit a nice fire to warm the building. He allowed us to add a bit of wood to keep the fire going

in the evenings, making our use of the bathroom in the shop
building more comfortable too. I liked to sit in the shop in the
evenings to write letters and journal entries as it was warmer by
that stove than in our trailer, unless we used an electric heater
and/or had the little kitchen gas stove lit for cooking.

Bald Eagle Survey Work

Thereafter followed a happy period of ranging outward from Camp
Verde to look for eagles, circling back to observe at our nest a
couple times each day, interspersed with periods of paperwork to
record our survey efforts and the mostly negative results of those
efforts. We spent time in the city library to read the reports of
previous surveys, talked to a ranger who could point out the
locations of previous eagle sightings on maps, and then organized
a series of outings over six days, 8-13 February. On two different
days, we did find one adult eagle each in two different locations.
One eagle, foraging a few miles from Kathy and John's nest, was
probably a member of that pair. We sighted the other eagle far
from any known nest, but despite making two lengthy hikes in that
area, our searches for a nest, or even a suitable nest site, were
unsuccessful. Nevertheless, both Peter and I thoroughly enjoyed all
the hiking and exploration involved in these eagle surveys.

As a side benefit of the eagle surveys, which were much more to
Peter's liking than sitting all day long beside a spotting scope
aimed at an empty nest, we enjoyed general exploration of the
Camp Verde area, finding a wild honey bee colony in a tiny cave
and a Great Horned Owl on a nest in another small cave. We were
fortunate that our eagle surveys took us to such interesting places
as Montezuma's Castle National Monument, Beasley Flats
Recreation Area, Dead Horse Ranch State Park, and Peck's Lake.
Both Peter and I enjoyed birding, especially along Clear Creek and
Beaver Creek, other places visited during our eagle surveys.

Peter discovered there would be a "send-off" breakfast for the all-female Pony Express commemorative riders on Thursday, 11 February, before they set off to ride from Camp Verde to Wickenburg, an event sponsored annually by the local saddle club. He and I attended the breakfast, ate biscuits, sausage and gravy (new for me) for $2.50 each, and listened to the entertainment: a western singer/guitarist accompanied by a bass player. We did not stay for the square dancers, going instead to the USFS office to sign out a pickup and head out for another eagle survey.

On Friday morning, 12 February, we were sent by the USFS to purchase sealant, and assigned to paint it on the roof of "our" trailer. However, at the local hardware store, the sealant was available only in five-gallon buckets—much more than we would need for the job—so we did not buy it. After spending most of the day doing an eagle survey, we went back to the office in the late afternoon to report. Fortunately for us, the coming weekend, our impending first period of days off (Mon. 15-Thurs. 18 February), and our subsequent re-assignment to another nest site prevented us from executing the unappealing task of painting sealant on the trailer roof.

Because Sunday, 14 February, was rainy, we observed our nest that morning from inside a vehicle parked at the closest point on the road, and then drove out to visit Kathy and John for 90 minutes. It was a pleasure to be able to observe an active nest and a pair of eagles. We saw a nest exchange between the adults, and learned how this observation was recorded. We also observed a small plane that flew by at a low altitude, and four kayaks on the river below, all of which had to be recorded as disturbances in the overwhelming paperwork. Kathy and John had been suffering from camping and observing their nest in the cold and wet weather conditions, and were amazed at all the different things we had been doing.

Back to Phoenix – Required Meeting, 19 February

During our 10-day observation period at Camp Verde, we saw no eagles at this nest, rainy weather continued, and the nest tree became surrounded by water. On 14 February, the day before we began our first four-day off-duty period, Peter called the Game and Fish office in Phoenix and was told we were to be re-assigned to another site called Orme, starting with our next 10-day duty period on Friday, 19 February. Accordingly, we borrowed the Biosystems Report from the USFS office to read about the Orme site. We were also to attend a meeting in Phoenix on the 19th. Eventually, we learned that a week after we left Camp Verde, another rainstorm and further flooding swept away the nest tree, which had been our first Nestwatch location. We produced a 7-page report for the Camp Verde nest assignment.

Peter typed the report we had written together, and we were invited to a pot luck lunch in the Verde District office on Tuesday, 16 February. We also had to turn in USFS equipment and our eagle survey report. Once both reports were completed and the equipment signed back in to the Forest Service District, Peter planned to use this first off-duty period to further explore the Camp Verde area since we would soon be leaving, and was joined in this by his friend, Sandy, for a couple days. I, however, decided to stay in the trailer until I had to drive to Phoenix for the meeting on the 19[th,] rather than do any exploring on my own.

The last two nights, 17 and 18 February, I was alone in the trailer, catching up on various tasks and enjoying a quiet time of reflection before our impending transfer to another nest site. I used this off-duty time to hike downtown to a laundromat, take change-of-address cards for both of us to the Camp Verde Post Office, shop for groceries and personal items, write letters, clean the shop bathroom and the trailer, and read. I also did "small laundry" with my plastic bucket-and-plunger method, working in the shop shower stall so any spills could drain away. I even put up a clothes line behind the shop and hung my t-shirts to dry. I liked visiting in the shop with Del—about teaching, "the wreck of the earth by humans," Arizona and the Verde valley—very interesting conversations. From Camp Verde, I called Mom and Dad to say Peter and I would be moving to another eagle site in another part of Arizona, and also called Gary. I told them I would have to give them my new mail address later, to write me in the meantime in care of the AZ Game and Fish Department's Phoenix address.

On Friday, 19 February, I woke early, ate a light breakfast, swept out the trailer, loaded the last items into my truck and drove it outside the gate, locked the gate, and walked the keys and my trash across the road to the USFS office before setting off down Interstate 17. It rained all the way to Phoenix, but it was warm enough not to cause ice in the pass. I made the drive alone, met Peter and the other Nestwatchers at Game and Fish. The meeting involved standing in a circle with the other Nestwatchers in the parking lot, asking questions about procedures, and learning from both each other's questions, and the boss's answers.

Reassignment

At the Phoenix meeting, Peter and I were startled to learn of a change in plan; it had been decided to send two other Nestwatchers to Orme, and to send Peter and me to Alamo Lake to team with Scott and GC, who were monitoring two nests there. This would allow our days-off to be staggered with those of Scott and GC so there would always be two Nestwatchers on duty to enforce the closed areas around the nests. Furthermore, Scott and GC had started work in early January, a month before us, and would both be leaving before nesting was completed for other summer jobs, while Peter and I would be able to continue as Nestwatchers into June as needed.

From my Journal: Friday, 19 February 1993
We followed GC and Scott to the Wenden AZ Post Office where we arranged for General Delivery mail, and then to Alamo Lake. Met the Army Corps people and drove to the Nestwatch campsite. Organized my truck for sleeping, and I made CJ's [1990 Peregrine hack site partner] *"Farmer's Breakfast" recipe, which we ate on tortillas. Put a tarp over the tailgate in a hurry and it rained all night and was windy.*

From my Journal: Saturday, 20 February 1993
We are now camped not in a gravel parking lot, as I was told, but on the sloping emergency spillway of Alamo Dam! My truck is in gear with the emergency brake on, and I have placed rocks under the front wheels; it also has two mousetraps in the engine compartment, per my teammates' advice. I seemed to hear mice in the night trying to get in.

First dawn-to-dusk day at Alamo: we lined four scopes up on the spillway near our row of parked trucks. The rain finally quit and the sky is clear, temperature 47°, and it is windy. The only discernable sound is the 5000 cfs outflow from the dam far below in the canyon of the Bill Williams River, loud enough to drown out most other sounds. Ate breakfast on duty, watched Ive's Wash eagles...

Spillway camp, with all four of our pickups at the edge.
Ive's Wash nest on left, a mile down the canyon

Spillway O.P., Ive's Wash Nest is down canyon. Jean
sitting under the shade tarp, camp kitchen area at her left

ALAMO LAKE AND IVE'S WASH – US ARMY CORPS OF ENGINEERS, BUREAU OF LAND MANAGEMENT and ALAMO LAKE STATE PARK

Alamo Lake

Alamo Lake is an impoundment, about five miles long and perhaps a mile wide at the greatest point, and covers approximately 5000 acres, although its size is highly variable, depending on annual rainfall and water releases through the dam. The lake is oriented northeast (the input end) to southwest (the dam and outlet end). A locked gate closed off the access road to the dam; the chain that bound the gate closed consisted of several short pieces held together with different padlocks. We Nestwatchers each had a key to one of the padlocks, the dam tenders had keys to a different padlock, and so on, a separate padlock for each agency that needed access. To reach our spillway camp, we drove across atop the dam.

The Alamo Lake dam is a 283-foot-tall earth-fill, flood-control dam, completed in 1969 by the Army Corps of Engineers at a cost of $15 million. The dam is located in La Paz County, at an elevation of 1266 ft. at the top of the dam. The data upon which plans were based proved, already in the first dozen years, to be inadequate, since in just those few years the area experienced three "100-year rains," one "300-year rain," and one "500-year rain," as defined by the data. I was told during a tour of the "dam house" (inside the dam) that the release gates and main spillway especially, are inadequate. During one period of flooding since the dam's construction, the water level in Alamo Lake rose a record eleven feet overnight. During my first night camped on the spillway, the lake rose eight feet. On 4 March, the day of my tour, the impoundment (lake) area was 46% full by volume. The dam manager explained that he planned to lower the lake level as quickly as possible, as soon as Painted Rock Dam on the Gila River stopped overflowing and causing flooding in Yuma AZ and

168

further downstream in Mexico. The Gila River enters the Colorado River at Yuma AZ, about 160 river miles south of where the Bill Williams River does. I found all this very interesting.

Alamo Lake is fed by the Big Sandy River from the north and the Santa Maria River from the east, and the latter river had a good "gallery forest" along its banks at the lower end near the lake. Gallery forests are those that grow as corridors along rivers (or wetlands) and project into adjacent landscapes that are otherwise sparsely treed—into the desert in this case—where without the water of the river, trees could not grow. After the confluence of the above rivers, the watercourse flowing into Alamo Lake and beyond the Alamo dam is known as the Bill Williams River, which eventually flows into the Colorado River downstream (south) of Lake Havasu City, Arizona. The lake itself is located on the border between Mohave and La Paz Counties of Arizona.

The presence of this lake and its rivers in the desert provides water for life, and good territories for nesting pairs of Bald Eagles, as well as enticing humans to the area for a variety of recreational activities. Alamo Lake had been stocked with several fish species, including large-mouthed bass, crappie, sunfish, channel catfish, flathead catfish, and tilapia. The Alamo Lake State Park campgrounds are large and well-used during the cool "winter" months. It was to study Bald Eagles and protect their nests from disturbances by all these human activities in the area that we Nestwatchers were assigned there.

One pair of Bald Eagles nested adjacent to Alamo Lake, and are designated herein as the Alamo Eagles. A second pair of Bald Eagles nested in the canyon of the Bill Williams River below Alamo Dam. The two pairs peacefully divided the lake and were never seen to dispute each other's rights to hunt and fish in their separate portions of the lake and its surrounding lands.

Ive's Wash

What does the term "wash" mean when used for a feature of the desert habitats where we worked? A wash is linear, as is typical of streams, but desert washes typically lack running water during long periods in average years. Nevertheless, the character of a wash, by its appearance, clearly indicates that it is a habitat chronically disturbed by water. Washes concentrate water and nutrients from the large areas that they drain, thus serving as good habitat and as dispersal corridors for both plants and animals. Ive's Wash, located on the south side of the Bill Williams River below Alamo Dam, was the feature used to name the Bald Eagle nesting territory below the dam. On the opposite side of the river, closer to the dam, was another, larger wash we usually referred to as "the big wash," which was important to us, first as an obstacle we had to cross in some of the long hikes necessitated by our work, and later as excellent birding habitat. A desert wash can also be dangerous if you are in one when a sudden rush of water comes down it from a cloudburst on its drainage area upstream. This never happened to us, but we knew about the danger and that we had to be aware of weather conditions in the surrounding area for our safety.

New Nests to Watch, More Partners

At Alamo Lake, Nestwatchers Scott and GC had been on duty since 5 January by which time incubation of two eggs in one of the tree nests by the lake was already under way, and they were able to alert the Game and Fish Department when heavy rains caused rising water levels in the lake to threaten this eagle nest as it became surrounded by the expanding lake. The two eggs were recovered by Game and Fish personnel on 8 January when water was only a few feet below the nest, and the nest went under on 16 January. The eggs were transported to Phoenix for incubation at the Phoenix Zoo, where one egg eventually hatched successfully.

Meanwhile, the Alamo Lake eagles had briefly tried to make use of their other two tree nests; however, both of those trees were also inundated by the rising waters. By 17 January, the Alamo Lake pair had begun a new nest on a cliff above the lake—the Alamo Cliff Nest. The female subsequently laid a single egg in the new nest, and was observed on 14 February to be incubating that egg.

Below the dam that holds back the water to form Alamo Lake, another pair of eagles, known as the Ive's Wash pair, were also nesting on a cliff, and as this nest had one hatchling of suitable age, it was planned to foster the eaglet from the zoo-hatched Alamo Lake egg into the Ive's Wash Nest to be reared by that pair along with their own eaglet.

When the Alamo eagles were using one of their tree nests beside the lake (nest #2 of three tree nests in the territory of the Alamo pair), GC and Scott were able to observe the nest from an O.P. above the dam, at an observation distance of about one mile. This observation point was fairly convenient to the spillway campsite from which they were also observing the Ive's Wash Nest. When the new Alamo Cliff Nest (designated nest #4 of this pair even though all three tree nests they had formerly used were destroyed by high water in January, 1993) was built, the observation distance across the late from a different O.P., was about three miles. A much closer observation point would need to be established, but this necessitated using a boat to traverse most of the length of the lake and across to the other side.

Because of all this unusual eagle activity, having two nests to monitor, and the abundant human activity on and around Alamo Lake, more Nestwatchers were needed to work with Scott and GC. The Nestwatch situation at the Alamo Cliff Nest was further complicated by the additional time and effort required to find a boat to borrow and to motor about five miles up and across the lake to reach the new O.P. within decent observational distance from the Alamo Cliff Nest. For these reasons, and because of the potential for fostering a zoo-hatched eaglet into the Ive's Wash Nest, AZGFD assigned Peter and me to work with Scott and GC, starting 19 February. Before GC and Scott left the team for their summer field jobs, they took their 4-day off periods in opposite weeks from Peter and me, ensuring that two Nestwatchers were always on duty at Alamo Lake in the early critical periods. Before leaving, they worked hard to bring the Alamo Lake and Ive's Wash paperwork up to date, and to start preparing the reports for both nests; Peter and I would be responsible for continuing observations through fledging of the three eaglets, and for finishing both reports.

The paperwork burden was heavy for Nestwatchers: there were forms on which to enter field notes, a daily summary form, a forage form, prey identification form, disturbance (to nest area or eagles) form, low-flying aircraft form, interaction (of eagles with other organisms) form, 10-day summary form, bird sighting form, and rare animal form. And, there were 23 pages of instructions for completing these forms! In addition, we were provided seven pages of instructions on Nestwatch report-writing, and these instructions informed us that we would be required to regularly submit preliminary data, and drafts of sections of our reports for critical comments and editing suggestions, and that changes had to be approved and reports completed before final paychecks would be issued.

Additional information provided to Nestwatchers included a 10-page article on the "Ecology of Bald Eagles in Arizona," a map of Bald Eagle nest locations in the state, a page of diagrams to help us identify fish being carried in the talons of eagles toward their nests, and 34 pages of information about Endangered, Threatened, and Species of Concern of native Arizona wildlife. It is from information laboriously recorded year after year on these many forms by Nestwatchers, and the information in the reports derived from all our notes and forms, that each year the Game and Fish Department could review the successes and problems of the Nestwatch Program, and work to improve it.

Although the gravel-covered spillway sounds like an unattractive place to camp for several months, there were several advantages: the sparse vegetation made it easier for us to spot and avoid rattlesnakes, the ground surface was fairly even for walking, and there were no large rocks or other obstacles. Journal comments written my first day on the spillway make it clear I already found the location attractive.

From my Journal: Saturday, 20 February 1993
There are saguaro and barrel cacti, paloverde and blooming brittlebush (Encelia farinosa) nearby. We hear hummingbirds courting and the swallows have returned. Wild burros called early this morning and Rock and Canyon Wrens are singing. It's very beautiful here, and certainly remote.

At our new assignment, Peter and I were plunged at once into the work of observing two nests, splitting the tasks with GC and Scott in pairs and alternating our days off. The dawn-to-dusk observation days were always on weekends (every Saturday and Sunday for all four of us plus, alternating pairs on Fridays); weekends were when the chance of human disturbances was greatest. Since Peter and I were new to the job at Alamo Lake, Scott and GC had to show us around. They had already set up camping on the spillway site and worked out some locations from which to observe the Ive's Wash Nest below the dam, and the Alamo Cliff Nest above the dam. Their original O.P., used for observing the Alamo pair's tree nest, was about a 3-mile distance from the new Alamo Cliff Nest. Therefore, GC and Scott found a new O.P. location with a viewing distance of about half as much, but it required us to look across the lake at the new cliff nest. Later, after the new egg hatched, it would be necessary for us to cross the lake by boat to yet another O.P., one from which it would be possible to more closely observe the development of the eaglet in the Alamo Cliff Nest.

The Ive's Wash Nest, located on a cliff above the Bill Williams River in its canyon below the dam, could be observed from our camp on the spillway about a mile away. An advantage of this site was that the eagles often caught fish or other prey, including birds such as grebes, from the lake and then flew right over our camp as they carried their prey to the nest, giving us the best possible chance of identifying the prey at least to type (fish, bird, mammal, or "other"), sometimes even to species. As the season progressed, we watched this nest often from a small beach of gravel along the south side of the river. The disadvantage of this gravel beach Observation Point beside the river was that we had to look up at the nest on the cliff from far below it, so we could not use it when the eaglets were small and huddled down in the cup of the nest.

We faced three critical periods of observation: first, determining that the Ive's Wash pair was finding plenty of food for their single eaglet, second, observation of the process of fostering the zoo-hatched Alamo Lake eaglet into the Ive's Wash Nest, and third, careful observation after the fostering to be sure that the adult eagles were finding enough prey to support two eaglets. To achieve these goals, we needed a much better observation point than either the spillway or beach. By the time Peter and I arrived, Scott and GC had begun pioneering routes across country to a couple of high places on the north side of the canyon; at these locations we were at a slightly higher level than the nest on the opposite side of the canyon, and about half a mile from it. Reaching this new O.P. involved first walking across the spillway, then up the men's latrine ravine to reach high ground, then carefully hiking down a treacherous scree slope to reach and walk along and across a deep wash—our so-called "big wash"—that at this time of year carried little or no water, and finally to find a walkable route back up onto high ground. The distance of this hike was about a mile and a half, but elevation changes of about 150 ft. up, followed by about 340 ft. down, then about 390 ft. up again on the way out (opposite elevation-change sequence and directions on the way back) made the hike strenuous work. My journal notes often mention how long the hikes took, the sore muscles I suffered in the first days, and the efforts we made on the first several trips to find improved routing, and to mark the best route.

From my Journal: Sunday, 21 February 1993
We hiked three hours and 20 minutes as GC and Scott showed Peter and me routes to the Observation Point across the canyon from the Ive's Wash Nest and we made cairns to mark the route. I pioneered one new trail section down the wash that wasn't really useful, but fun and I took a photo. We ate lunch, which we had carried along, as soon as we reached the O.P., and I found the first California poppy in bloom. At 4:35 PM we started back and made it in 1¾ hour, a new record they said, and much more acceptable.

Eventually Peter could make this hike in just under an hour, but I was not as fast; after the route was familiar, we walked alone. We always carried water and food, stayed on or near the marked route, and told our partners when we expected to return. I also always carried a snake-bite kit. Remember, this was before cell phones and towers were ubiquitous. Because the hike took so much time, we tended to stay at the O.P. across the canyon to observe several hours, leaving when there would be just enough daylight to get back to the spillway before dark. During the crucial days of the fostering and the long, dawn-to-dusk hours of observation required of us Nestwatchers during this critical period, we set up a small tent below this hilltop O.P. in which we could shelter from rain. We carried extra water and left some at the O.P. to stock up before the zoo eaglet was delivered. On the day of fostering, as soon as there was sufficient light, we hiked out with heavily-loaded backpacks, prepared to stay all day and to take turns camping overnight at the O.P., two Nestwatchers at a time. Our plans involved alternately going back to camp for a night and to resupply.

Jean, hiking along the "big wash" to reach a scalable slope up to the Hilltop O.P. on top of the hill at the right

Staying in Touch

The year 1993 was pre-cell phone, at least from my perspective, but even had I had one of the early cell phones, there would not have been a tower "in reach" at Alamo Lake. While I was stationed in Camp Verde, at the office in Phoenix, or traveling around during my days off, I could generally find pay phones to use for required calls to check in with the Nestwatch boss, and for calling home. We were supposed to call the Game and Fish office if we had any serious problems or questions, but at our Alamo Lake/Ive's Wash assignment there was no pay phone readily available at first, the nearest being nearly 40 miles away in tiny Wenden AZ. In a couple of desperate situations, we were grudgingly permitted to use the Alamo Lake State Park phone, but only if we used our personal phone credit cards. The Kingman AZ Bureau of Land Management issued us radios, and, if we walked up on the dam, we could call that office, about 73 line-of-sight miles away from us and in the opposite direction from Phoenix, with our concerns and have them relayed to Game and Fish in Phoenix. Alas, the AA batteries that powered the radios did not last long after hot weather arrived, so using the radios was almost as problematic as finding phones. It was almost too late to be useful, but a new pay phone was installed at the state park store near the end of May.

To stay in touch with family and friends during the four and a half months I was on the Nestwatch job, I wrote many, many letters and postcards. Periodically, I also called home. When I learned we would be relocated after only two weeks at Camp Verde, it was necessary to notify the Post Office there to forward our mail. Not having a definite new address at first, I called my parents and gave them the Game and Fish office address in Phoenix. Eventually, I received mail "General Delivery" at the Wenden Post Office. I was regularly writing letters to my parents, to Gary and both our daughters, to other relatives and assorted friends, and to colleagues at the UW-L Biology Department where I would be teaching again in the fall. When my 4-day time-off periods arrived, I typically drove to Wenden, parked in the shade by the Post Office, went in to get my mail, sat in my pickup to read the mail, added comments to the letters I had started, sealed them into envelopes and put them in the mail. Wenden had a laundromat, but it was small and in poor condition, so I usually did laundry in Wickenburg, a bigger town 47 miles from Wenden, and also did most of my shopping there. Wenden, however, sometimes had a small farmer's market where we could get fresh produce.

Phoenix was 66 miles beyond Wickenburg. We were required to report in at the Phoenix office periodically, and to deliver preliminary data and rough drafts of sections of our final reports. We took turns at this duty, but it was most often undertaken by whoever was traveling in that general direction on their days off. Whoever had this duty could also collect any mail for the group that had come to the Phoenix office and, every two weeks, could pick up all our paychecks as well.

News from home was always desired. Being out of touch for each 10-day period meant that mail waiting at the Post Office was very important, and so were those pay phones. For me specifically, the discomfort of being so far from home and so out of touch was exacerbated by worry about my dad's failing health. On 14 February, the day we learned we would be moving from Camp Verde to another location to watch two different nests, I called my parents in the evening for Valentine's Day.

From my Journal: Sunday, 14 February 1993
I was very dismayed to learn Dad isn't doing so well, fainting and falling, "losing ground" as Mom put it. I slept poorly this night, feeling guilty for being far away, unable to help, worried about both Dad and Mom.

Camping Life at Alamo Lake

At Alamo Lake, we had two main campsites, the one we used first and longest, was on the emergency spillway. On the spillway, all of us slept most nights under the toppers covering the cargo areas of our pickups—the weather in February and March was cool and rainy, making these weather-proof shelters desirable. The spillway site was in full sun, and as dryer, warmer weather conditions developed, shade became more necessary, both in which to park our vehicles, and to sit in to make the hours of observation more endurable. Accordingly, by the end of April we had dismantled the spillway camp and moved our trucks to the Gauging Station down in the Bill Williams Canyon below the dam. We also had lesser camping places, to be described later, and used small tents or slept on the ground, when we needed to camp at these for brief periods.

Camping on the spillway was primitive—there were no amenities at all to start with. In the cool, early months we each slept in the back of our individual pickups. Later, when the weather warmed, the three guys sometimes laid their sleeping bags out on the ground. Stories were bantered back and forth about people who, sleeping on the ground in the desert, woke to find a rattlesnake or other critter had crawled into their sleeping bag with them to keep warm; these stories mostly kept me from this activity. However, the requirements of the job did cause me to sleep on the ground a few nights. Happily, I have no sleeping bag invasions to report. For the Ive's Wash Nest, our main Observation Point was near where we parked our trucks in a row at the downslope edge of the spillway, just before the slope dropped off steeply into the canyon. As the weather began to warm, the Bureau of Reclamation provided us with a shade tarp, which we set up on 7 March. It was the type of tarp that allowed air to pass through so that it flapped minimally in the wind and was therefore quiet. Scott provided a smaller blue plastic tarp that we could hang vertically along the south side of the shade tarp, and we set up our camp kitchen against that blue tarp, keeping the kitchen, coolers, water jugs, and us as comfortable as possible in the increasingly warmer weather. In a rainy spell, we spread another tarp over the shade tarp to keep us and our equipment dry.

Generally, we each prepared our own breakfasts and lunches, but sometimes took turns cooking the evening meal for the whole group when we were all on duty, or just for our partner (in my case, Peter) when the other two Nestwatchers were off duty and away from Alamo Lake. All three of the guys were nutrition-conscious and tended toward vegetarian, high-fiber foods. My version of camp cooking did not impress them much at first, but they were thoroughly pleased by my varied, pan-fried bannocks, and by the foods I produced with my Bake-Packer™.

What kinds of foods did we eat in the spillway camp? How did we keep our foods? Where did we get our supplies? How did we cook? As I had done for Peregrine jobs, in preparation for this Nestwatch job, I stocked up and brought along canned and packaged foods for the kinds of meals I liked to cook in camp, knowing that it is generally cheaper to buy supplies at my regular stores at home than in small towns near fieldwork locations. I prepared bannock (pan-fried biscuit) mixes ahead of time at home, and pancake mixes too. We could get fresh fruit and vegetables sometimes at a "freight-damaged" outlet at Wenden. Kathy, Nestwatcher at the Ladders nest near Camp Verde, visited her grandfather who lived in Arizona and had several citrus trees. She came to see us at Alamo Lake a couple of times, and on one of those visits, timed after seeing her grandfather, she brought us two plastic grocery bags full of citrus fruits: oranges, grapefruits, lemons and others, all deliciously tree-ripened and therefore thoroughly enjoyed by all four of us, even the lemons. Scott taught me how to choose oranges that were ripe. He liked to eat an avocado nearly every day, and would bring several of them at the beginning of a duty stint, all carefully chosen so that one would ripen for each day.

At my home in Wisconsin, in preparation for the Nestwatch job, I had dehydrated a supply of several kinds of fruits and vegetables, and packaged these in plastic bags inside a metal can with a tight lid, successfully keeping out insects and rodents. Other foods were in cans, the cooler, or in a second big metal can. I had learned on Peregrine jobs how crucial it was to protect my food supply from ants and rodents in these ways. I remember how upset GC became when he found mice had gotten into some of his food.

Often in my journal, there are notes about what we ate in camp; each teammate had a different cooking style and considerable experimentation occurred over the course of the months we were there. Peter made a good vegetable curry that he served on couscous, for example. I made meals based on commercial, flavored noodle and rice packets, adding canned meats and/or rehydrated vegetables. One of my Introductory Biology students during fall semester 1992, upon learning that I would be doing fieldwork instead of teaching this spring, gave me a few MRE (Meals-Ready-to-Eat) packets. This gift allowed me to sample some of the food supplied to our military in the field; I found the MREs interesting, and liked some better than others, but was also intrigued by the little heater provided with the packets. Ramen noodles formed the basis of other meals. GC bought hamburger to make into chili; another time he prepared sauerkraut and kielbasa. He caught a big channel catfish below the dam in a little bay, thereafter referred to as GC's Catfish Bay, and fried that up for our supper, supplemented with rice and vegetables prepared by Peter. One supper Peter made us burritos and I provided cookies I had purchased. Peter also made a delicious meatless spaghetti sauce, though I admit to being startled the first time to find raisins in it.

GC had a two-burner Coleman white-gas camp stove. The single-burner camp propane stove I started the job with burned out its O-ring in late April, something that tended to happen with these little stoves after several weeks of daily use. I had encountered this problem repeatedly in Peregrine summers, so I had brought along a second stove of the same type. I could run such a stove either directly off one-pound, single-use fuel cylinders, or attach it to a stand my husband had made and fuel it from a refillable eleven-pound propane tank.

Under the shade tarp, Spillway O.P., Jean with spotting scope, camp kitchen area in background

Peter's 30th birthday occurred soon after our arrival at Alamo Lake and GC made French toast and fried eggs for the three of us (Scott was off-duty and off-site) that morning. When I learned of his approaching birthday, I told Peter that if he bought a Jiffy™ cake mix in his preferred flavor, I would make him a cake. He looked doubtful, but complied and I baked his chocolate cake in the Bake-

Packer™. Having no previous experience with the capabilities of this device, Peter was suitably impressed with the resulting cake's texture and flavor. I also made supper of curried fruit and ham over brown rice that evening. We celebrated Scott's birthday just before he left for his summer job—Peter made hominy soup for supper and I made a yellow cake in my Bake-Packer.

We did have coolers along and could purchase ice when we went to town or, more expensively, at the Alamo Lake State Park store. However, as the weather warmed, the ice melted so fast it was not worth trying to keep it for a whole 10-day work stint. We would come in with ice and use the perishable items out of our coolers first. In the very hot temperatures near the end of Peter's and my time at Alamo Lake, the lack of ice and cold drinks was a hardship.

Our spillway camp was located behind a locked gate, which tended to prevent unannounced visitors and to give our camp security and privacy. At the state park campground, we could fill our water jugs. We were also permitted to take our showers at the park campground and I did some of my small laundry there, with the bucket-and-plunger method, in order to reduce the number of trips I had to make to Wickenburg.

From my Journal: Thursday, 4 March 1993
Pinned up my laundry (shirts, socks & undies that I had washed with bucket and plunger in the campground shower stall) on a line I strung between the canoe rack on Scott's truck and the one on mine. Made and ate lunch. Laundry dried in two hours.

Latrines were an individual responsibility. I asked right away where I could go for female privacy and we settled that one particular ravine adjacent to the spillway was for male latrines, and I was assigned a different ravine. I had brought along a shovel and a wooden "potty seat" so I dug a large hole, piled rocks around it to support the seat and used this "facility" whenever I was at the main camp on the spillway. However, we also had four other Observation Points that we used less often, so it was necessary to individually carry toilet tissue and at least a trowel wherever we went.

Alarm clocks were rarely needed: when you live outdoors in primitive conditions for a while, you tend to become attuned to daylight hours, waking at dawn and going to sleep soon after dark. A plentitude of exercise most days ensured that we usually slept well. Additionally, at Alamo Lake, the wild burros, descendants of escaped or abandoned burros used by miners in the past, often woke us with their hee-haw greetings to the dawn: the "five o'clock hee-haw," as we called it. Sometimes their "chorus" was joined by coyotes and owls.

Wild burros were often seen and heard during our Nestwatch time at Alamo Lake

From a letter: Thursday, 25 March 1993
About 2 PM the clouds got really dark & we could see rain coming
so Peter and I packed up and went down to Scott's tent on the
hillside below the O.P. After two hours, the rain let up some and
we put on our ponchos for the long hike back from Hilltop O.P. to
the spillway, noting that water was beginning to trickle in the big
wash and rock pools to fill. This late winter rain is supposed to be
the last boost needed for best desert bloom. We got wet on the hike,
so made hot drinks and soup right away for early supper and
retired to our trucks. GC returned while I was writing this in the
cab, and drove up close to hand me my mail from his truck window
to mine. I've been cozy in my truck, but the rain has lessened and
I'm tired, so I'm going outside to brush my teeth, etc. I often go to
bed soon after 8:00, almost always by 9:00 or shortly after!!

Each Nestwatcher was required to have his/her own transportation.
The four of us at Alamo Lake each had a pickup; mine was a small
Toyota with aluminum, cab-high topper. Scott's truck was also
small and it was older, sometimes causing Scott to be late back to
work, once because the clutch failed at the start of his return trip
after his days off. Scott's truck was towed back home that day (he
lived within Arizona), the clutch was replaced, and Scott returned
to us as soon as he could. This was another incidence when lack of
phone service was difficult—there was no easy way for Scott to let
us know he would be late and why. GC had to do some
maintenance work on his pickup during his off days.

Though I was fortunate not to have any vehicle problems, we were
on the job so long, and I had driven so many miles just to get to
Arizona, that it was necessary to have the oil and filter changed. I
had this done in Wickenburg at the end of March during one of my
times off, walking around town doing various errands while the
truck was being serviced.

Sickness, Injury and other Troubles

All of the hiking required at Alamo Lake was welcomed exercise since such a large part of our job involved sitting still for hours at a time to observe the eagles and their nests. I wrote home about brushing against a cactus and how painful the spines were before I could remove them, and my journal includes complaints about suffering muscle soreness until I became used to the strenuous hiking. I did fall several times, once on 11 March on the hike back from the O.P. on the cliff across from the Ive's Wash Nest, when a loose rock rolled under my foot. The result was a gouge in the palm of my right hand as I tried to break my fall and my hand came down hard on a sharp rock. On that occasion Scott bandaged my hand with pinyon sap! Later, when my hand was almost completely healed, I fell twice on the same day, 23 March, while carrying things across the spillway, carelessly having left my boot laces loose; this time cutting the palms of both hands on the loose gravel of the spillway. These rock cuts were very painful, but healed well.

From a letter: 10 April 1993
In early April, the black flies (gnats) hatched out and I have welts on ears, neck, hands, wrists. So itchy!

My journal notes from 20-21 May refer to several blisters that developed on one of my ankles, on one hand and on my torso. I never figured out what caused them, but they developed on several parts of my body during those few days.

From my Journal: Thursday, 20 May 1993
The blister on one ankle is hugely full of fluid, and one blister on the back of my hand has burst. The ones on my ankle are a problem mainly because they are irritated by the footgear I need to wear, and by the action of walking.

From my Journal: Friday, 21 May 1993
The blisters emerge just like those from poison ivy, but without the
maddening itching component. This morning the newest blisters
are small so I think I'm over the peak, but now there are some on
my torso.

One member of the team had a serious, chronic health issue and
carefully warned the rest of us how to spot if he was in trouble, and
how to help. There were a couple of worrisome occasions in the
health of this individual—neither occurring when I was present—
and both were handled well by one of the other guys.

Most of us had at least one spell of digestive trouble through all
these experiences, and my journal mentions rice and chicken broth
being prepared to help a partner recover from such a situation. One
of us came down with a cold, but in general we were all able to
stay remarkably well throughout our months as Nestwatchers.

One team member misplaced his driver's license and had to send
in a request for a replacement; one needed new eye glasses,
requiring him to make trips to Phoenix on his off days to first order
the glasses, and later to pick them up. Difficulties such as these and
car repairs are a nuisance for anyone in regular life, but such things
are more serious problems during long periods of fieldwork in
remote locations, away from our usual suppliers, car-repair shops,
and healthcare providers. Fortunately, all four of us were
experienced fieldworkers, had prepared well in advance, and were
capable of handling such complexities and unexpected situations
while away from home. I was the only teammate with a spouse and
offspring, so perhaps my situation had more scope for complexities
to occur. One teammate was at the time living in Arizona, so he
could go home during his days off. The rest of us were from
further away.

Altitudes, Weather Conditions, and Lake Levels

The altitude at Camp Verde was 3147 feet, which contributed to
the lower temperatures and a few mornings of frost on our vehicles
that we experienced there. Nevertheless, it was clear to me that I
had escaped the winter my family was still enduring in the upper
Midwest. During the ten days of duty at Camp Verde, Peter and I
recorded morning low temperatures ranging from 30-44 degrees
Fahrenheit, and a daytime high temperature range of 45-65°F. We
had more days there with rain than without. Once we left Camp
Verde for Phoenix, and then Alamo Lake, we were living at lower
elevations and in warmer temperatures.

It was not until April that dry, spring-like weather arrived at Alamo
Lake. Before April, the morning low temperature range had been
32-50 degrees Fahrenheit, and the afternoon high temperature
range was 50-70°F. Then, during April and May, morning lows
were 50-70°F and afternoon highs were 74-98°F. By 14 June, our
last day at Alamo Lake, the daytime high temperature was ranging
between 105 and 110°F.

The wide range of temperatures (30-110°F) I encountered during
my four and a half months as a Nestwatcher, required a wide range
of clothing types too. On one of my off-duty periods I visited a
second-hand clothing store in Phoenix to find a long-sleeved, light-
weight cotton shirt that would cover my arms against excess
sunlight, yet not be uncomfortably hot, the one clothing item I had
failed to bring. No clothing, however, would be cool enough for
sitting in the sun the last few weeks of the job, so the shade we
found at the Beach O.P. and in the Cave O.P. was essential. Peter
went swimming in the river during some of the hottest days, but I
was afraid I might not be a strong-enough swimmer to deal with
the current in the Bill Williams River below the dam, even during
low-discharge levels. Scott taught me the value of having a spray-

bottle of water, what he called an "Arizona air-conditioner." I bought one and used it to moisten exposed areas of skin so I would be cooled by the water's evaporation in the dry desert air. My journal records another technique I applied against the heat.

From my Journal: Monday, 3 May 1993
In the hottest part of the afternoon, I took off my yellow t-shirt and soaked it in the Ive's Wash cove's cool water, then put it back on.

Alamo Lake elevation on maps is given as 1108 feet, but this was a sort of average figure, with the lake usually being lower in late summer and higher after winter rains. Alamo Lake was higher than average during most of the 1993 Bald Eagle nesting season. According to the U.S. quadrangle topographical map for the area, the elevation at the top of Alamo Dam is 1266 ft. and our spillway camp was below that, at approximately 1200 ft. The several nesting locations used over the years by the Alamo Lake and Ive's Wash eagle pairs were the lowest-elevation nest sites of any Arizona desert-nesting Bald Eagles. The new Alamo Cliff Nest, which was on a cliff near the upstream end of the lake, was at 1570 feet. The Ive's Wash Nest was on a cliff about 300 feet above the river and about a mile below the dam; the river just below the dam is at about 1000 ft. elevation, thus that nest was at about 1300 ft.

Rains were exceptionally heavy during January, February and March, 1993. The lake level rose 62 feet between 6 and 20 January as a result of rain on the watershed areas of the Big Sandy and Santa Maria Rivers above Alamo Dam. Because this dam is operated by the Army Corps of Engineers as a flood-control dam, the level of the lake fluctuates not only by the amount of rainfall upstream, but also by means of the cubic feet per second (cfs) allowed through the dam by the engineers. When Scott and GC arrived on 5 January, the flow rate was zero, but because of the two-week period of heavy rainfall immediately after their arrival, the engineers had increased the flow to 5000 cfs by the time Peter and I arrived there on 19 February. Each time the flow rate was changed, a member of the Army Corps of Engineers came to inform us of the change, and to warn us any associated dangers.

From my Journal: Sun. 14 March 1993
Ken (dam guy) stopped by: dam release is at 6000 cfs now, but is going to 7000 cfs tomorrow! The high rate of release of recent weeks has already caused the concrete weir to break.

When the flow rate was reduced to 300 cfs near the end of February to protect downstream areas, we were specifically warned not to try to wade the river, that even though the flow would look so much less than it had recently been, it was still unsafe. Because the rains continued, however, it was necessary to increase the flow again in March as soon as high water in the Bill Williams River below the dam would not threaten downstream areas with serious flooding. The peak release rate was 7000 cfs for a week or so in mid-March. By early April the flow from the dam could be reduced to 250 cfs and remained in the 200-400 cfs range or less during the remainder of my time at Alamo Lake.

Although this warning about wading the river was important, it was not long before Peter tried it. We did wade the river below the dam several times, always with attention to the cfs release rate.

I found all this flood-control process very interesting. Growing up in an area of rural Iowa where the rivers and creeks are small, I had no experience with, and little understanding of flood-control dams. In the part of Iowa where I was raised, floods happened, towns and homes were threatened, fields were flooded, fences, roads and bridges were damaged, but most of these floods were relatively small and just had to be endured and the damage repaired after the flood-waters receded. After I moved to Wisconsin and settled near

190

the Mississippi River and one of its tributaries, I became aware of the river levels being announced daily on weather reports and the importance of this information to boaters, fishermen, and even to me for my occasional canoeing outings. I visited some of that big river's lock-and-dam installations, but it was only at Alamo Lake that I really experienced the flood-control usage of a dam up close. In fact, on 20 April an Army Corps engineer came to our spillway camp and asked if we wanted to help him re-set the release flow.

From my Journal: Tuesday, 20 April 1993
Three of us went down in the bowels of the dam by elevator, about 24 stories down, watching through the elevator roof in darkness as we descended. Alternating, we turned the small release valve (25cfs) closed, and toured the "gates" area inside the dam. We saw the ladders and emergency (dim!!) lighting. Ken opened the larger gate by motor to 200 cfs and we hurried outside to see the river, which we had helped shut off, begin to flow again.

Perhaps it is hard for you, the reader, to visualize the amount of water in the aforementioned release amounts, especially to understand the difference between the 25 cfs and 250 cfs minimums we saw, and the peaks of 5000 cfs and 7000 cfs. Let me put it this way: At 25 cfs, it would take an hour for the water flowing through the dam gates to fill an Olympic-sized swimming pool, while 250 cfs will fill such a pool in about 6 minutes. At 5000 cfs, the pool would fill in just under 18 seconds and at 7000 cfs, the pool would be filled in less than 13 seconds! Since we were camped above the outlet of dam, I commented in my journal about the noise so much water makes coming out of the dam gates. It basically became the only sound we could hear on the spillway unless we spoke to each other up close.

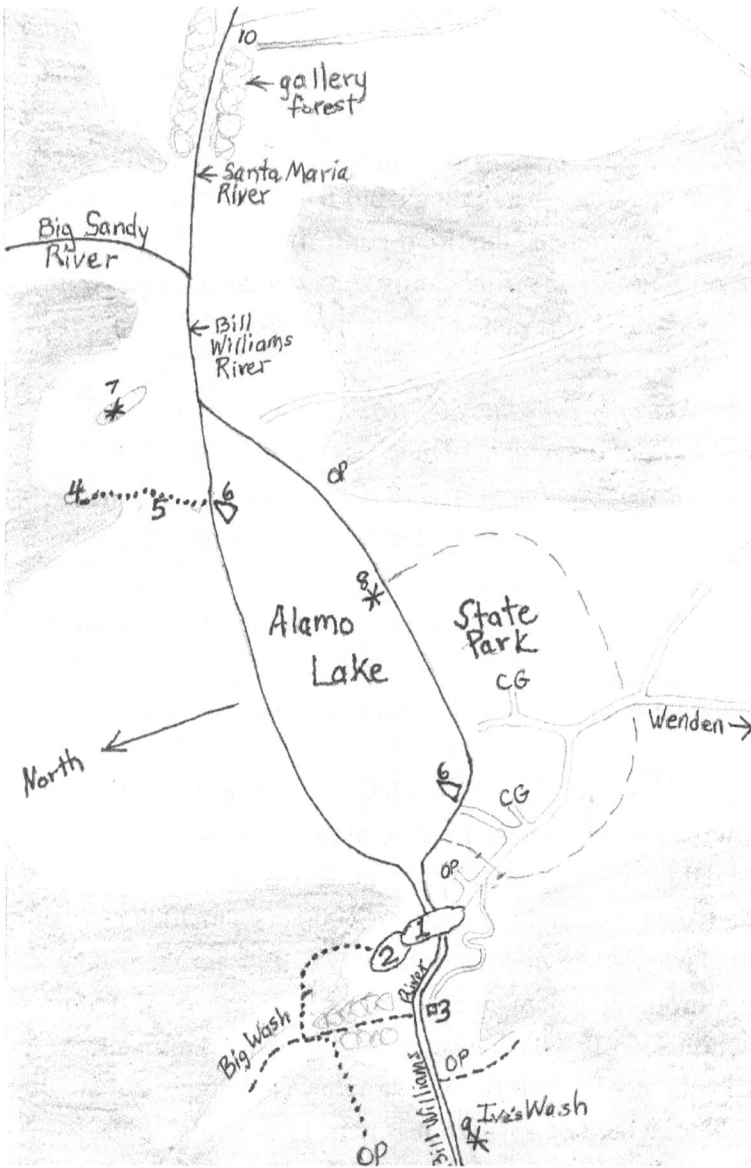

1-Alamo Dam, 2-spillway, 3-gauging station, 4-Cave O.P.,
5-lakeside campsite, 6-boat landing sites, 7-Alamo Cliff
Nest, 8-Alamo pair's tree nest that flooded, 9-Ive's Wash
Nest, 10-sandbar camp. Shading=areas of higher elevation,
dashes=intermittent waterways, dots=main hiking routes

THE EAGLES OF IVE'S WASH

By 26 February, after a few days of observing the Ive's Wash Nest from the Hilltop O.P., Peter and I were quite sure that neither of the adults was banded. After the careful days of observation, we could also be certain this pair had hatched only one eaglet, and they were bringing plenty of food to the nest.

From a letter: Saturday, 6 March 1993
The female eagle stands on the prey, tears off a piece, and holds it in her beak near the eaglet, now about 4+ weeks old. We can see his head above the nest edge as he bobbles around awkwardly. It takes the adult 15-20 minutes to stuff the eaglet now. At first, he was fed quite often, offered tiny pieces, and it only took 5 minutes.

Bill Williams River Canyon below Alamo Dam, a small arrow indicates the Ive's Wash nest promontory on south canyon wall, Hilltop O.P. further up the hill on right

The Ive's Wash Bald Eagle pair built their nest on a small promontory in the steep-walled canyon below the dam. They could of course catch fish in the river, but they also fished in the waters of Alamo Lake. The Alamo Cliff Nest was about six miles from the Ive's Wash Nest, and the two pairs of eagles, seemed to have peacefully divided the territory of the lake, and we did not see altercations between them. The Ive's Wash eagles flew over our spillway camp location when they brought prey from the lake to their nest, a situation that made it possible for us to more-exactly identify at least some of the prey species being carried toward the nest over our heads, than at any of the other hunting or fishing places and return-to-nest routes of either pair.

Prey

What kind of prey were we able to identify in the talons of the eagles passing overhead on their way to their nest—largely fish, of course, including largemouth bass, catfish, carp, crappie, and sucker. We saw the Ive's Wash adults bring in a few kangaroo rats, several American Coots, and a grebe of unknown species.

From my Journal: Wednesday, 24 February 1993
We went up the big wash to the northwestern of three hilltops, from which we saw two fish brought in to the nest, very clearly the second one was alive in the eagle's talons. The female stands on the fish, tears off bits with her beak to offer to the eaglet. On the way back to the spillway, we again made route errors and had to backtrack—need more cairns to mark the trails so we can avoid this waste of time. On the last downhill stretch, I could feel blisters starting to form on my heels—I hope they toughen up.

From a letter: Sunday, 28 March 1993
Yesterday GC and I went to the O.P. opposite the Alamo Lake Cliff Nest and observed there all day. I saw the eagle catch a great,

194

huge fish (probably a catfish) at the edge of the lake. It was quite a struggle, and the eagle could barely fly with the fish after finally subduing it.

Interactions

Besides the food the eagles brought to the nest, we also had to record interactions and disturbances. The former term refers to responses by the eagles when other birds flew into the territory around the nest. Sometimes the eagles pursued such intruders, but on other occasions the intruders pursued the eagles. Most of such interactions were with Common Ravens and Red-tailed Hawks. Because both species were nesting nearby, the ravens, hawks and eagles frequently intruded in each other's territories, resulting in interactions between the eagles and the other two species.

The most dramatic interaction occurred between the adult male Ive's Wash Bald Eagle and an immature Bald Eagle. The adult male took off from the nest heading north before the other eagle came into our view, but when the intruder approached the vicinity of the nest, the adult stooped (dived) on it twice. The immature rolled over in the air and the two touched talons. The immature returned the favor, stooping on the adult and we could hear vocalizations throughout this "dogfight." Eventually, the adult chased the immature out of the area, but the immature's departure took it directly over our O.P. only 30 feet above us—what a sight!

One of my favorite interaction observations was very low-key—a hummingbird of unknown species hovered near the adult eagle while it was perched on the nest—the eagle just watched the hummingbird without making any threatening moves toward it. A more worrisome interaction involved three raccoons wandering near the nest, causing alertness in the attending adult; this interaction is described elsewhere herein.

An eagle pair tends to have more than one nest over the years, to rotate among them in different breeding seasons, and to keep adding sticks to whichever nest they are using in a given year. One of my most striking memories of eagle behavior involves the male and female of the Ive's Wash pair. I observed the male flying low over the ground and strongly downslope on the south side of the Bill William's River, heading toward the river. When he reached the drop-off at the edge of the canyon, the eagle extended his talons and grabbed a large stick of a tree, the branches of which stood up above the cliff edge. The eagle's intent was for his forward momentum to crack the stick loose from the tree, but on the first attempt this did not work and the eagle's flight was abruptly limited and he had to quickly release the stick and recover his altitude. The eagle circled around to try again; the second attempt did crack the stick loose and the male carried it down canyon and upward to the nest on its cliff pinnacle. Landing on the nest, the male chose a spot to lay the stick near the edge of the big nest the pair was using in 1993. The female walked over and picked up the new stick, moved across the nest and placed it in a different location. This action seemed so like a human female, moving a piece of furniture that was carried in by her husband, to her choice of location!

Disturbances

The term disturbance was used for human activities that might interfere with the breeding success of the eagles. Off-road vehicle travel through the Bill Williams River Canyon had been a serious concern in the previous year. Such access in the 1993 breeding season was prohibited by high water. Water release rates from the dam were well above 25 cfs from 13 January through 14 April, and then above 200 cfs from 20 April through the end of the breeding season. Hikers, horseback riders, campers, anglers and others were also absent in the canyon during our watch. The most frequent type of disturbance we observed was low-flying aircraft (within one kilometer of the nest and below 2,000 feet). A few of these were private, single-engine planes, and military helicopters, however, most (107 recorded) were military jets. On 6 May, F-16 jets engaged in mock dogfights, releasing a number of flares directly over the nest area in the morning and again in the afternoon. In most cases, these aircraft elicited no response from the eagles, but the lower ones caused the adult to stop feeding its young, and we observed the eaglets crouch down on two occasions. A 2000 ft. minimum altitude advisory was in effect for the immediate nest area, but it was often disregarded by the pilots, subjecting us and the eagles to ear-shattering noise, and once a sonic boom. I learned to recognize F-16 (Falcons) and F-15 (Eagles).

From my Journal: Saturday, 6 March 1993
Today two guys came to camp while I was on duty alone. They had shot several jackrabbits and wanted to put them out for the eagles. I was concerned there would be lead shot in the meat and refused for the safety of the eagles. Seems these guys are in the habit of putting such food out for coyotes.

Fostering

All indications were that the Ive's Wash adults would be able to raise the Alamo Lake pair's first offspring, the one hatched in the Phoenix zoo from one of two eggs rescued just before flood waters rose over their early-season tree nest. The plan was to foster the zoo-hatched Alamo Lake eaglet into the Ive's Wash Nest for that pair of eagles to raise along with their own eaglet. The two eaglets were of similar age and size, but we would generally be able to differentiate them by small plumage differences.

The zoo-hatching and eaglet-fostering events were big news in Arizona, good media opportunities for the Game and Fish

Department to promote its work in the Nestwatch Program. Accordingly, on 9 March we were to expect delivery of the zoo eaglet by helicopter, and its placement into the Ive's Wash Nest by two AZGFD biologists. Also present, would be our Nestwatch boss as Bald Eagle Management Coordinator, individuals from the sponsoring agencies, and cameramen.

Our preparations for this momentous day had included the aforementioned searches for hiking routes and an observation point on a hill across the canyon from the nest, as well as the careful observations that supported the chances of success for the fostering. To gather this information, our team had already spent several days observing the Ive's Wash Nest from the Hilltop O.P.

On Tuesday, 9 March, I woke at 5:10 AM, having set my alarm. The afternoon before I had packed my big backpack and, during the evening of the 8[th,] our team of four had discussed how to cover the fostering event by observing from both the Hilltop O.P. and from the spillway. I added a few items to my pack in the morning, things that had occurred to me during a restless night, for example, my second camera. I was ready by 5:50 AM, after a washup and changing to clean clothes. Scott and I were to have first duty at the Hilltop O.P., but since I was ready first and the slowest hiker, I started out from the spillway as soon as I could, knowing that Scott would use the same route and catch up.

From my Journal: Tuesday, 9 March 1993
In place barely in time, I watched while vehicles arrived across the dam. The helicopter from Phoenix, which first circled the area, then picked up people from the dam and landed a total of seven people above the nest in two trips. Our boss followed the two biologists almost to the nest, only the last few yards being difficult terrain. The biologists hooded (to calm it) and removed the Ive's Wash eaglet for weighing, measuring and banding. (The zoo eaglet

had, of course, already been banded at the zoo.) One biologist held the eaglet while the other removed prey remnants from the nest for study, and placed several trout in the nest. After the zoo eaglet, that we began to call Foster, was in place, the Ive's Wash eaglet, called Junior, was returned to the nest to join it. The photographer & others were conveyed back to the spillway, but the two AZGFD biologists, a USFWS biologist, and our boss came by helicopter to our Hilltop O.P. to observe with us until the adults had returned to the nest and a feeding had occurred (Foster got about three bites), and the adult male was seen perched near the nest. ... It was a long watch, but the "stepsister rivalry" between the eaglets eased, prey was brought to the nest, and more feeding occurred. Peter came out with a supply of water, joining Scott and me at the O.P. for the afternoon only.

Jean, at Hilltop O.P., with scope aimed across the canyon at the Ive's Wash Nest; it is also the Hilltop camping site

I had been recording very detailed notes about the fostering process and the boss asked to look them over. I noted his comments as follows: "A+, Great work—very complete & succinct." I was proud of this, and kept a photocopy of the three-page timeline fieldnotes I recorded from 8:09 AM, when I arrived to begin note-taking, until 6:43 PM when Scott and I ceased observations for the day.

I cannot include in this book pages of fieldnotes or any of the Nestwatch forms or reports since these are the property of AZGFD. However, I will provide a brief sample of the event sequence from my fieldnotes. The helicopter had arrived and circled over seeking a landing area at 8:58, the biologists and our boss arrived at the nest at 9:24, having flushed both adults, and the fostering process was complete, with both eaglets in the nest at 9:55 AM. By 10:59 the helicopter was lifting off from the nest area with the second load of people, bringing the four biologists to our O.P. at 11:04. At 11:54 the adult female returned to the nest, and at 12:35 she began to feed the eaglets, Junior first.

Because of the need for very careful observations of the Ive's Wash Nest to ensure that the adult eagles were able to care for and provision both eaglets, we worked out a plan to have two of our team at the Hilltop O.P. nearly continuously for several days, starting at 8 AM on 9 March. That evening Scott and I were prepared to camp out at the Hilltop O.P. He had brought and set up a small tent below the crest of the hill that we could use if/when it rained, but this was one of the situations when I slept out on the ground, removing rocks from an area up there on top of the hill above the canyon, and spreading a tarp on which to lay my sleeping bag. That first night, Scott lit a tiny campfire and cooked supper for us: rice, carrots, tuna.

The next morning, I woke just before sunrise and began observing the eagles. I heard a strange squealing sound from across the canyon and watched as the adult male eagle stood up in the nest on alert, then flew to land near the female on a rock they frequently used as a perch. I discovered the eagles were watching a large raccoon at the base of the rocks, and I wondered if it had caught a ground squirrel that was the source of the squealing.

From my Journal; Wednesday, 10 March 1993
The male eagle watched very intently as the raccoon ambled uphill, seeming to sniff toward the rocks where one biologist, the three photographers, and the pilot sat yesterday. Two more raccoons appeared on the trail of the first and all three disappeared behind the rocks, where those four people sat during the fostering. I watched anxiously, fearful that the raccoons would trail human scent to the nest. Fortunately, they did not. I theorized that the group of observers had had food with them—not a good idea—and that food odors had attracted raccoons to the area.

Camping at the Hilltop O.P.

Peter replaced Scott to camp with me on the Hilltop O.P. the second night after fostering; Scott decided to sleep partway down the hill in his little tent. On the afternoon of 11 March, I packed up, but wrapped my sleeping bag, pad, and a few other items in my plastic ground cloth to leave at the O.P. I also left my scope for Scott to use. I returned to the spillway to join GC. He walked up on the dam to radio Scott and Peter, learning all was well with them. On 12 March I put jugs containing 1½ gallons of water in my pack along with food and other supplies and returned to the Hilltop O.P., using a rope to lower my heavy pack in the steepest spot in the hiking route. I found a Black-throated Sparrow nest in an Ocotillo plant in the big wash. En route, I met Scott heading out. In Scott's pot on a tiny fire, Peter and I cooked supper of instant mashed potatoes, cubes of spam, plus asparagus (the latter rehydrated from my home-grown and home-dehydrated supplies).

On the 13th, Peter opened observations, then handed over to me, packed up and hiked out. GC called for a radio check, finished packing and headed in, but I had the watch alone for a couple of hours. In the afternoon, I headed back to the spillway, and met Peter on his way in to join GC. In this very organized way, we kept a close watch on the Ive's Wash adults with their suddenly-doubled parental duties.

From my Journal: Saturday, 13 March 1993
I was glad to get back to base camp on the spillway and took a sponge bath, but my hair is stiff *with dirt from camping and sitting on the ground, and with sweat from sitting out in the sun all day, so I really don't feel much cleaner.*

We still had the Alamo Cliff Nest to monitor as well. On 14 March, when Scott arrived back at the spillway, he and I drove over to observe that nest from across the lake. The observation-distance would have been essentially unworkable had we not been loaned the very high-power Questar™ scope. On this day, a coyote walked right through the field of view, behind the perched eagle I was looking at through that fabulous scope. On our way back to the spillway camp, we stopped at the park campground for showers—it was wonderful to get cleaned up after camping and sitting in the dirt all those days.

After the intense ten days of dawn-to-dusk observations out at the Hilltop O.P., I no longer camped out there, though I think the others may have done so a few more times. My notes indicate I hiked out again, carrying a water supply, and leaving what I had not used when I headed back. The 15th and 29th of March, days on which my next two off-duty periods began, mark also two very stressful periods in my Nestwatch career, but the events of those periods will be covered later in this story. It is because of these unusual, stressful events that my notes are somewhat less complete for a few days in the second half of March.

Gauging Station Camp, Beach O.P.

By the end of April, the weather was getting too warm for us to want to camp in full sun on the spillway. Since the eaglets in the Ive's Wash Nest were now big enough to see from a position below in the canyon, Peter, Scott and I (GC left for his summer job 21 April) moved our pickups down a switch-backed half-mile road to the gauging station along the Bill Williams River below the dam.

Gauging Station, in Bill Williams River canyon, below Alamo Dam, Jean slept in her pickup parked at door

The gauging station was a small, square building with a door in one side and a ladder up to the flat roof. Cables ran from the roof to a tower on the other side of the river and the purpose of the gauging station was to measure the rate of water moving in the river below the dam. Peter and I met the Gauging Station maintenance man one day in May and he gave us a tour of the inside of the station. Later we would separately use the station's flat roof as an occasional sleeping platform—well out of reach of rattlesnakes—and referred to it as "the Penthouse."

Our new O.P. for the Ive's Wash Nest was on a gravel beach beside the river about a half-mile walk from our vehicles parked by the Gauging Station. In the morning there was filtered shade from willow, mesquite and paloverde shrubs at the edge of the gravel bar, and in the afternoon, the nest cliff itself provided excellent, deep shade.

Peter, beach O.P. and his beach camp; Scott and GC also slept out on the beach

We carried my camp kitchen and other gear in to this O.P. so that we could make our lunches and suppers while on duty. Peter carried in his sleeping bag, pad and ground cloth and often slept on the beach, but I walked back out each evening and slept in my truck. On the first of May, Peter and I used rocks to create a little bay in the river next to our O.P. wherein we could set foods and drinks for cooling without the current carrying them away. Sometimes I ate my breakfast at my truck before walking in to the Beach O.P., other times I carried food in to eat at the beach, especially on the "dawn-to-dusk" duty days. We used the Beach O.P. for observation of Ive's Wash Nest and eagles into mid-May, until both eaglets successfully fledged from that nest.

This move of both camp and O.P. meant we each had to dig new latrines; I needed one in at the O.P., but another out by my truck at the Gauging Station. This is an aspect of wilderness living and of fieldwork that no one likes to think about, but that does not mean the problem does not exist. We had to consider both privacy (not readily available in a desert), and sanitation in the placement of our latrines.

THE EAGLES OF ALAMO LAKE NEST and CLIFF NEST

The Alamo Lake pair of eagles had formerly varied their reproductive efforts between three different nests in trees beside the lake, but these were all swept away by the unusually high water of 1993. The Alamo eagles built their new nest on a cliff on the northwest side of the lake. The tree nest in which they had begun their 1993 nesting season and which was inundated by rising water levels on 10 January, after the dramatic rescue of the pair's first two eggs of the season (8 January), had been on the southeast side of the lake, where two observation areas reached by dirt roads were close enough for Nestwatchers to observe the nest quite well.

The new nest, on a cliff that stood out by itself as a kind of "land island" was much farther away and on the opposite side of the lake; from those observation points, at best we could tell if the eagles were present at the nest or perching on the cliff near it. There were, of course, places on the cliff where the eagles could perch out of our sight. The better of the two observation points was on high ground beside a dirt road and required us to aim our spotting scopes across the lake, and to observe the nest from at least a mile and a half away. Fortunately, we had been loaned a Questar, an excellent-quality, mirror-type scope, which helped make our long-distance observations possible. We parked one of our trucks beside the little road, rigged a tarp off the truck's topper, and set up our camp chairs and scopes in the shade patch thus formed.

From my Journal: Saturday, 20 February 1993
GC took Peter and me to see the Alamo Cliff Nest from the southeast side of the lake. From the spillway camp, it is a drive of 18 miles one way to this Observation Point, via rather indirect, mostly gravel roads and my little truck may not be able to do the

Jean in temporary O.P.; the Alamo Cliff Nest was across
the lake, well over a mile away

*last bit on a barely-there dirt road. After we got back to camp,
kangaroo mice ran all through camp while Scott and Peter
prepared Mexican food for supper.*

Eventually, as this breeding pair hatched their new egg and began
care of their eaglet, it became necessary to find a closer O.P. for
better observation and better record-keeping. To that end, we made
arrangements several times to borrow a small boat and motor, and
crossed the long lake diagonally, from the state park's boat landing
on the southeast side near the dam, almost to the northeast end, a
trip that took approximately an hour each way. Landing and
securing the boat on the northwest side, we then hiked about half a
mile along an old dirt road, uphill of course, and observed the nest
from a small cave we found that gave us much needed afternoon
shade as the temperatures rose with the arrival of summer
conditions.

These boat trips fell mostly to Peter and me after Scott and GC had left for their summer jobs. It was a major inconvenience to try to schedule the use of a boat, but we were very grateful to Bruce, a member of the park staff, who was willing to loan us his small aluminum boat with its 6-hp motor. Peter did an excellent job of dealing with the motor and piloting the small boat, including restarting the motor the day it quit in the middle of the lake. In May, Peter and I arranged to take Bruce and his wife out to supper in a café in the area as a thank-you gesture. In late May, Peter met with the new managers of the Alamo Lake State Park store and made arrangements for us to use one of the park's rental boats when we needed to cross the lake to observe the Alamo cliff Nest during the last couple weeks of the season.

Alamo Cliff Nest (top center of cliff), photographed from near Cave. O.P. at nearly half a mile distance

Our reports on the development of the eaglet in this nest eventually led the Game and Fish Biologists to come to Alamo Lake (5 May), cross it with us in a much bigger boat, hike up to the cliff, climb it and access the nest to weigh, measure and band the eaglet that we called "Solo," and to collect prey remnants from the nest area for analysis. The purpose of this analysis was to help provide more information about what prey items the parent eagles were bringing to the nest for food, thus supplementing the observations of Nestwatchers—there was no way we could watch for prey deliveries during all the daylight hours, every day. Seeing the bag of prey remnants collected by the biologist—assorted fish tails and fins, feathers, legs of water birds, bones, and other scraps—made me glad I was not going to have to do the analysis! Peter crossed the cliff all the way to the nest and so got to help hold the eaglet during these processes. I stopped before the last chasm-crossing in the cliff and took on the role of photographing all of this event, including the overhead circling of the upset adult eagles. The Game and Fish Biologists left some fresh fish at the nest after this disturbance and the adults settled down and returned to the nest soon after we all left.

Toward the end of our stay, when Solo, the Alamo Cliff Nest eaglet was showing signs of being ready to fledge, Peter and I took camping gear and supplies along in the borrowed state park boat and camped on a flat place above the lake, in order to save transit time, have more time for observing the eagles.

Peter cooking in camp above the lake; he slept out on the ground; Jean set up her tent

Jean and Peter in the Cave O.P., looking toward Alamo Lake Cliff Nest

<u>Hiking, Wildflowers, Wildlife</u>

During the first days of our Camp Verde assignment, hiking was not at all part of the Nestwatch job. Once it was evident that the eagles had abandoned the Camp Verde nest, however, our hunger for hiking and exploration was realized for a few days by the Forest Service's request that Peter and I search for Bald Eagles in the general Camp Verde area.

In contrast, at Alamo Lake hiking was often a major part of the job. We still spent hours, even entire days, sitting by spotting scopes on the spillway, or at another O.P., observing eagle activity at the Ive's Wash Nest, watching for eagles returning to the nest carrying prey, being alert to note disturbances to the eagles and their nest by human activities, and recording interactions between the eagles and other birds, or between eagles and other animals. This kind of duty could be tedious when no eagles were present, and we often spent hours at a time barely speaking. On the other hand, we also spent time getting to know each other, and sometimes developed strange and interesting entertainments.

From a letter, Thursday, 8 April 1993
This afternoon a caterpillar crawled toward me. I got it to crawl onto my flyswatter, bent the swatter back and released it to shoot the caterpillar off into the vegetation as by a catapult. When it returned, this time crawling toward Peter, I handed him the flyswatter to try again.

Because of the important fostering process, however, we often took the long, strenuous hike to the Hilltop O.P. across the canyon from the nest. This long hike made possible small side-jaunt explorations en route by one Nestwatcher at a time.

Sitting time was reduced on any day when we observed the Alamo Cliff Nest, at first because of the necessity of driving the 18-mile back-road route to and from the O.P. located across the lake from the nest. Later, sitting time was reduced by the need to boat the length of the lake, then hike half a mile uphill to the Cave O.P. that gave us a much closer view of this nest. Again, the hiking in itself was welcome, but the exploration of new territory enhanced the pleasure of it. On that side of the lake there were remnants of mining attempts of the past. On those occasions that we camped overnight on a level area above the lake, we were well away from the nest cliff.

The pleasure of identifying wildflowers, trees and other plants was taught to me in my childhood by my mother, who knew many of the native wildflowers that grew along the railroad right-of-way running through the Iowa farm where I grew up. I furthered this interest while earning my Master of Science degree in Biology by taking several botany courses. My mother also sparked my lifelong interest in birds by giving me a small bird guidebook when I was 10 or 11 years old. I saved my small allowance and bought a more advanced bird field guide when I was in junior high, the first of many bird books I would eventually own. Birding became a life-long interest. I also studied Ornithology in graduate school, and later the undergraduate Ornithology course was part of my teaching assignment at UW-La Crosse for eight years.

Gradually in adulthood I accumulated a variety of other identification books, including wildflower, mammal, reptile and amphibian books, and I brought appropriate ones with me to Arizona. Since we were required to keep records of birds, mammals, reptiles and amphibians sighted in the areas around our eagle nests, these books were very useful. I also tried to identify as many wildflowers as I could, photographing some of them. The many kinds of cactus growing in the area were especially interesting to me, since cacti are rare in the Midwest. I stood on a ladder at Hassayampa to take a picture of saguaro cactus flowers. I was astonished when the brittlebush plants came into bloom, surrounding us with mounds of golden flowers, and the taller paloverde shrubs also turned golden when they bloomed. I especially enjoyed ghost flowers (*Mohavea confertiflora*) for their interesting name, as well as for the translucency of the pale, cream-colored flowers decorated with purple dots. Ghost flower plants grow about one foot tall and the species is classed with snapdragons and penstemons in the figwort family (Scrophulariaceae), though their flowers have an open cup-shape, one and a half inches across. So much of the vegetation I lived among that spring in Arizona was new to me!

From a letter: Thursday, 25 March 1993
One of the interesting plants here, called Tackstem (Calycoseris wrightii), has tiny, tack-shaped glands on its stem and a pretty white flower that looks something like "goatsbeard" back home. Evening Snow (Linanthus dichotomus) is a white phlox that blooms at night—very pretty. I discovered this when I went to the latrine in the night.

The lists of birds and other animals we accumulated were attached to our reports, and we included some of the more interesting wildlife observations in the text of the reports. The scope of this effort can be summarized in a small table as follows, with reptiles and amphibians grouped together as herptiles:

	Camp Verde	Ive's Wash	Alamo Lake
Bird species	33	97	90
Mammals	2	16	13
Herptiles	0*	22	10

*Our 10 days at Camp Verde were in early to mid-February, when reptiles and amphibians were very unlikely to be active.

Another aspect of our duty to record our bird and other wildlife sightings was the state's concern for threatened or endangered species and the need to gather more data about such organisms, including species with declining populations that should perhaps be considered for listing as endangered or threatened. To justify applying for these candidate species to be listed, it was necessary to study them, and our observations and reports on such species would help provide needed information.

Nestwatchers were each provided with a copy of the 1988 Arizona Game and Fish Department's "Threatened Native Wildlife in Arizona" document, which provided lists of species already on the endangered or threatened lists, and those of concern for which more data was needed. The chart below shows the number of species in each category according to this document:

	Endangered	Threatened	Candidate	Total
Fish	17	7	2	26
Amphibians	4	1	4	9
Reptiles	2	1	7	10
Birds	11	11	20	42
Mammals	14	4	6	24
Totals	48	24	39	111

It was necessary to read this document and familiarize ourselves with the many species described in the Threatened Native Wildlife (TNW) lists so that whenever we observed one of these animals, we could fill out the required report. Most of the fish we observed were being carried in the clutches of our eagles toward their nests to be food for the eaglets. Sometimes we could identify the species of a large fish an eagle was carrying in its talons as it passed by near us or overhead, but none of the ones we could identify were rare fish. Likewise, the big fish we sometimes saw in still areas of the river were not rare species.

The only rare herptile Peter and I saw and reported was a Desert Tortoise (*Xerobates agassizii*). This candidate for listing in Arizona, according to the 1988 TNW document, stunned us by suddenly walking into view when we were on duty up at the Hilltop O.P., across the Bill Williams River from the Ive's Wash eagle nest. We had no idea where it came from, how it was able to climb to the top of that big hill, a hill that was a difficult climb for humans (at least for me). Certainly, we never came up the side the tortoise appeared to have come from, the cliff side of the hill.

From my Journal: Friday, 12 March 1993
Suddenly a desert tortoise crested the O.P. ridge right in front of Peter and continued on a path that passed four feet from his camp chair, the tortoise munching vegetation as it walked. How interestingly it walked! Peter and I sat very still, smiled at each other in shared pleasure at our good fortune in this sighting. He photographed it several times, later more closely, and we gently measured its carapace for our report.

Ferruginous Hawks, designated a state threatened species, and Belted Kingfishers, on the state endangered list, were observed in the vicinity of all three of our nest sites. Around Alamo Lake, we saw both Snowy Egrets (state threatened list) and Great Egrets (state endangered list), but like the Bald Eagle, these species were limited in the state to a few nesting areas near water sources, and therefore threatened by recreation activities and various human-initiated damage to the habitats they require.

Of particular interest to me were my sightings of Peregrine Falcons in the Ive's Wash and Alamo Lake areas, as I had already served several times as a Hack Site Attendant in The Peregrine Fund's program to reintroduce these falcons into the Rocky Mountain west, and I was scheduled to be a Hack Site Attendant again in summer 1993 after I finished my Nestwatch job. The Peregrine was a candidate for Arizona state listing, and was on the federal Endangered Species List at the time. A Peregrine was even observed twice stooping on the Ive's Wash Nest on 6 May.

Arizona abounded in poisonous creatures; camping, hiking and sitting outdoors day after day, we lived among them. By early March we were finding scorpions in and around camp. We were thrilled to observe a Gila Monster (*Heloderma suspectum*) a few times, but they were shy and slow-moving so it was easy to avoid their poisonous bite.

One evening as I hiked out, from the Beach O.P. to the gauging station, to make supper at my truck, I found a big brown tarantula (female) right in the path; I had seen her three evenings already and thought I had located her burrow. I was carrying my water pan and hiking stick so I tried to gently push the tarantula under the pan to trap it so I could show it to Peter, when he came out to eat. At first this did not work and I got rather a fright when the tarantula grabbed onto my walking stick and began to climb it! However, I successfully trapped it for Peter to see. It was too dark for me to take a photo, and Peter did not want me to keep it trapped overnight. I am not sure of the species—apparently 30 species of these largest of spiders are known to inhabit Arizona—but knew enough to tell it was a female. I wish I had been able to take a photograph.

Mohave Rattlesnake in the rocks along the trail to the
Beach O.P.

Rattlesnakes, both the Western Diamondback (*Crotalus atrox*) and
Mohave Rattlesnake (*Crotalus scutulatus*) were found in the area
around Alamo Lake and, after the weather warmed, we saw them
fairly often, especially the former species. Peter had told me it was
often the second person hiking in a line that got struck, but one
morning as I followed him up the old mine trail to the Alamo Lake
Cave O.P., I saw him step right over a small rattler without
noticing it resting in a crack in the ground. I noticed, and, being
second in line, made sure to step carefully around it.

From my Journal: Tuesday, 23 March 1993
Peter took a walk up on the dam while I was cooking supper, and I
saw a rattlesnake when I went over to the water jugs to get a
sponge. The rattler buzzed at me from about eight feet away!

From a letter: Monday, 5 April 1993
*On the way back to Alamo, I saw a rattlesnake just starting to
cross the road just outside of Wenden, and I think I may have run
over its head. I was sorry about that as I don't want to build up
any "bad Karma" or anger the "Rattlesnake Spirit." Two of my
partners assured me I was okay since it was an accident—intent
matters. The third was more scientific and said, "I must meet this
Karma sometime, I've heard so much about her."*

Even insects in Arizona can be deadly. Chagas, a disease caused
by a parasite, is spread by the bite of triatomine bugs (more
commonly called kissing bugs). The parasite is actually present in
the feces the bug may leave behind on your skin; the parasite then
may enter you through the site of the bite. We did encounter
kissing bugs, in particular in the Cave O.P., but were not bitten.

From my Journal: Saturday, 5 June 1993
*We were being plagued in the cave today by a kissing bug. Peter
finally captured it in the scope's lens cap and dumped it into the
chasm at our feet.*

Plants were hazardous too—the many species of cactus threatened
us with their sharp spines. I was especially warned not to touch the
cholla species, because first the spines pierced you and then a piece
of the plant would break off and be attached to you. If you tried to
pick it off with your hand, it too might become attached to the
cholla fragment. Desert plants in general tend to have evolved
thorns to deter animals from grazing on them. Several of the
shrubs, such as paloverde, acacia, mesquite, ocotillo (*Fouquieria
splendens*), and cat's claw (*Senegalia greggii*), had thorns. When
we needed to grab onto a plant for support in our hikes over steep
terrain, we tried to use creosote bush, aka greasewood (*Larrea
tridentate*), which was one of the few thornless shrubs in the area.

Besides the familiar House Wren, there were four other species of wrens in the Alamo Lake area: Bewick's, Rock, Canyon, and Cactus Wrens. In my journal I describe the song of Canyon Wrens as "liquid waterfalls of song." During several mornings on observation duty in the Cave O.P., Peter and I were joined in the cave by a Canyon Wren apparently practicing his song with the cave as a megaphone or echo chamber.

Birds I particularly enjoyed up on the Hilltop O.P., overlooking the Ive's Wash Nest, were the White-throated Swifts (*Aeronautes saxatalis*). Despite appearances, swifts are thought to be more closely related to hummingbirds than to swallows, sharing the characteristic of very tiny feet. Though swifts cannot perch on wires as swallows do, both are aerial predators of flying insects. This species, at about 6.5 inches, is a bit larger than the Chimney Swifts I knew from the Midwest. One of our fastest-flying birds, White-throated Swifts, nest in crevices in cliffs and zoom along cliffs and canyons in the western states. While we were perched atop the hill over the Bill Williams River's canyon, watching the Ive's Wash Nest across from us, these swifts often flew, in small "chattering" groups, very rapidly past us and the cholla cactus plants amongst which we sat. I wondered if they ever misjudged their flight paths and, as if in answer, once one of the swifts, as it sped past, brushed lightly against the wide brim of my hat. Another day I was distressed to receive an even more definite answer to my question about the accuracy of swift flight.

From my Journal: Thursday, 6 May 1993
While Peter was swimming in the deep water at the base of our wash, I found a floundering, injured White-throated Swift on the gravel of the beach and trapped it under my hat to calm it. When Peter finished his swim, I pointed to where my hat lay on the gravel and asked him, "Would you like to see me pull a swift out of my hat? He looked at me strangely, but gamely replied, "Sure,"

*and then said, "Wow! You weren't kidding." He held the bird
carefully, while I gingerly pulled seven cholla cactus spines out of
the swift's flank and back! We placed it in the shade in a crack in
the cliff away from our areas of activity so we wouldn't disturb it
during our work. It was able to cling to the rock in the crevice.*

From my Journal: Monday, 24 May 1993
*Alone at the Gauging Station, I woke very early and couldn't
return to sleep despite it being my day off. ... Sat in my truck to
work on reconstructing a truck log for the early weeks from notes,
gas log, journal and maps. Heard a noise in my truck engine (last
night too, but I've been too tired/too lazy to set traps lately).
Opened the hood and found a woodrat (nocturnal, packrat) had
started to carry in sticks to make a nest in my truck's engine
compartment. Found some truck wiring had been chewed, and an
orange peeling carried in by the woodrat. Set traps. Left the hood
up to discourage the critter. Hope the wiring still works!* [It did.]

The Alamo Lake area was rich in wildlife; the many different
lizards posed identification challenges that I enjoyed and we were
able to identify 12 different species. Peter, though, saw lizards as
another kind of challenge and my journal notes that, on 26 May, he
caught a small side-blotch lizard by hand. We saw eight species of
snakes, including the two kinds of rattlesnakes, and four kinds of
amphibians (toads and frogs). Our sightings of mammals included
at least two species of bats, three of mice, two kinds of woodrats,
two kinds of ground squirrels, one each of cottontails and
jackrabbits, porcupine, coyotes, javelina, burros, mule deer,
beaver, a ringtail (*Bassariscus astutus*) that only Peter got to see,
and domestic cattle.

From my Journal: Thursday 25 March 1993
Collared Lizards (Crotaphytus collaris) *sometimes run fast enough
to get going "upright" on their hind legs. I saw one, about 7-8"
long, do that today and thought it looked like a tiny, fast dinosaur!*

Gila Monster trying to hide among rocks

Enjoying Arizona on my Days Off

On our days off, Nestwatchers were free to leave our assigned
locations, and many of us used these 4-day opportunities to travel
around the state. This was also when we could find a laundromat,
stock up on groceries and other needs, and visit friends or family
who lived in the state. Since there were four of us camped out on
the spillway of Alamo Dam and monitoring the two nests in that
area, our days off were staggered so there were always two of us
on duty. I tended not to go far on my own. Peter was quick to make
his own travel plans or team up with other Nestwatchers whose
days off matched ours.

I did not always spend my days off away from Alamo Lake, sometimes I just continued to camp there and enjoy that area. The opportunities for hiking and birding there were excellent and almost unlimited. Plus, camping was free for us at our Nestwatch sites, and I had free access to water and the showers at the Alamo Lake State Park campgrounds. I did nearly always leave at least once during each of my 4-day off periods, if only to pick up and send off mail at Wenden, and to purchase some fresh supplies.

From my Journal: Tuesday, 2 March 1993
It's my day off. Scott & GC are going to watch today from the Ive's Wash clifftop O.P.; I hiked with them as far as the big wash and, leaving my pack above, went down the "chute" with them to show them the Costa's Hummingbird nest I found, then climbed back to my pack as they went on to the O.P. I sat near a bush with fresh berries and another with flowers and just enjoyed the birds a while: Phainopepla, Black-tailed Gnatcatcher, Costa's Hummingbird, White-crowned Sparrows. Read a while and ate the lunch I had packed along. After lunch, I hiked up the wash to a huge waterfall (dry at this season, of course) but going up it seemed too risky while wearing a pack and without someone to "spot" for me. I climbed instead a narrower, but just as tall, waterfall from a tributary wash, then went up the ridge on my right and looked down on the course of our big wash as it made a big curve coming from the west. I reached a high point from which I could see GC and Scott on the O.P., and I took some photos of the O.P., the dam, and Lake Alamo.

Peter introduced me to his friend, Sandy, and the Hassayampa River Preserve where she worked near Wickenburg, and I visited there several times on my days off. It was a wonderful place to watch birds and I was able to enjoy several species I had rarely seen in my non-fieldwork life, including the beautiful Vermilion Flycatcher, Lucy's Warbler, Anna's Hummingbird, and Hooded

Oriole. Because I enjoyed this place so much, I began volunteering there when I visited. A few times I was allowed to sleep in the back of my truck in the Hassayampa parking lot overnight. Among the adventures I enjoyed there were picking and tasting wild figs, eating pizza baked in Sandy's home-made solar oven, and helping Sandy move a rattler off the property—she captured it near one of the staff cabins with a long-handled snake gripper and put it in a big metal garbage can. I quickly put the lid on the can and we loaded it into the back of her pickup. She drove and I rode in the back to make sure the can stayed upright and the lid stayed on! Elsewhere on the property, but well away from the buildings, the loop hiking trail and most of the visitor activity, we released that snake, hoping not to encounter it again.

One of my cousins and some friends were living in Tucson at the time, and I planned to visit them. The way it turned out, I stayed with the friends in conjunction with flying "home" to Iowa because of my dad.

I also had a cousin in southern California that I wanted to visit; at first, I had hoped to avoid driving in the Los Angeles area and investigated the possibility of making the trip by Amtrak. However, the 3-days-a-week train schedule was not convenient for my times off, so I left Alamo Lake in my pickup at 5 PM on a Sunday (25 April) afternoon and arrived in my cousin's suburb of L.A. about 10:30 PM, having had no traffic problems in the city at all, though I had found the fast and heavy Interstate 10 traffic intimidating. I was especially concerned about the amount of traffic, and the speed at which all the vehicles were traveling, on the long descent, which I drove after dark, of about 30 miles from Chiriaco Summit (1700 ft. in altitude) to below sea level on the desert valley floor east of Indio, itself at an altitude of only 13 ft. above sea level.

I had a wonderful visit with my cousin, Janis, her husband and daughter, and got in some excellent birding while I was there because of their advice on local places to visit, even adding three new birds to my Life List: Wandering Tatler, Black Turnstone, and the endangered California Gnatcatcher. Nevertheless, I was anxious to find out how the eagles were doing, and to escape the busyness of L.A. for the quiet of the desert. I chose to depart the L.A. area at 4:00 AM on Friday, 30 April, to again avoid the worst of the area's commuter traffic. The sun came up as I reached Riverside CA and on this daytime drive back to Arizona, I saw the huge wind farm near Indio and the jojoba plantations at Desert Center. It was less intimidating to do that long, Interstate 10 slope in daylight—less frightening than it had been in the dark and the heavy traffic when I was L.A.-bound on Sunday evening.

After my early start for the trip back to Arizona and several hours of driving, I felt sleepy and stopped at a rest area for a 30-minute nap, waking when I began to "roast" in the locked truck in the hot Mohave sun. I stopped in Salome AZ for ice, groceries, and gas for my truck, and in Wenden to pick up our General Delivery mail. After stopping at one of the Alamo Lake State Park campgrounds to fill my water jugs, I arrived at the spillway to find Scott and Peter, and most of their gear gone, with no obvious note of explanation.

From my Journal: Friday, 30 April 1993
Tired from rising so early and the long drive, I parked on the
spillway and crawled into the back of my truck for another nap,
but was wakened by a BLM archeologist, visiting from Kingman,
who wanted to see the eagles. I set up my scope and gave him
brochures, provided to us for that educational purpose by AZGFD.
I found a note from the guys, held down by a rock. While I was
away, Scott and Peter had moved camp from the spillway to a spot
down by the river where it will be possible to have some shade

while watching the Ive's Wash Nest. After Scott came back, we loaded up my camp kitchen and other gear and I moved down there too, except that I plan to sleep in my truck by the gauging station, rather than out on the ground at the beach with them.

Other Fieldwork Experiences in Arizona

Peter was skilled at networking. In order to enrich his experiences during the 1993 Nestwatch months, he searched for other bird-related fieldwork opportunities, discovered two, volunteered for both, and asked if I wanted to participate. He made the arrangements, and I agreed to help.

In 1993, Arizona was just starting its first state breeding bird atlas project (1993-2000). Although I would later be involved in two Wisconsin Breeding Bird Atlases, in 1993 I was as yet unfamiliar with the scope and purposes of these huge undertakings. Breeding Bird Atlases (BBA) were developed, and first undertaken, in Europe. By the 1970s, researchers in North America had also begun to use these multi-year studies to document the presence of breeding bird species within given geographic areas, such as states in the U.S., or provinces in Canada. Each area is sampled in uniformly-sized survey blocks distributed across the state or province, according to a random or systematic method, depending on the agency and geographic entity involved. The observations and data-recording work are done by people able to identify the species birds of the area by sight and sound, and who know the nesting places and breeding behaviors of those birds. These may be either paid atlasers, or volunteers.

Peter discovered that our spillway location was within one of the Arizona Breeding Bird Atlas survey blocks. His friend, Sandy, was also volunteering for a BBA survey block that was located along the Hassayampa River near the preserve where she worked. We spent a couple days helping Sandy in her atlas block, and she came to Alamo Lake on her days off and returned the favor as we searched for birds and their nests, observing them to note behaviors that would indicate they were breeding in our survey blocks even if we could not find a nest for a particular species.

From my Journal: Monday, 17 May 1993
I wore a small backpack, with a special waterproof bag inside to protect my optics, bird-song tape & tape-player, and used two hiking sticks to cross the Bill Williams River above our Beach O.P. At 350 cfs, the river was very powerful and deep enough to get me wet almost up to my waist by the route I chose. The bottom was uneven and composed of slippery rocks, and I had to brace myself with the poles, feeling my way one cautious step at a time. Keeping my balance against the current was difficult and I felt panic in an adrenalin-rush at mid-stream, but finally made it across. Birding in the bosque [riparian/floodplain forest] *was excellent and we added nesting breeding behavior evidence for the atlas. Sandy has arrived to see the eagles, camp with us, and bird with us tomorrow. Sometimes I feel so old working with these younger people; at their age (30) I'd already been married nine years, borne two children and was probably about to potty-train the second.*

From my Journal: Friday, 25 May 1993
Woke at 4:45 AM, dressed, took my pre-packed daypack, water, snake bite kit, binocs. Peter, Sandy and I birded upriver on the Hassayampa and entered a wash. I found two Cactus Wren nests, an empty Mourning Dove nest, and a White-winged Dove nest with one egg. We also found fledglings of various species, and some Verdin nests in four hours of birding.

Sandy kept the atlas records for her Hassayampa River survey block and Peter kept the records for our Alamo block, but I

226

enjoyed helping and learned a lot about breeding bird atlas projects. Later we met the AZ BBA leader; he was pleased with our records of 24 species of breeding birds in the big wash area.

Willow Flycatchers are one species of a group of confusing small flycatchers in genus *Empidonax,* most of which can be confidently identified only by voice. There are several subspecies of Willow Flycatchers; one of them, the southwestern Willow Flycatcher, *Empidonas traillii extimus,* found in New Mexico, Arizona, southern California, southern Nevada, and adjacent portions of Colorado, is rare.

Sandy, Peter, and I participated in the first southwestern Willow Flycatcher survey in Arizona. Concern that populations of this subspecies were declining, had led to plans to conduct statewide surveys for it in appropriate habitat, and the bird was being considered for listing under the Endangered Species Act. The three of us drove north for a training session to be held 13-14 May (one of the off-periods for Peter and me), at a site in Coconino National Forest east of Camp Verde, where we all camped the night of the 13th.

About 30 people were present for this training session conducted by two biologists from the Nongame Branch of Arizona Game and Fish Department. Training included information on the bird and its status, design and procedures of the survey, and proper use of the survey forms. We also divided into groups and went into the field to learn about features of typical southwestern Willow Flycatcher habitat.

After the training was completed, we three volunteered to survey the Bill Williams River just below the dam, the adjacent big wash, and the section of the Santa Maria River directly above Alamo Lake. We were issued the required forms and a tape of the Willow

Flycatcher's rather unmusical song, *"fitz-bew."* I had seen, heard and identified this species in the upper Midwest, and was one of the few people present with direct, previous experience with it. Nevertheless, there were more than 70 people concerned and interested enough to participate in one or the other of the two training sessions, and to sign up for survey areas.

On Wednesday, 2 June, Peter and I met three AZ Game and Fish guys, two from the Yuma office and one from Wickenburg, who were present to monitor livestock damage to vegetation along the river, and the extent of livestock access to the river. We loaded our gear into their big 4WD truck, the better to get through the sandy access "road" without getting stuck, and rode with them in to the mouth of Date Creek. Once there, we set up camp on sand under cottonwoods near where the creek joins the Santa Maria River.

We were shown the damage that cattle had done to the river-side vegetation, and a fenced study plot—filled with dense, green plant growth—as a clear illustration of what vegetation in the area would look like without grazing cattle. We hiked downstream to a small wetland area with cattails, saw a Zone-tailed Hawk nest and several peccaries. Toward evening we built up a campfire and another Game & Fish guy arrived with chicken and roasted it over the fire as supper for both agency people and volunteers.

I spread my light-weight sleeping bag on a tarp on the sand, but the nighttime temperature was cooler than I expected and I was chilly during the night despite wearing all the clothes I had brought along when I crawled into my sleeping bag. The gallery forest trees filtered the bright moonlight—lovely. In the morning, I had a piece of left-over chicken and Grapenuts™ for breakfast.

Jean, at sandbar camp during southwestern Willow Flycatcher survey

By 6 AM on 3 June, Peter and I were crossing the river to begin our Willow Flycatcher survey in the area of possibly suitable habitat that we had scouted the day before. The bed of the Santa Maria River was a very wide sheet of sand, but the actual channel of water was narrow—about 20 yards wide— braided, and only a few inches deep when we were there. Walking in the water and water-soaked sand was hard work. The survey procedure involved trudging along or in the river in these conditions, and at a temperature of about 100°, stopping every 50 yards or so, and playing the tape of the Willow Flycatcher song. Since a male Willow Flycatcher on a breeding territory regards another singing male as an intruder, if a territorial male was present in our survey area, he would be expected to approach, perch in the open, and reply to the tape.

Peter and I spent much of that day following these survey procedures, covering long stretches of possible habitat beside the Santa Maria River. In the late afternoon when we were almost back to our starting point, standing before a patch of willows, we finally had an *Empidonax* flycatcher appear while the tape was playing, hop from branch to branch in agitation, and sing *"fitz-bew"* back to us when I shut off the tape! This was very exciting, but it meant we would have to return about a week later and try to prove the male had stayed on territory.

We returned to this difficult-to-access area on 8 June and again found the Willow Flycatcher in the same location, and again it responded when we played the tape. On neither occasion were we able to observe a second bird or find a nest. We called AZGFD with our exciting news, filled out the paperwork, which included describing the habitat, drawing a map of the location, noting the presence or absence of cattle, and listing all the other bird species we identified. In some of the habitat areas we saw cowbirds and livestock, as many as 30 head of cattle, plus some wild burros.

The replacement of riparian native vegetation, such as willows and cottonwoods, with non-native tamarisk was considered indicative of habitat degradation, and possibly a contributing factor in the suspected decline of the southwestern Willow Flycatcher population. We therefore had to record the presence and quantity of tamarisk in our survey areas. Personally, we both despised the thick, dusty, prickly tamarisk, especially in areas where we had to crawl through it to reach the river bank.

We also surveyed for Willow Flycatchers on 7 June in some possibly suitable habitat along the Bill Williams River below the dam, and in a couple washes (dry at that season) that emptied into the river. However, in those locations we found no additional Willow Flycatchers. No cowbirds or cattle were seen during this survey either, but we had seen both in the same areas on other days, as well as wild burros. In May, we had seen an *Empidonax* flycatcher in the big wash, but since it was not singing, we were unable to definitively identify it.

The presence or absence of cowbirds was of particular importance in regard to the southwestern Willow Flycatcher. We observed both Bronzed Cowbird, and the far more common Brown-headed Cowbird, in the Alamo Lake area. Both are generalist nest-parasites; as such, the Brown-headed Cowbird, especially, poses a serious threat to the survival of several species and subspecies of birds. Kirtland Warblers are a well-known example, but concern for the rare southwestern subspecies of Willow Flycatcher included a need to study whether cowbirds, as well as habitat degradation, were a threat to the flycatchers' ability to successfully reproduce.

Rather than building their own nests, the female cowbirds lay their eggs (as many as 40 eggs by a single female in one breeding season) in the nests of a variety of other birds, typically species that are smaller than the cowbirds. This disrupts breeding success of a host bird, such as a Willow Flycatcher, in several ways. The cowbird female may toss out an egg of the host species when she lays her own egg in the host's nest, reducing the possible number of offspring of the host. Cowbird eggs usually hatch in fewer days than the host's eggs, giving the cowbird nestling a head start. Since it is then usually bigger than the nestlings of the host species, it can beg more effectively, and get more of the food being brought in by the parent birds, thus causing some or all of the host's young to starve. Not all species of small birds are appropriate hosts for cowbird eggs. Some species are able to recognize cowbird eggs and either destroy them, eject them from the nest, abandon the nest, or rebuild their nest on top of the cowbird egg. In other cases, the host birds might be too big, and break the cowbird egg during incubation, or bring the wrong kinds of foods for cowbird nestlings, as in the case of hummingbirds, which bring nectar for their young. Another poor-choice host species might lead hatchlings away from the nest, as ducks do, rather than bringing food to the nest. Being altricial (helpless young) in the nest, cowbirds that hatched in the nest of such birds would starve.

I was curious whether the Willow Flycatcher surveys, in which Peter, Sandy and I played a small part, had any results. An internet search during this writing, revealed that the U.S. Fish and Wildlife Service successfully listed the southwestern Willow Flycatcher as a federally endangered subspecies in 1995. The plan for its recovery was completed in 2002, by which time it was estimated that only 900-1110 pairs existed. By 2007, further surveys raised the estimate to 1299 territories. The primary reasons determined by USFWS for the decline of the subspecies were loss and degradation of dense, native riparian habitats. Contributing factors to these habitat issues are water impoundment projects, water diversion for agriculture, and groundwater pumping. All of these factors alter water flow in the streams, thereby also causing changes in riparian vegetation. Other negative impacts were stream bank stabilization projects, riparian vegetation control efforts, livestock grazing, off-road vehicle use, increased fires, and urban development. Willow Flycatchers can successfully nest in tamarisk, but this non-native plant species is generally detrimental. And, finally, cowbirds can significantly threaten some Willow Flycatcher populations by reducing the flycatchers' reproductive rates. Brown-headed Cowbirds have increased significantly in both range and abundance, because of increases in irrigated agriculture and livestock grazing.

Outreach, Public Education

As Nestwatchers, part of our responsibility was to educate members of the public about the biology and reproduction of Bald

Eagles, and conservation efforts on their behalf. We had to explain the Nestwatch Program and the need for closed areas around eagle nests located in areas vulnerable to disturbance by humans, and could hand out special brochures about the eagles. We were visited by other Nestwatchers on their days off, by family and friends of Nestwatchers, by employees of the three agencies active in the Alamo Lake area, and their friends and families. On many occasions, Army Corps of Engineers, Bureau of Land Management, and Alamo Lake State Park personnel brought visitors through the locked gate to our spillway camp to talk to us, learn from us, and look through the spotting scopes at the eagles and the Ive's Wash Nest. Sometimes groups were brought to us by appointment, including members of the staff of Hassayampa River Preserve, where Peter and I frequently visited and volunteered on our days off. We had a teacher visit who was doing a project about the Nestwatch Program, and a scout troop. Rich and Colleen, a couple working as hosts in one of the state park campgrounds, brought their visiting family to see the eagles.

From my Journal: Thursday 25 March 1993
After a morning on duty at the spillway alone, Peter returned from the Hilltop O.P. and gave me a break. I went to the campground for a shower and walked over to talk to Rich, letting him tell me story after story of his colorful life—air crashes, horse throws, rattlers, and the grenade he just found. I had been especially interested when he told me that earlier he had worked on predator control at Gray's Lake, Idaho, during the project involving fostering Whooping Crane eggs into Sandhill Crane nests. [This early conservation effort on behalf of Whooping Cranes was less successful than later attempts to establish a breeding population of the species in the upper Midwest with a migration route to Florida.]

Toward the end of our Nestwatch days, Peter and I both spent some time at Hassayampa during our last off-duty period. I had gone to Phoenix to photocopy our field notes at AZGFD for the boss and pick up our paychecks. After arriving at Hassayampa, one of the staff and I picked mulberries and baked two pies. I slept in my truck in the parking lot that night.

From my Journal: Wednesday, 26 May 1993
Went out to my truck after dark, hearing voices in the visitor's parking lot, a man & woman arguing. Became worried about my safety, got into the cab of my truck to close and lock myself in. That startled the arguers into silence; they then pushed their vehicle into position, snapped on lights, started the engine and left quickly! Relieved, I made descriptive notes about their vehicle, opened the tailgate for fresh, cool air, crawled in the back and slept.

The next day, I told my intruder story around the office and strongly suggested they close the Preserve gates at night. Peter arrived, borrowed the preserve's 35mm slide projector and, in the evening, showed the slides of our Nestwatch work for the staff of Hassayampa River Preserve and a few of their guests and visitors, in appreciation for all the kindnesses of the staff to both of us. I asked for copies of a few of Peter's slides, and made copies for him of my slides taken while he was involved in the weighing, measuring and banding of the Alamo Cliff eagle on 5 May.

The End of my Dad's Life

Gary celebrated his birthday in 1993 by attending the Canoe Show in Madison. Daughter Janis and her boyfriend, my sister and her husband, all went to enjoy the Canoe Show with him. I planned to call to wish Gary a Happy Birthday, but waited until the next day when one of my 4-day off periods would begin and I could go out to find a pay phone. It was my intent for this time-off period to visit friends in Tucson. I started this off-period by getting my mail in Wenden, finding only a letter from my brother bringing me the news that Dad's health was continuing to worsen. Next, I called Phoenix to check in with our boss at Game and Fish, and then friends Stan and Virginia who lived in Tucson. I had written these friends I would be working in Arizona and hoped to visit them; when I called, they welcomed me and I drove on to Tucson. Since they already had houseguests, I was bunked in their RV, parked beside their retirement home in a trailer park.

After reaching Tucson, I called Gary and learned Dad was back in the hospital with fluid in his lungs. Patti, my sister, was planning to drive to Iowa the next day to see Mom and Dad, and my brother, Paul, was thinking about making the trip (by plane) to Iowa from his home in Michigan. There was other, less dismal, family news in that phone conversation, for example, news about the job searches of our son-in-law.

From my Journal: Monday, 15 March 1993
Our son-in-law got a seasonal job with Wyoming DNR. Gary plans to help Gayle (daughter) and her husband move at the end of the month.

From my Journal: Tuesday, 16 March 1993
It is 1 AM and I woke to coyotes calling. Sleep eludes me. Dad lays dying in a hospital, Mom is coping, Paul and Patti are rallying, Gary has soothed my concerns. I have a plan to call each day to stay in touch until I go back to Alamo. Dad is dying, but I am alive. The fieldwork perspective sustains me. I'm alive, I'm here, I'm now. Life demands I live though death is all around. None of this is more real than the hospital, none of this is less real. There are the mountains, the desert tortoise, eagles, wildflowers, sunsets, teammates, the physical use of my body and intellectual use of my

mind. There is clean air. There is work and the smallness of
humans in the immensity of the universe. I am alive. I will live.

I spent that day quietly with my friends. Stan took me to a mall to
get a couple things I needed, and to a park with desert plants and
plantings. There were birds, and the park was wild and peaceful,
albeit in the city. In the evening I called Gary and together we
decided I would go "home" to Iowa the next day if he could get me
plane tickets.

From my Journal: Wednesday, 17 March 1993
Gary called at 7:30 with arrangements all made except pickup. I
called and claimed the last seat on the Tucson-to-Phoenix airport
shuttle. ... Stan and Virginia took me to the shuttle depot. At the
terminal in Phoenix, I paid $452 by charge card for the plane
tickets and called the AZGFD boss's voice mail about my plans.

I changed planes in Minneapolis to reach a smaller airport closer to
my parents, where my brother-in-law met my flight. That night I
called Gary. My sister and brother had arrived ahead of me. To
pass the time, I asked my brother, Paul, an accomplished artist, to
teach me how to draw an eagle in "going away overhead"
perspective so my drawings for the data sheets would not be so
clumsy.

I was very glad to have those few days in Iowa with my family.
Gary came from Wisconsin (on the 19th) and I spoke by phone with
both daughters. Iowa, still in winter, was a big contrast from the
desert, where flowers were blooming and birds nesting; twice
while I was at Mom's, I helped shovel snow off her driveway.

Several times I visited my dad in the hospital, saw Dad's brother,
some cousins and other relatives as they visited Dad, or stopped by
the house. Mom and Dad's neighbor lady very kindly helped by

preparing food for all of us several times. I was with Mom when Dad's doctor told her his lungs were not clearing as hoped, and the doctor provided us with Hospice and Home Care information. We went to the bank's trust office to ask questions about probate. It was awful, all of it, yet we were together in it.

From my Journal: Saturday, 20 March 1993
I made plans with Gary's help, and calls to reserve flights back to Arizona, for the shuttle from Phoenix to Tucson, for Stan to meet the shuttle and take me back to my truck at his and Virginia's home. Paul was also making calls for his flights home to Michigan.

On the 22nd, after shoveling snow for Mom, Gary drove Paul and me over very slick roads to the "local" airport to catch a flight to Minneapolis, where we separated. Our plane got in late, so I had to run from one end of the terminal to another, and my next flight was boarding when I reached the gate. Back in Tucson, Virginia made me a lunch and I set off driving, stopping for gas, cash and groceries, and to call Mom that I'd had good flights.

From my Journal: Monday, 22 March 1993
Tired only in the last hour of driving, sustained by lunch, cake, Indian flute music on the tape player, and my memories. Stopped briefly in Wenden to mail letters written on the planes, and to write a note to send Stan and Virginia. Got water at the Park office, put a new padlock on the gate, and "set up camp" by the rock wall.

Another 10-day work period went by. At my next time off, I followed Peter to Wickenburg, planning to visit Hassayampa River Preserve, a Nature Conservancy property where his friend, Sandy, worked. Peter introduced me to the manager, before continuing on his way to Phoenix to make photocopies, give the Nestwatch boss a set of our latest data sheets, and to pick up mail and our paychecks. I dropped my films off at the Wickenburg camera shop for developing, bought a sheet of plastic and some groceries, did laundry and wrote letters. In the evening I called Patti to keep her apprised of my plans and where she could reach me, and learned of the safe arrival of Gary, Gayle, her husband, their cat, aquarium of fish, and household goods in Wyoming, that they would next begin the search for a place to live. Also, that Dad's lung involvement makes him too weak for home care, and his need for an IV precludes the hometown nursing home. It seemed clear he did not have much time left, and I was very glad I had gone to see him.

That evening, 29 March, I drove out in the country to a brushy place GC had recommended as a free place to camp, and Peter showed up about 9 PM from Phoenix to join me, bringing our paychecks and some old letters that had been mailed to Game and Fish. The next day I returned to Hassayampa and spent several happy hours birding along the preserve trails. When I got back to my truck just before noon, I found a note to call Patti.

From my Journal: Tuesday, 30 March 1993
 Dad died this morning peacefully—his heart just stopped. I'm so glad for him not to suffer longer. I called the airlines & made arrangements to fly home Thursday and back Sunday, called Patti back with this info. I'm grateful Gary gave me the information about using his frequent flyer miles leftover from work. Patti had reached Paul in Seattle [where he and his wife had gone for a conference]*, but not Gary, Gayle and her husband in Wyoming, nor Janis (daughter) in Wisconsin. Patti was about to leave for Iowa and we made plans for calls tonight after she reaches Mom's house. Fortunately, she had a key to my house—I had to ask her to bring along clothing suitable for me to wear to the funeral.*

I spent the afternoon reading, birding and writing letters at the Preserve where the manager, upon learning the circumstances, kindly offered to let me stay. I slept in my truck in the parking lot.

The next day I began to volunteer at the preserve, cleaning the bathrooms, emptying the trash, washing dishes, washing and refilling the hummingbird feeders, sweeping the visitor and gift store areas. I also packed a bag for the trip to Iowa.

From my Journal: Wednesday, 31 March 1993
In the evening I called Patti at Mom's, Janis in Wisconsin, Gary and Gayle in Wyoming. Today they found a mobile home for Gayle and Dean to buy and a court to park it in—which is why Patti couldn't reach them—the Wyoming sheriff found them last night at a motel. The trailer will be delivered and set up tomorrow, which is also when Dean starts his new job <u>so they can't come. Paul & Ann can't get a flight from Seattle, nor for their son to come from Michigan. Janis is reluctant to drive alone from Wisconsin.</u> How very strange for such a home-body family to be so scattered at this crucial time. Of Dad's immediate family, only Mom, Patti, her husband, and I will be there, the other seven will be unable to come for the funeral.

.

Not long after midnight I woke, rearranged my pickup and began driving from Wickenburg to Phoenix. It was lovely driving in the desert night and the Carefree Hwy was empty, the city traffic easy. I became utterly confused by the airport parking directions and had to ask a security guard. After parking my truck in a ramp, I tried to rig sunshades in the front, closed the curtains in the back, and wrapped my cameras and optics in sleeping bags to cushion them a little against temperature extremes. I took the shuttle into the airport, slept an hour on the floor with my arm through the handles of my bag, and ate a light breakfast from my supplies while waiting for the ticket office to open. I flew the same route from Phoenix to Minneapolis, then to a local Iowa airport. A cousin picked me up at the local airport and took me to Mom's. Mom's good neighbor prepared supper for all of us and afterward I went to the funeral home. We had one day together before the funeral.

From my Journal: Friday, 2 April 1993
*We sat in the front rank, Mom, Patti, her husband, and I, only four
of Dad's immediate family (seven absent), plus Dad's brother and
sister. The service was by a new minister who didn't know Dad.
The couch creaked ominously under the six of us. It was finally
over and we followed the hearse to the cemetery for a very brief
committal, sitting in blanketed comfort while others shivered. We
went to the lunch served at the church and it was a relief, almost a
party. There was so much food. I tried to avoid people I didn't
recognize, and to talk to the ones I cared about. A cousin's wife
told a funny story about Dad that I had never heard. We went
home to relief, loss, silence. Ate more donated food. The flowers
were delivered by the funeral home per Mom's decisions and we
started lists of cards, memorials, food donations, etc. per the
undertaker's advice, and arranged to pay the bill when he
delivered the guestbook, thank-you cards, etc. This was my first
experience with the "business" of death. Ugh.*

From my Journal: Saturday, 3 April 1993
*Funny how everyone comes before the funeral, when you think you
can't face seeing them, brings food, sits with you. Then no one
comes after, and you are alone to face loss. Mom was amazingly
controlled and strong.*

I had one more day in Iowa to help wash pans and containers from
the foods people had brought, to help Mom with writing thank-you
cards, and other tasks, such as sorting Dad's clothes for donation to
Goodwill. She gave each of us a shirt of Dad's for a memory. Patti
and I went with Mom to pay the funeral home bill, and tried to see
the lawyer (he was not in).

The next day, Patti and her husband took me to the airport before
heading back to Wisconsin. She looked so tired. I was so grateful
she and her husband had been able to be there with Mom right

away when Dad died, to help Mom with choosing the casket and deciding on other arrangements. I caught my flights back to Phoenix, this time feeling like a competent airline traveler, yet disoriented to be so. I found my truck in the parking ramp to be in good shape and headed out of Phoenix at once. I stopped briefly at Hassayampa to pick up the food I had left in the refrigerator there, to say thanks and good-bye to the staff there, and also at Wenden to mail a letter and to call Mom.

From my Journal: Monday, 5 April 1993
How strange, and yet how peaceful to be back in the desert, unchanging, blooming, quiet, soothing. For me this first day back was a day of adjustment, of trying to reconcile loss and relief, winter in Iowa and summer in Arizona, attending to grief and leaving it behind (in a sense). My teammates had purchased a bottle of wine and we toasted all our fathers around the campfire.

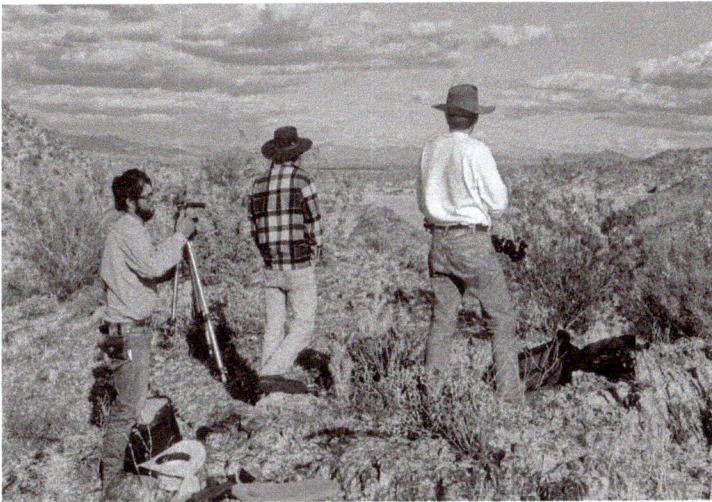

Nestwatch teammates in the rugged Alamo Lake country: GC, Scott, Peter

Teammates

I do not think I could possibly have been more fortunate in the three men who were my teammates during my season as a Nestwatcher. GC was easy to talk to. Scott was desert-wise, and gently entertained us in the evenings by playing the second-hand guitar he bought in Phoenix and restrung. Peter bore the brunt of report-typing without complaint, was as avid a birder as I was, and an excellent wilderness camper. All of them were serious about the job and hard-working. Even early in the Nestwatch season, I was impressed with my good fortune in working partners.

From my Journal: Saturday, 20 February 1993
I feel lucky to be assigned to this place and with all these guys. I'm glad to already have had experience working with Peter. Though I've just met Scott & GC and they are very different, I like them both. Because they have been observing nesting eagles for six weeks already, GC & Scott are able to show Peter & me how to do the daily summaries, and to give us tips on the other forms we have to work with, many of which we had no experience with at our first assignment, the abandoned Camp Verde nest.

Fledging

Before fledging, the young eagles of both nests did a lot of wing-flapping to exercise their flight muscles. Sometimes their flapping was vigorous and coordinated enough to lift them off the nest, but if a strong gust of wind did not come just then, they were able to settle back down on the nest. Actual fledging, the moment when a bird leaves its nest for the first time and lands elsewhere, can be a deliberate act on the part of the bird, or it can be precipitated accidently by a wind gust coming along just when the young bird is practicing flapping, even hovering just above the nest. The gust of wind may then carry the bird away from the nest, forcing it to find somewhere else to land. When both Ive's Wash eaglets and the single eaglet of the Alamo Lake cliff nest had officially fledged by this definition, our Nestwatch duties would be finished and we could leave as soon as our reports were completed, delivered and accepted.

Scott had really hoped to observe the fledging of at least one of the eaglets in the Ive's Wash Nest, and accordingly watched very diligently right up almost to the minute he had to leave to start his summer fieldwork job. He even hiked out to the Hilltop O.P. the day before he left; it was a windy day and there was a lot of wing-flapping by both eaglets in the Ive's Wash Nest, but neither fledged. Scott worked a full day his last day on site, ate supper with us, said good-bye and headed home to prepare for his next job. Scott's last day was also the day that the new Alamo Lake eaglet was banded, but Scott's devotion to observing the Ive's Wash Nest, although not rewarded with a fledging, allowed both Peter and me to witness the Alamo eaglet banding process. The Ive's Wash eaglets both fledged on 10 May out of our view; we found them both perched in the canyon away from the nest only five days after Scott left, and we were able to individually identify them as Foster (offspring of the Alamo Lake pair's first nesting attempt) and Junior, whose parents actually were the Ive's Wash eagles. We could then finish the Ive's Wash Nest report.

The Alamo Lake Cliff Nest eaglet fledged while we were watching on 13 June. We were able to complete the last details in that report the next day, say good-bye, and depart Alamo Lake.

Report-writing

Nestwatch reports had to be typed, and there were very specific instructions about the format we were to use. Peter had brought along a word-processing typewriter. Because I was unfamiliar with its functions, Peter did all of the typing, leaving for me much of the work of compiling the data from all the forms into summary sheets and doing the writing for many of the remaining sections of both the Alamo Lake and Ive's Wash reports.

Peter and I had some experience in writing a Nestwatch Report, but the Camp Verde report was brief and easy because we saw no eagles and had no prey deliveries, interactions or other behaviors to report. We did record disturbances, but as we were on site at that nest for only one 10-day work period, these were limited, albeit numerous and varied enough for us to think this nest, which was later destroyed by the flood, was not a location conducive for Bald Eagle reproductive success.

The reports for the Ive's Wash Nest and Alamo Cliff Nest were another matter, much more complex, and lengthy, the more so because of the flood-caused rescue of eggs from the first Alamo (tree) nest, subsequent re-nesting by that pair, and the fostering of the zoo-hatched eaglet from the first Alamo nesting attempt into the Ive's Wash Nest. The Ive's Wash Nest report ran to 21 typed (single-spaced) pages, the Alamo Cliff Nest report to 17 pages. Added to both reports were maps, a chronology of events, tables of interactions, disturbances, foraging attempts, and prey deliveries, as well as lists of wildlife sightings (birds, mammals, reptiles and amphibians).

Besides having two nests to observe, report-writing was complicated by several other factors: there were four of us gathering data, different individuals writing separate sections of the two reports, and, on any given day, different members of the team might be observing the same nest from separate observation points. Nevertheless, all the data had to be compiled according to the correct nest, and duplications guarded against. Both GC and Scott had worked diligently to complete early sections of the two reports, and to compute subtotals up the point of their departures, for the various kinds of data we were required to collect. After they left, Peter and I continued data collection until all three eaglets fledged, updated the tables, computed new totals, and completed the reports for both nests. This was made easier after the Ive's Wash eaglets fledged, as that report could then be completed while we had only one nest with one eaglet in the Alamo Cliff Nest to continue to observe.

Peter and I had noted when we wrote up the report on the Ive's Wash Nest, that the most serious disturbance to that pair of eagles was the intrusion by AZGFD biologists into their nest on 9 March, and our boss commented on this section of the report as follows: "Good—often people do not include this, but as you say—it is often the most serious disturbance." He also noted again our careful observations during long hours for eight consecutive days immediately after the fostering: "again—nice succinct section." At the end of section one of our report he wrote: "Nice first section— [you] summarized succinctly what was observed and explained in detail the big events." It was very gratifying to receive these positive comments from the boss on our reports.

Because we were required to submit some sections of the reports early for review, and to turn in periodic summary tables of various categories of data, a great deal of the report-writing work was done gradually as the weeks and months went by. We were given criticisms and suggestions on the advance sections so corrections could also be made as we went along. In practice then, it was possible to finish the reports in a day or two of hard work after fledging at each nest.

From my Journal: Friday 7 May 1993
I wrote the text for the disturbance and fostering sections, the
acknowledgements, management and program recommendations.

Peter did the rest and has done all the typing because he didn't teach me how to use his word-processing typewriter. That's fair, because I did hours and hours of "dawn to dusk" observations alone while he typed in the park office.

From my Journal: Monday 14 June 1993
Sat at the park office picnic table with Peter. He ate lunch & assisted me in finding the last foraging info & re-doing some percentage calculations. We said good-bye with hugs: "It was a fruitful association; there isn't another Nestwatcher I'd rather have worked with," Peter told me. And, I felt the same about working with him. Gary and I filled our water jugs at the office, turned in a forwarding card at the Wenden Post Office and headed north.

My Husband Gary's Visits to Alamo Lake

Gary parked his pickup beside mine on the spillway
when he came to visit in April

To help daughter Gayle and her husband—the latter was to start a new job with Wyoming Game and Fish Department—move from Iowa to Wyoming in late March, Gary drove from our Wisconsin home to the little town in central Iowa where they had been living and working while finishing some schooling. He helped them load their vehicles, his pickup, and a 7x14-foot cargo trailer with their household goods and trailed them to Wyoming in late March. After they found a used mobile home to purchase and a trailer park to place it in, Gary helped them move in. Leaving the cargo trailer in Wyoming, Gary then set out to drive to Arizona to visit me.

Gary was involved in this Iowa-to-Wyoming move when my dad died and was buried; after the funeral, I was back in Arizona by 4 April. Gary arrived at Alamo Lake on 8 April, and parked his big pickup on the spillway, but away from the row of the trucks of my teammates. We moved some of his gear into my truck so we could share his at night. I introduced him to my teammates and we all had supper, cooked by GC, together that first evening.

From my Journal: Friday, 9 April 1993
Woke at Gary's side, how wonderfully warm, familiar, loving, content. We talked, got up, walked up into the "ladies latrine ravine" and found a wounded jack burro on the ridge above the spillway, which we watched for a couple hours that day. After breakfast Gary watched the Ive's Wash Nest with us from the spillway. After lunch we moved down by the river.

Peter watched the nest while Gary and I hiked up Ive's Wash, a lovely place of rocks, with a trickle of water, a pool of tadpoles, and a few cattails. Then I watched eagles while Peter went swimming in the pool at the base of our wash after wading the river. Gary took his camp chair to sit by the river and just rest after all the stress and traveling he's been doing lately. GC caught a channel catfish in the river and cooked it for our supper.

From my Journal: Saturday, 10 April 1993
In the evening we finally had our bonfire, and baked foil-wrapped
foods in it. Gary and I shared a yam and each had a potato, carrot
and half an onion. Others had an apple stuffed with raisins or a
green pepper stuffed with rice, tomato & garlic. All very tasty.
Scott played his new guitar by the fire for us—lovely.

Gary was thus on site with the Nestwatch team for a dawn-to-dusk
weekend of observations. Peter and GC borrowed a boat and
motored across the lake to observe the Alamo Cliff Nest on the
11th while Scott and I kept watch on the Ive's Wash Nest. Since
Monday, 12 April was the beginning of a 4-day off-period for
Peter and me, Gary and I planned to do some Arizona sight-seeing
together, using Gary's truck, and leaving mine parked on the
spillway. Scott encouraged us to set off about 5:30 PM on Sunday,
so we dumped camp trash at one of the park campgrounds, mailed
letters in Wenden and headed for Robbins Butte Wildlife Area near
Buckeye AZ, where we camped that night. I had saved the last
MRE, (scalloped potatoes and ham), given to me by one of my
biology students, to share with Gary and we ate it that night. The
next morning, we went for a walk just after dawn. Robbins Butte
was managed for doves and quail and those are the birds we saw,
plus White-crowned Sparrows.

Determined to make the most of these few days together, while I
was off duty, we planned to see some of the southeast corner of
Arizona, which we had missed during our 1982 family vacation in
the state. Taking turns driving southeastward, we stopped in
Wilcox AZ for gas and groceries, then went on to Chiricahua
National Monument to camp one night. We enjoyed the scenery
there, toured the visitor center, and Faraway Ranch. At the latter,
we joined a tour of the ranch house of Emma and Neil Erickson,
which their daughter, Lillian later made into a guest ranch. We
learned the couple also had a son, Ben, who ranched in the area as

248

well and eventually met his second wife, a birder and concert pianist, when she was a guest at the ranch, and another daughter, Hildegard. Hildegard's granddaughter, from Sonoma County, California, was present in our tour group with her husband and two younger sons, telling a family anecdote and thereby making the tour more personal for all of us. The pianist kept a grand piano in an old, sunken cellar of the ranch house; she would play concerts for the family when they retreated to the cellar during lightning storms.

From my Journal: Monday, 12 April 1993
From Chiricahua I was able to call Mom. Paul [my brother] and his wife were there to visit her and help write more thank-you cards. Mom reported the amount of memorial money she had received in Dad's memory, that she had been to the lawyer twice to get the probate process started, had gotten insurance and Social Security information—so much for her to deal with—I'm glad Paul is there. Gayle had written to her, and Mom had talked by phone to Paul's son, Avery, and to Patti, so we caught up on news of most of the family in this one call.

Chiricahua National Monument, and the locations we visited on 13-14 April were in the Cochise County portion of Coronado National Forest. Because of my interest in birding, my journal notes of this time of exploration often include the special birds that I saw in the places we visited.

From my Journal: Tuesday, 13 April 1993
After making pancakes for breakfast in camp, we drove up to Massai Point for the view, and walked the nature trail—the rocks are spectacular! Next, we drove a gravel road into Rucker Canyon, but took one wrong turn so saw some extra back-country. Because of the long gravel access, we had few other tourists to detract from our sense of exploration. After an afternoon rest in the back of the

truck while it rained, we hiked in Bear Canyon within the
Chiricahua Wilderness, seeing Painted Redstarts and Yellow-eyed
Juncos. There was only intermittent water in the canyon.

We spent Tuesday night in a Rucker Canyon campground, seeing a
Common Black Hawk the next morning before going on to
Cochise Stronghold campground for Wednesday night, where the
Clivus Multrum composting toilets were a new experience. Band-
tailed Pigeon and Scott's Oriole were interesting bird sightings in
this location.

On Thursday, 15 April, we moved on into Santa Cruz County and
visited Madera Canyon, a birding hot-spot, where I found four Life
Birds, three of them hummingbirds: Magnificent, Broad-billed, and
Black-chinned Hummingbirds were seen at the campground
feeders. The fourth Life Bird was a beautiful male Elegant Trogon,
which we found only after taking two long hikes on trails
recommended by the park naturalist.

On Friday, 16 April, I was due back at Alamo, so we stopped in
Benson AZ on the way to get my 11-pound propane tank refilled,
and in Tucson to do laundry and shop for groceries. Arriving at
Alamo, we stopped first at the campground so Gary could meet
Rich and Colleen, the Cholla Road Campground hosts, who had
been unfailingly kind and friendly to me. There we were glad to be
able to take showers and change to clean clothes before I had to go
back on duty.

During the next three days, Gary shared more of the Nestwatch
experience. One day he hiked with me to the Ive's Wash Hilltop
O.P. to experience that vigorous hiking route. He took photos and
endured the long hours of eagle observation in the hot, relentless
sunshine. Scott and Peter were also at the O.P. and Scott planned
to camp out there. By great good fortune, Gary was treated to the

sight of a Gila Monster that visited the O.P. that day. GC had stayed at the spillway to work on the reports and observe from there. To add to Gary's Alamo experience, Peter showed us the way down to the river from the Hilltop O.P., and the three of us waded the river (25cfs), each choosing a slightly different route. On the other side, Gary and I encountered a rattler on the road. On this hike, Peter and I also saw two rattlers in a den, asleep.

Another day, Gary joined GC and I as we motored across the lake in Bruce's little boat, the interminable trip made more interesting than usual by terns, courting grebes, and its newness to Gary. That day the boat trip back to the Alamo Lake State Park landing was against the wind and Gary contributed to our safe return.

From my Journal: Sunday, 18 April 1993
At the eroded bank, we tied the boat, shouldered our packs, encountered a rattler, and hiked the long, tiringly-uphill route by eroded mining roads to near the top, from whence we could observe the nest. GC refused to stop at a place that would get deep cliff shade after 1 PM, so I sat in the thin shade of a paloverde. We had good observation luck. The walk down was easier, but the footing bad; Gary fell once. The afternoon west wind made the ride back across the lake slow and <u>very wet</u>. GC drove the boat, I tried to shelter the optics and other gear, Gary continuously bailed. We were all wet and chilled, so after we reached shore, we went directly to the campground to take hot showers.

On the last day of Gary's April visit, we repacked his truck and I sorted through my gear to send home with him things I no longer needed, making my truck much easier for me to live in during the remainder of the job. On 20 April, Gary set out after we shared breakfast, to drive to Wyoming to check in with daughter Gayle, and to hitch onto the cargo trailer to take it back to Wisconsin.

On 9 June, Gary used some frequent-flyer miles, left over from his business travel, to fly down to Arizona to share the last few days of my Nestwatch duties, and subsequently to help with driving for the long trip home. During my last off-period, I volunteered at Hassayampa in order to be handy to meet Gary's flight in Phoenix. I went first to AZGFD to photocopy our latest data-summary sheets for our boss, and then went to the airport. Returning to the Game and Fish offices, I was able to introduce Gary to my boss, and to chat in person with the southwestern Willow Flycatcher survey project leaders about Peter's and my reports of our two sightings of a territorial male Willow Flycatcher along the Santa Maria River above Alamo Lake.

Returning to Hassayampa where Peter was also visiting, Gary and I were offered a small apartment—with an actual bed—for the night, and I enjoyed the opportunity to show Gary the great hiking trails, involve him in a bit of my volunteer work, introduce him to the staff, and to get him to sample one of the wild, white-fleshed figs I had previously savored there. Before returning to Alamo Lake, I also showed him the places in Wickenburg where I did laundry and purchased supplies. Back at the gauging station, I made sweet-and-sour pork on rice for supper, also serving cabbage salad and muskmelon, and Peter joined us for the meal.

From my Journal: Thursday, 10 June 1993
When Peter walked in to sleep on the sandbar, Gary and I set up pads and covers to sleep under the stars on the gauging station roof, a lovely night in our Nestwatch "penthouse."

The next day was our 28th wedding anniversary. Gary and I woke early and, after a pancake breakfast, packed and organized for camping across the lake. At the park store, we filled our water jugs and were given free ice to put in the 5-gallon, insulated water jug. After loading the boat, Peter and I took our trucks up to the closer campground to leave them and saw a fox during our walk back, a mammal that did not make it into either of our reports, I suppose because it was not near either nest.

The three of us set out across the lake with a fully-loaded boat, lugged all our gear up to the flat area where Peter and I had camped before, prepared our packs and hiked up to the Cave O.P. to observe the Alamo Cliff Nest most of the rest of the day. In the late afternoon, Gary and I set up my tent using the same tie-down rocks at the camping location that I had used before. Peter made curried chicken with rice, apples and raisins for our anniversary supper and I baked a pineapple upside-down cake in the Bakepacker for dessert. Peter gave us a copy of REFUGE by Terry Tempest Williams, and a bag of M&M's™. It was a very unusual anniversary celebration for us!

From my Journal: Saturday, 12 June 1993
What a noisy night last night! Peter was troubled by mosquitoes (we could hear them outside our tent's window screens) since he hadn't set up his tent; our sleep was also disturbed by bullfrogs and Lesser Nighthawks calling all night, and there were other sounds the identities of which were less certain—owl, heron, coyote and/or fox, perhaps. We packed lunch and gear and hiked up to the Cave O.P. After a look at the cramped space therein, Gary elected to sit through the morning shade period in the mining chasm just below. It was a very long and tedious dawn-to-dusk day during which it was my turn with the scope and fieldnotes duty, and very little happened. "Solo" didn't fledge though he did hover once in the evening, which Gary got to see. I was very sleepy today, had to actually lay down & sleep for half an hour; woke very sweaty and with a small kissing bug walking on my face! Ugh!

We hiked down to camp after seeing a big chuckwalla (exact species unknown) lizard with deflated belly—chuckwalla after laying eggs? —and a rattler. Peter put up his tent and we drank cool water from the orange jug, but the ice was already gone. Supper was cabbage salad, "Farmer's Breakfast," and wafer cookies.

Sunday, 13 June, was our last dawn-to-dusk day, but it was a great one because Gary, Peter and I all got to see the Alamo Cliff Nest eaglet fledge. I read nearly half the new book during the long, dull morning in the cave. It was very hot—we learned later it was 109° at Alamo Lake that day. We also observed burros mating, a young chuckwalla, and a pack rat; these few unusual sightings helped break up the monotony of sitting in that little cave, in the awful heat, with only ambient-temperature water to drink, waiting, waiting.

From my Journal: Sunday, 13 June 1993
At 1:25 PM Solo suddenly hop/flapped up to the nest, paused, spread his wings and took flight, circling above the nest for 30 seconds and sort of crashing down just north of the nest. At 1:31 PM he flew as deliberately again and left the nest for good. We saw him fly in the nest-side canyon twice more briefly during this afternoon.

Despite seeing the Alamo Cliff Nest eaglet fledge, we continued our dawn-to-dusk duty and did not return to our tent camp until just before dark to eat supper and crawl into the tents for an uncomfortably hot night. Before dawn the next day, we woke, ate breakfast, broke camp, packed our gear down to the boat, and hiked to a high spot beside the trail to watch for Solo for a few hours. During this time, I was also calculating percentages and updating tables and text on our data for the Alamo Cliff Nest report.

Boating across the lake, hiking up to get our trucks, returning the boat, gear and motor to the park office compound were our next tasks. Then we badly wanted showers and clean clothing. Afterward, Peter and I sat at a park picnic table to complete the last report sections at 110° in the shade.

At mid-afternoon, Gary and I filled our jugs with cold water at the park office, turned in my forwarding-address card at the Wenden Post Office, and left the area. We camped that night, 14 June, in forest pines at a tiny Kaibab Lake campground, where we took the time to unload and clean the dirt and dust off my gear and truck. It was 48° that night and I was chilly in my light-weight sleeping bag—what a contrast to the temperatures at Alamo Lake!

We stopped in Flagstaff the next day to see Scott and meet his girlfriend, then headed east into New Mexico. We were appalled at the $155/night fee for a hotel in Santa Fe, so continued driving and found a $45 place to stay. The night of 16 June was spent in a motel in Sutherland, Nebraska, where we were awakened repeatedly to the sound of trains and thunderstorms. My journal ends with the Nebraska driving day, but on the 17th, we drove from Sutherland NE to the small town in Iowa where my mother lived. We stayed with her for a few days to visit and to provide assistance, before continuing to our Wisconsin home.

From my mother's diary: Thursday, 17 June 1993
Jean and Gary came about 4:30, unpacked and we had supper and talked. To bed, as they were weary from their trip.

Friday, 18 June 1993
Gary and Jean did their laundry. Jean and I did business in the morning with the lawyer and farm elevator, and sorted files. We made calls to Paul & Janis. Jean and I visited Roy [Dad's brother] in the evening.

Saturday, 19 June 1993
Gary and Jean cleaned the gutters, Gary left for Wisconsin [in Jean's truck]. *Jean and I visited Ethel* [Dad's sister], *and Nook* [neighbor who did so much cooking for us in the last part of Dad's life and at the time of the funeral].

Sunday, 20 June 1993
Jean and I left for Wisconsin at 7 AM [in Mom's car]. *Stopped at Patti's and had supper there. Tired.*

Mom stayed with us, visiting, and helping with gardening and the landscaping business of my sister and her husband, until Monday, 28 June. On that date, she drove back to her home in Iowa alone.

Meanwhile, Gary and I had only a few weeks for unpacking, catching up on tasks around home, and visits with friends and family before it was time to tend to our gear, repack, resupply and head west. We would be on site near Pinedale WY by 14 July for another in our series of Peregrine Falcon Hack Site Attendant jobs. (See our previous book, *Seven Summers with Peregrines: Finding Midlife Adventures.*)

Nestwatcher Jean, in the "chute" shortcut down into the "big wash" on the long hiking route to the Hilltop Observation Point

Closing Comments

Looking back over the files, photos, copies of letters, and my journal from my Arizona Bald Eagle Nestwatch experiences in order to write this story has been a nostalgic return to those days and places. My fieldwork adventures are many and varied, all of them greatly treasured, and I am immensely grateful for all of these experiences. The majority of my fieldwork jobs took place in either Wisconsin or in the Rocky Mountain states of Idaho, Montana, Wyoming and Colorado. The geographic outliers were my 1997 Aplomado job in Texas (also covered in this volume), which at least had the familiar hack site structure, and this Bald Eagle Nestwatch job in Arizona. In both these latter two, I worked in habitats much less familiar to me, which meant I had a lot to learn just about how to live and work in the different environmental conditions of Texas and Arizona: different temperatures and weather, different plants and wildlife. The Nestwatch job was also challenging because, including travel time, I was continuously away from home 147 days, by far the longest period for any of my fieldwork jobs. Wenden AZ was also the farthest from home I ever worked, about 1800 miles.

From my Journal: Friday, 26 February 1993
A dawn-to-dusk day: we observed from the Hilltop O.P. from 9:30 to 4:30. Peter finds it hard to sit all day, but this is what I like—to sit and read, think, write, observe wild organisms in a beautiful, natural place with few people anywhere around. I think we're very fortunate in this site: it has little disturbance and is quite remote this year because of the flooding. We're camped in a spot that is secure and private. I'm very happy here. All my partners are easy to get along with and work with.

REFERENCES

Arizona Game and Fish Department, 1988, "Threatened Native Wildlife in Arizona," Arizona Game and Fish Department Publication, Phoenix, Arizona, 32 pp.

Arizona Game and Fish Department Bald Eagle Nestwatch Program, https://www.azgfd.com/wildlife/speciesofgreatestconservneed/bald eagles/nestwatch-program/

Ebert, Jessica. "The Other Bald Eagle?" Field Notes section, *Audubon,* January-February 2005, pp.8-10.

Hunt, W. Grainger, Daniel E. Driscoll, Edward W. Bianchi, and Ronald E. Jackman. 1992. Ecology of Bald Eagles in Arizona. Part A: Population Overview. Report to U.S. Bureau of Reclamation, Contract 6-CS-30-04470. BioSystems Analysis, Inc., Santa Cruz CA. https://www.nps.gov/articles/southwestern-willow-flycatcher.htm

"Ornithological Newsletter" #91, December 1992, published by The American Ornithologists' Union, OSNA, 810 E. 10th Street, Lawrence KS. Access requires membership in OSNA, Association of Field Ornithologists, Cooper Ornithological Society or Wilson Ornithological Society. http://www.osnabirds.org/Newsletter.aspx

U.S. Fish & Wildlife Service Bald Eagle Fact Sheet: https://www.fws.gov/midwest/eagle/Nhistory/biologue.html

Bald Eagle population estimate for 2020: Bald Eagle Population (Estimates For Each State) - Wildlife Informer

Part 3 – Jean

Aplomado Falcon Reintroduction

Texas

1997

PREFACE

Having spent several summers as Peregrine Falcon Hack Site Attendants, we were hoping to experience the same process working with another species. Accordingly, for the summer of 1996, Gary and I applied with The Peregrine Fund to work as Hack Site Attendants for the reintroduction of endangered Aplomado Falcons in Texas. However, tragedy struck that summer at the World Center for Birds of Prey in Boise, Idaho, in the form of a virus, apparently introduced in the falcons' food supply. The virus caused illness in the captive Aplomado Falcons, and resulted in the loss of many of the young falcons being reared in the breeding facility for 1996 release sites. Therefore, we returned that summer to serving in the Peregrine Falcon reintroduction program. (See our book *Seven Summers with Peregrines: Finding Midlife Adventures.*) We repeated our applications to be Aplomado Falcon Hack Site Attendants and were accepted for 1997.

At the beginning of the summer of 1997, I was scheduled for a week of training in bird banding techniques; provided by The Institute for Bird Populations of Point Reyes, California, the banding school was to be held in North Carolina. Before leaving home, it was necessary for me to prepare for both the banding training and the summer job in Texas, as there would not be time to come home in between. I set out for North Carolina on 12 June 1997, with my small pickup fully loaded. As was my habit, I made use of the long road trip to make a visit en route, spending the first night in the Indiana home of my friend Helen and her family; she and I had known each other since our undergraduate college days.

The next day as I continued driving, my mind was shadowed with worry for my brother who was undergoing surgery for a tumor on his head. I stayed the second night, 13 June, in a Motel Six in Wytheville, Virginia, and called home to learn my brother had come through surgery fine, but my 80-year-old mother, distracted with worry about her son, had fallen from her raised garden bed and broken her hip! [Some 18 months after my dad's death in 1993, my mother had sold their home in Iowa and moved into a new mobile home in an attractive court in Wisconsin, about fifteen miles from the homes of my sister and me.] Her neighbors saw that Mom had fallen and went to her aid; she asked them to call Gary. He drove over at once, called for an ambulance, then called my sister, who met the ambulance at the hospital. Gary had all this to report to me at the start of my summer away from home. Having paid for the banding training, I continued to North Carolina and attended the first class in the evening of Saturday, 14 June, at Hill Forest Camp near Rougemont NC.

The bird banding course is taught in different locations each year by experienced banders from the Institute for Bird Populations, who are also trained in teaching. The purpose of the course is to increase the number of trained banders, and to upgrade the skills of practicing banders. To improve the value of banding as a research technique for gathering information about bird populations, we were trained in methods to collect data on reproductive status and plumage details such as coloration, wear, and molt status. We also learned to determine age class and sex of each bird, and how to record all this information for reporting to the North American Bird Banding Program. During training we used a detailed instructional guide prepared from information previously learned by bird banders; this manual was undergoing major revision in 1997.

To band birds, the bander must qualify for and obtain a federal banding permit. The U. S. Geological Survey (USGS) Bird Banding Lab produces and updates the *North American Bird Banding Manual*, which provides among other information, the correct leg-band size for each bird species. The other essential reference used by banders, and during the banding training course, is a book by Peter Pyle, *Identification Guide to North American Birds*. This book is filled with amazing detail about the plumages and other characteristics of birds, including differences based on sex and age. With skill, training, and careful use of these references, it is possible not only to identify the species of a bird caught in the bander's mist nets, but to determine the age, sex, and breeding condition of that bird.

The full week of banding training consisted of both classroom instruction and experience at banding nets set up in various habitat types in several locations, and ended on the following Saturday, with a final early-morning banding session. Extensive practice as well as lectures, provided each of eleven students with knowledge and skills in setting up, furling, and taking down mist nets, removing birds from the nets, handling these delicate creatures safely, determining the correct band size from the Bird Banding Manual, and placing the band on the bird.

I would eventually receive by mail a "Certificate of Achievement" signifying that I had completed the introductory bird-banding course. Additional training and experience would have been required for me to obtain a banding permit. However, my primary purpose in taking the course—to learn more about these ornithological research techniques so as to incorporate information about them in the Ornithology class I taught at the University of Wisconsin-La Crosse—was well served by this week of training. By the date the banding course ended, 21 June, my mother had undergone surgery to repair her broken hip and was expected to recover, with a couple weeks of physical therapy scheduled in a nursing facility before she could go home. After several fraught phone conversations with Gary during the week of banding training, together we decided I would go on to Texas for the Aplomado hack site job. He would stay at home to, along with my sister, be available to help my mother during her recovery, and to deal with other family issues. Gary called The Peregrine Fund, and our boss, Bill, contacted one of the alternate Hack Site Attendant candidates to meet me in Texas in Gary's place.

Leaving North Carolina, I was amused by the Gaffney, South Carolina, water tower that resembles a peach from one direction— look it up—and appears to be something less attractive from another direction. One of my fellow banding training classmates had warned me that weather in the Carolinas could include sudden heavy downpours. I did encounter a very heavy rain, and benefitted by her advice to get behind a big truck, slow down and follow the truck's lights. Keeping moving in this way, she said, would be safer than pulling over and confusing another driver who, in the poor visibility, might think my vehicle was in motion on the road rather than parked on the road shoulder, try to follow, and hit it.

I spent the night of 21 June in a Motel Six in Atlanta, Georgia. Horrified by fast-moving freeways with six lanes for each direction in that big city, I dealt with the traffic the next morning by avoiding it, leaving town at 5:00 AM, and with the problem of driving alone all day by stopping in rest areas twice for brief naps. By evening, I had crossed the border into Texas and was tired and desperate to stop driving. Not being able to find a place to camp, I stopped at a motel in a tiny town. That motel room was very dirty and dingy, one the worst dives—i.e., disreputable motels—in which I have ever stayed.

The next day, 23 June, having a relatively short distance to go to Aransas National Wildlife Refuge, I stopped in Bay City, Texas, for fresh foods and a few other supplies.

Arriving and checking in at the Aransas headquarters, I asked questions, found out how to receive mail while I would be working there, was permitted to do laundry in refuge housing, and went to Rockford, Texas, for more supplies based on answers to my questions. Finally, I got cleaned up and spent the night in refuge housing, organized and prepared to begin my stint as an Aplomado Falcon Hack Site Attendant the next day.

Young Aplomado Falcons newly installed in hack box, camera lens held at observation peephole for a photo

INTRODUCTION

Aplomado is Spanish for leaden, referring to the blue-black coloring on the backs of adult Aplomado Falcons (*Falco femoralis*). These falcons are about 15-16 inches in length, compared to 16-20 inches for Peregrines, but they are also slimmer and much lighter in weight. Their prey includes birds and insects, which are caught on the wing by this fast-flying falcon. Aplomados are also fast when they move about on foot on the ground, where they hunt insects, lizards and various small mammals.

Aplomado Falcons were native to southern Texas, New Mexico, and Arizona, and on southward into Mexico, Central and South America. The species was mostly extirpated from the United States after about 1930, the last breeding pair being found in New Mexico in 1952. Causes of its disappearance from the United States were habitat loss as grasslands were converted to various agricultural purposes, and widespread use of DDT. This powerful insecticide directly poisoned falcons and their prey, but short of poisoning, also bioaccumulated in the tissues of insects against which the DDT was used, then in the tissues of birds and other prey animals that ate the insects, and finally in Aplomado Falcons. Even if not present in quantities to directly poison predators at the top of the food chain, such as Aplomados and other raptors, DDT caused harm by reducing reproductive success through interference with normal breeding behavior, and by resulting in production of thinner-than-normal eggshells that could easily break under the weight of the adult during incubation.

Inhabiting mainly grasslands, Aplomado Falcons usually nest in yuccas, shrubs, or trees, but may nest on the ground. The species can also be found in woodlands or wooded areas near marshes. Rather than constructing their own nest, an Aplomado pair takes over an old stick nest built by other birds such as crows, ravens, jays, or other raptors. The pair remains together all year and often hunts together, one bird flushing prey for the other to intercept. The male may transfer food to the female in flight. These falcons are fast enough to outfly Mourning Doves, but often hover while hunting, thus appearing more like over-sized American Kestrels than Peregrines.

In 1986 Aplomado Falcons were placed on the Endangered Species List in the United States and, as early as 1977, efforts to breed the species in captivity were underway, with the goal of reintroduction into suitable habits within their former U.S. range. Between 1985 and 1989, 224 captive-bred Aplomado Falcons were released in south Texas through the combined efforts of the Santa Cruz Predatory Bird Research Group and The Peregrine Fund, as captive-breeding ramped up and release techniques were adjusted to the specific needs of this species.

By 1992, The Peregrine Fund, headquartered in Boise, Idaho, had reached its goal of developing a captive population of 30 breeding pairs, was raising Aplomados in captivity, preparing to release fledging-aged young by a modification of the "hacking" process that was being used so successfully for Peregrines. The entire 1993 captive-production of 26 young was released at two sites in Laguna Atascosa National Wildlife Refuge in south Texas. In 1995 the first nest since extirpation was found in south Texas; both adults were banded, indicating they had been released by The Peregrine Fund. The Matagorda Island portion of Aransas National Wildlife Refuge was in its second year as a release site for Aplomado Falcons in 1997, when I participated there.

An inhibiting factor to the ability of those government agencies tasked with endangered species conservation efforts to form cooperative arrangements with private landowners, is the concern of the property owners that they will lose control over management of their property, or even be liable to lawsuits if the endangered species are harmed on their property. To encourage public-private partnerships, the Safe Harbor Agreement (SHA) policy was developed: "In exchange for actions that contribute to the recovery of listed species on non-federal lands, participating property owners receive formal assurances from the U.S. Fish and Wildlife Service that if they fulfill the conditions of the SHA, the USFWS will not require any additional or different management activities by the participants without their consent. In addition, at the end of the agreement period, participants may return the enrolled property to the baseline conditions that existed at the beginning of the SHA." [from the USFWS website, listed under References at the end of this section]

Often, as in the case of Aplomado Falcon reintroduction at Laguna Atascosa and Aransas National Wildlife Refuges, endangered species reintroduction work takes place on federal lands. However, neighboring private landowners, even if they have positive attitudes about efforts to recover listed species, may be concerned that such conservation projects might interfere with their plans for management of their lands. Safe Harbor Agreements have been useful in allaying landowner concerns since first developed in 1995.

In 1997, a total of 108 young Aplomado Falcons were released in Texas, most on public lands such as National Wildlife Refuges, but some by arrangement, on private ranchland. Of those, 74 (68%) were considered successful in reaching independence. Also, by 1997—still early in the recovery effort for this species—at least four established pairs were known, and one pair was observed to fledge one young, bringing the known wild production, since reintroduction began, to five total individuals.

The term "hacking" refers to a process of releasing young raptors, in this case, captive-bred young of fledging age, from a special "hack box" and then providing them with food for a period of weeks while they learn to hunt for themselves. No adult birds are present to provide food and protection; to the extent possible, these functions are filled by humans known as Hack Site Attendants. Small, domestic quail were raised in Boise as the food supply and, for the Matagorda hack sites, stored in freezers at the mainland Refuge headquarters.

Hack Site Attendants for Aplomado Falcons, selected by The Peregrine Fund, had to travel to their assigned hack site on their own, and were "grantees" rather than employees. We were provided with a list of suggested personal equipment to bring, a detailed booklet about the hacking process, and instructions for notetaking and for writing the required reports. The Peregrine Fund also loaned us a few equipment items, including the large coolers we would need for transporting the quail that would be supplied as food for the young falcons while they learned to hunt for themselves. My partner, for example, was loaned a spotting scope and tripod, but I was able to provide my own.

Matagorda Island Unit of Aransas National Wildlife Refuge, near Austwell, Texas

MATAGORDA ISLAND UNIT OF ARANSAS NATIONAL WILDLIFE REFUGE

The headquarters of Aransas National Wildlife Refuge (NWR), established in 1937, is close to the Texas coast of the Gulf of Mexico, with the small town of Austwell, Texas (only a couple hundred people), located several miles away. The nearest places for us to obtain supplies were in Rockport, Texas (about 5000 population), almost 60 miles from the refuge headquarters. Aransas NWR rose to prominence in the conservation movement because of the Whooping Crane, a species thought in 1923 to be extinct. Realization in 1941 that only 15 of the majestic birds remained in the wild, aroused national and international concern, and inspired efforts to save the species from extinction. The few remaining Whooping Cranes were breeding in remote Wood Buffalo National Park and adjacent areas in Canada and coming to the marshes of Aransas NWR to winter. At Aransas, efforts were made to protect the cranes, and the salt-marsh habitat they needed during the non-breeding part of their life cycle. Encouraging interest and concern for Whooping Crane conservation, a tour boat company based in Rockford, Texas, was allowed to take members of the public to view the cranes from a safe distance.

As a birder, I was deeply interested in Whooping Crane conservation efforts, and in fact, was able to take the boat trip out of Rockford to see the cranes in 1982 while in Texas visiting a friend. The fact that there was only this one flock of Whooping Cranes raised concerns that one hurricane, or one outbreak of disease, could wipe out all of them at once. Eventually, through captive breeding and releases, the Wood Buffalo-Aransas population increased enough for work to begin on establishing an eastern flock that would breed in the upper Midwest and winter in Florida. This, in itself, is a fascinating conservation story, which included teaching the young cranes their migration route and stopover sites by leading them with piloted ultralight aircraft. As of 2020, the eastern flock was estimated at 84 cranes, the Wood Buffalo-Aransas flock at 504. There were additional birds in captivity, and in small non-migratory groups as well. In October, 2020, I was thrilled to see a pair of Whooping Cranes in Necedah

National Wildlife Refuge in Wisconsin. The species is still on the U.S. Endangered Species List.

Because Aransas NWR was already so deeply involved in the Whooping Crane conservation effort, it must have seemed only natural that the Refuge would help Aplomado Falcons too. Aransas also administers Matagorda Island State Park and Wildlife Management Area. Matagorda is a 38-mile-long coastal barrier island, one in the chain of barrier islands that shelters the Texas coastline from the Gulf of Mexico. The island varies from ¾-4 miles in width, has a total surface area of about 57,000 acres (i.e., 89 square miles), and is located about five miles away from the mainland. There is passenger ferry service to the state park portion on the north end of the island.

In 1942, Matagorda Island Air Force Base was built with concrete runways, roads, and various structures; the base operated until closing in 1978. The runways and some structures remain on the island. Other legacies of the period of Air Force presence on the island, are many large depressions, the results of bombing practice. The island also had a long history of private ownership and ranching, which ended with Air Force acquisition of the island during World War II. The large, old ranch house was still standing in 1997, impressive, but deteriorating from neglect, humidity, and salt air.

For the purposes of Aplomado Falcon reintroduction, three small hack towers had been built, each with hack box on top. These towers are similar to towers used at some Peregrine hack sites, but instead of being about 30 feet tall, Aplomado hack towers are only about 8-12 feet tall. Two of the towers on Matagorda Island were placed close together as Hack Site One, located several miles north of our residence, which was in one building of a cluster of former Air Force and ranch buildings, now the island refuge facilities. The single tower at Hack Site Two, was a few miles to the south of the refuge buildings. A small 2x4 frame structure with canvas top and back, was constructed about 200 yards from the towers at each hack site, to provide a shade-shelter for the attendants during their long hours of observation duty in the Gulf Coast summer heat.

Two Hack Site Attendants were assigned for each hack site and the four of us, all females in 1997, were allowed to live in half of an old duplex near the runways and other old structures on the island.

Also living on the island, in another of the old residences, were Wayne, known as "Doc," and Martha McAlister, Environmental Education specialists and naturalists, who introduced us to the island lifestyle and shared much information about Matagorda Island and its history. Doc was a retired biology professor from a Texas junior college, and told me the work he was doing on Matagorda was "the best of teaching—just the field trips." He also served as general handyman for the island, performing this duty especially on evenings and weekends.

Refuge personnel came by boat to the island daily, Monday through Friday, on a regular schedule. Their work commute involved taking a refuge truck from the mainland headquarters to a boat dock on the coast, then a 30-minute boat ride across the intracoastal waterway to the island boat dock, and finally another, shorter, truck ride to the island refuge buildings. When they took a refuge truck from headquarters to the mainland dock to come to the island in the morning, the truck was left at the mainland boat dock until they returned in the afternoon. Likewise, when the staff left the island each afternoon, they parked a truck at the island boat dock for their use the next morning. The distance across the water between mainland and the island was five miles, but the boat ride was about eleven miles long because the cove with the island boat landing was not straight across from the mainland Refuge boat landing, but further south along the length of the island.

Besides the McAlister house and "our" duplex, the island refuge complex included a classroom building and bunkhouse used by visiting environmental education classes, a community kitchen, a refuge office, large workshops, an old hanger in which the vehicles were kept, and a big diesel generator under a roof. On the weekends, we Hack Site Attendants were isolated on the island except for the McAlisters; if the latter wished to be away overnight or for a weekend, one of the mainland refuge staff had to come out to the island to stay in case we had problems.

Island terrain was generally flat, and my notes say there were "only ten trees around the buildings, none of them very tall." Two of these trees were picturesque live oaks with permanently-leaning shapes because of the onshore winds, but there were also a few palms and salt cedars. We could not actually see the Gulf from the cluster of buildings or from our Hack Sites because of intervening vegetated, secondary (isolated inland) dunes, but we could sometimes hear the Gulf surf.

The coastal island environment was very different from any I had ever previously experienced, yet the longer I was there, the more interested I became in the habitat. Basically, a big sand dune with grasses, sedges, various forb species, yuccas, prickly pear cactus, and mesquite shrubs covering most of it, the island has a nice cove with a boat landing, and is edged in some places by salt marshes, especially on the intracoastal (northwest) side.

Besides the boat dock in a small cove close to the south end of the island, and the buildings now in use by the Refuge, the other notable manmade features at our end of the island were the large, old ranch house (closed and empty), and the two long, concrete runways crossing each other at right angles in the form of a plus. There was also a road the length of the island, in some places hard-surfaced, in others reduced to two tracks with gravel or crushed shells as the surface of the tracks, and with grass growing in the middle. A short side-road, about a mile long, led from the cluster of buildings down to the Gulf beach. Another mile-long side road connected the building complex area with the island boat landing.

From a letter: Thursday, 7 August 1997
I've grown to quite enjoy the fast boat rides each week to commute to and from the island. The best parts of the weekly mainland visits are the privacy I usually have in the refuge apartment, and the chance to call home.

ISLAND PERSONNEL

The only full-time residents on Matagorda Island were Doc and Martha McAlister. Sometimes Refuge personnel stayed overnight, but generally two or more of them came by boat Monday through Friday mornings, and went back to the mainland at the end of each work day. There seemed to be a couple of staff members assigned to regularly work on the island, but occasionally others also came.

Hack site personnel in the summer of 1997 consisted of four women. MHI and IMI arrived first in mid-June and were responsible for Hack Site One with its two towers, each with a hack box, located about seven miles north of the cluster of buildings. One of the women was in her early 20s, the other almost 30. The two had not met before they were assigned to be partners on Matagorda Island, but both had some previous fieldwork experience.

Arriving next, I reached the Refuge on 23 June, and Matagorda on the 24th, where I was assigned to release Site Two, which had a single tower and hack box. Originally, I had expected to work with my husband, Gary, as my hack site partner, but when he withdrew because of family circumstances at home, The Peregrine Fund assigned an inexperienced young woman of college age from their alternate list of applicants to be my partner. JCW was not able to reach the island until 30 June, by which time the first group of Site Two falcons had been installed, and I had been observing them in the hack box through the peepholes drilled for that purpose, and feeding them for several days on my own; their planned release was only two days away when JCW arrived. In my first days on the Island, I was also able to observe with the attendants at Site One; their first group of falcons had been released a couple of days before my arrival, their second and third groups were released during my first few days on the island. This was a good opportunity for me to gain some experience with the species before our Site Two birds were to be released.

As a veteran Hack Site Attendant of eight Peregrine Falcon release sites over seven summers, I was far more experienced, and definitely older (53) than the other three attendants. This did not necessarily endear me to them, but they sometimes found my knowledge useful. As was usually the case for hack site jobs, The Peregrine Fund had not given any of them enough information about what equipment and supplies to bring to suit the specific conditions the attendants would encounter while living and working on Matagorda Island. This meant they had to cash their first grant check soon after arrival and do quite a bit of shopping. Being used to arriving on the job without adequate information from The Peregrine Fund, and because of my experience of a wide variety of hack sites and on-the-hack-job living conditions, I had come pretty well prepared, and had asked some useful questions when I checked in on the day that I reached the Refuge.

Doc McAlister had apparently developed a tendency the year before to "parent" the hack site attendants who served on Matagorda, but we asked the Release Specialist to show us how to fill the 3-gallon water jugs ourselves from the osmosis filter system, instead of having to ask Doc to bring us another jug when needed. We also asked Doc to show us where to dump our garbage and our kitchen fruit and vegetable wastes, so he would not come into the duplex to get them. We thought the kitchen wastes were being composted, but they were just dumped near the incinerator, located half a mile from the cluster of buildings, for the coyotes and raccoons to pick through at night. Burnable garbage was incinerated on the island, but non-combustibles had to be washed, then taken to the mainland and sorted into recycling containers. I did appreciate that Doc wanted to check in the evenings to make sure all of us had arrived back from the release sites.

Early on, I put up a bulletin board—I found it in the duplex—hanging it via a bent clothes hanger over the top of the entrance door, which was always in the open position. I kept the bulletin board supplied with scratch paper and encouraged the others into the note-leaving habit. I also put up a manilla envelop at the door labelled OUTGOING MAIL so anyone going to the mainland would remember to take the mail along. On the back of our door, I hung a bag in which we could accumulate the plastic grocery bags, or take one when needed. "You are an organizer," commented IMI.

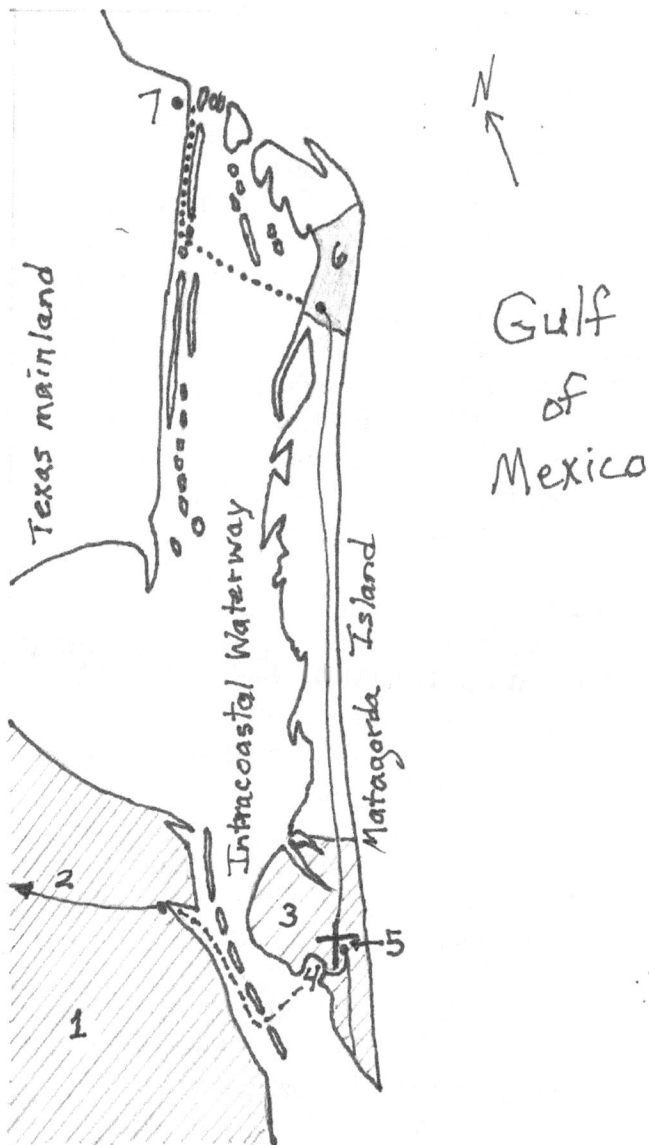

1-Aransas NWR, 2-road to mainland Refuge headquarters, 3-Matagorda Island Unit of refuge, 4-cove & boat landing, dashes show boat commute route, 5-Island building complex & runways, 6-Matagorda Island State Park (shaded), dots show ferry route, 7-Port O'Connor TX

LIVING CONDITIONS ON A COASTAL BARRIER ISLAND

The apartment in the west half of the old duplex where we four attendants lived, was essentially one large, L-shaped room, with a small bathroom and tiny closet in the angle of the L. The leg of the L at the back of the building was nominally a bedroom, with two single beds. It was not really separated from the longer room across the front of our apartment because the connection was an archway. The front room had two more single beds in the left half, and a small kitchen in the right half. Awkwardly, access to the bathroom from the front room was through the bedroom or, to avoid intruding on MHI and IMI, I could go through the tiny closet! Across most of the front of the duplex, there was a narrow, screened porch, accessible to both apartments. Although the kitchen was small, each of us generally cooked for ourselves.

Because power on the island depended on a generator that normally ran only in the daytime, power availability was limited, and sometimes undependable. There was no air conditioning, which would have been welcome, but it hardly mattered since we were out on duty observing the falcons during most of the daytime hours for many of the weeks we were there.

There was a sandy beach on the Gulf side of the island where the other three attendants went swimming, also jogging and sunning. I, however, found the beach uninviting, in fact disturbing—it was littered with the debris of human activities. "Everything except the kitchen sink" is a saying, but it applied to this beach. I collected seashells and "sea glass," but also a "hard hat." Lumber was found and used to create falcon perches, and a plastic lawn chair was picked up by our Release Specialist for one of us to sit on in the shade-shelter. My partner and I found plastic milk-bottle crates and a piece of plywood to make a useful little table in our observation shelter. There were oranges, onions—all kinds of food items on the beach and, all kinds of plastic containers—a very great variety and quantity of litter. Oil rig platforms off the coast were surely the source of some of the debris, but there were fishing boats and pleasure craft on the Gulf waters also.

The island amenities I appreciated most were the showers I could take daily (brackish water from a well), refrigerators, an ice machine in the community kitchen that produced a plentiful supply of potable ice we used to stock our coolers to keep our lunches cold, and to ice our beverages in thermoses. Also valuable were the screened porch that extended across the front/south side of the duplex, and a ceiling fan located above my single bed that I could run all night long, making the room comfortable enough for sleep.

Drinking water was produced by treating the brackish, sulphury, deep-well water with reverse osmosis, and decanted into three-gallon plastic jugs. We collected one jug at a time and set it into a wire-framed stand in our kitchen that allowed us to tilt the jug with one hand and pour into a pan or water bottle held with the other hand. Untreated, the well water was safe for dish-washing and showers, but it tasted too vile for drinking. JCW and I each had a small water bottle nested in a "can cooler" and each carried a half-gallon jug of water on ice in the cooler, using it to keep refilling our water bottles during long days on duty.

From a letter, Thursday, 10 July 1997
Last night (Wednesday) we got "home" to find all the water faucets would run only a trickle—the water pump quit and Doc says it may not be worked on until Friday. I took a trickle shower. The big tank must contain water then, as Doc says we'll continue to have water as a trickle by gravity. The work boat wasn't scheduled to come today, he also told us. Why they can't tell us these things in advance, I don't know! JCW and MHI are deeply disappointed; they were planning on going over tonight to call home and coming back Fri. AM. This is the second Thurs. in a row this has happened to them. [Note: Someone did come by boat on this day to fix the waterworks, so JCW and MHI were able to go to the mainland after all. The pump failed a second time that summer, and on that evening, I was the only one that got a shower because I happened to go first.]

In the apartment in the old, decrepit duplex we inhabited, MHI and IMI, arriving first, had claimed the beds in the so-called bedroom. That left the beds in what should have been the living room for late-comers, for me, and for JCW who did not arrive until a week after me. Continuous with our living room sleeping area was a small kitchen. The screened porch across the front of both halves of the duplex was wide enough for a few chairs and end tables. The kitchen was supplied with a gas stove and refrigerator, since electricity was normally minimal, but the gas refrigerator did not work even though it was new. The diesel generator was supposed to be off overnight because it was loud and located next door to the resident caretaker; however, with only electric refrigerators in the duplex, we needed the generator on all the time. And, that meant I could run the ceiling fan over my bed every night. Fresh air came in well through the porch and the door and south windows of the apartment, all of which were open all the time I was there.

Island duplex, (our apt. in left half), screened porch
across front (south side), framed by two leaning live oaks

The duplex was dirty when I first reached the island and the two attendants who had arrived ahead of me had not done much to improve it, so I spent quite a bit of time during my first three days on the island cleaning the bathroom, kitchen, and the front room area that would be my "bedroom." Further, one of the attendants
280

was careless about spilled food and they had not noticed that ants had gotten into their food supplies. I admit to exerting my seniority to demand a greater degree of cleanliness and showed them the kinds of containers I used to store my foodstuffs so ants, other insects, and rodents could not get into my food.

Because the ant problem was severe by the time I arrived—I saw a quarter inch-wide column of ants coming and going across the kitchen floor and up into the cabinets and shelves—it was necessary not only to do serious cleaning to disrupt the ant trails, but to purchase and put out ant poison and traps. The two attendants who had arrived about a week before me, did not believe that ants could get into their food until I showed them ants crawling around inside their plastic bag of brown sugar. The ants were also in their supplies of dried beans, nuts, and several other kinds of foods.

IMI insisted there were fleas in her bed, bought flea powder and doused her bedframe and mattress with it. I was horrified and refused when she tried to insist the rest of us use the powder—imagine breathing the stuff when you rolled over in the night! The Release Specialist was also concerned, fearing that we would transfer some of the powder onto the quail and endanger the falcons. He took the flea powder away and disposed of it.

Later I wondered if the suspected fleas were in fact ants biting IMI in the night, because one by one, each of us suffered ant bites during the nights. MHI especially was plagued by the tiny, biting ants, and we traced the ants' preference for her to the "oatmeal soap" she favored. I had to pull my bed away from the wall so the ants were less likely to climb onto it. Eventually, as the other attendants did a better job of securing their food from ants (more and more of it had to be kept in the two refrigerators), the ants became desperate and began attacking us, and even eating holes in our dirty laundry. Each of us had been doing a little hand-laundry some evenings and hanging the items on the porch to dry overnight—after ants started chewing our dirty undies, we had to be sure to wash things out every single night. I started collecting the different sizes of ants (at least four, from tiny to large) that infested our house, and arranging one of each size under pieces of scotch tape stuck to letters I was writing!

From a letter: Tuesday, 23 July 1997
The ants moved into the beds in the front room last night (mine and JCW's). I woke at 3:30 AM with them crawling on me, especially on my head and in my hair, but everywhere, and biting me. Fortunately, their tiny size means tiny bites; I got up, pulled the head of the bed away from the wall, vigorously shook out and brushed off myself, sheets and pillow, finally got back to sleep.

The other half of the duplex was to be kept open for Bill, our boss, or Brian, our Release Specialist, when they came to install, release, or otherwise deal with the falcons. Because access to the island was complicated, when one of these experts came from The Peregrine Fund for falcon duties, they typically stayed over a night or two. Brian tried fishing several evenings, caught a species he called red fish. On one of his visits, Bill barbequed supper for us of sausages and, for the vegetarians, eggplant "steaks."

These visits were interesting changes in our routines, but also had a cost in lost privacy, something already, chronically, in short supply with four women trying to complete all the tasks of living in 60-90 minutes each morning and evening. Due to the long summer days, and the siesta-tendency of the falcons in the hottest part of the day, the most useful hours of observation were early morning, and early evening. During the middle of the day, the heat waves made identification of individual falcons by their colored leg bands essentially impossible, so it was just as well the falcons were inactive and sleepy during those hours. These circumstances meant that we all got up early and got ready for work at the same time, with the same congestion in bathrooms and kitchen in the evening. We tended to all get back to the residence around 9;00 PM, just before dark, and all wanted to prepare food for an evening meal, get a shower, do hand-laundry, and make preparations for the next day of work, while still getting to bed well before midnight. I tended to make a pasta or rice-based concoction and divide it into containers for three or four meals before cooking again. I often ate a serving for my lunch, not minding that it could not be rewarmed out at the O.P.

After the intense observation period ended, we split the work into two shifts, each about six and a half hours; a morning shift for one attendant at each site, and a late afternoon/evening shift. The person on morning duty, would drive back to the residence at mid-day, and their partner would take the truck to go out to the hack site for the "second shift."

Eventually we were allowed to use the bathroom and refrigerator in the other apartment whenever neither Bill nor Brian was staying therein. This required another bout of cleaning to make the condition of the shower acceptable, and the refrigerator fit to hold our food supplies. A fault in the door of that refrigerator meant we had to put a big brick in front of it to keep it closed, but this second refrigerator gave us more area for ant-free food storage. The second shower speeded up our evening preparations.

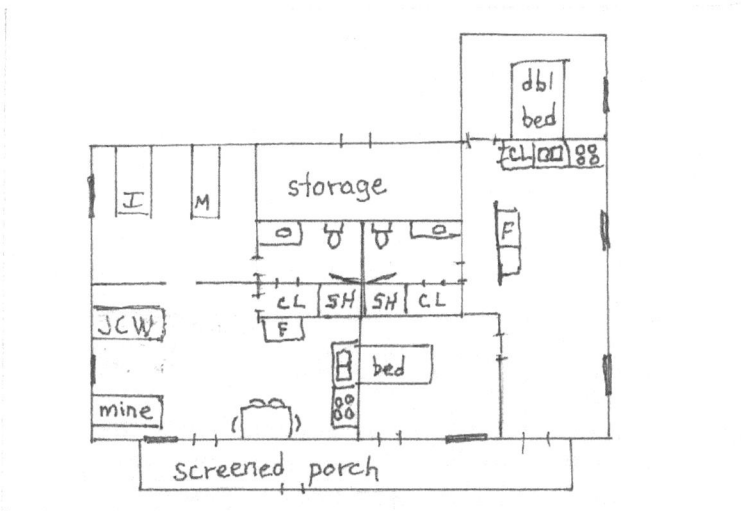

Duplex floorplan - Hack Site Attendants used left half
SH=shower, CL=closet, F=refrigerator

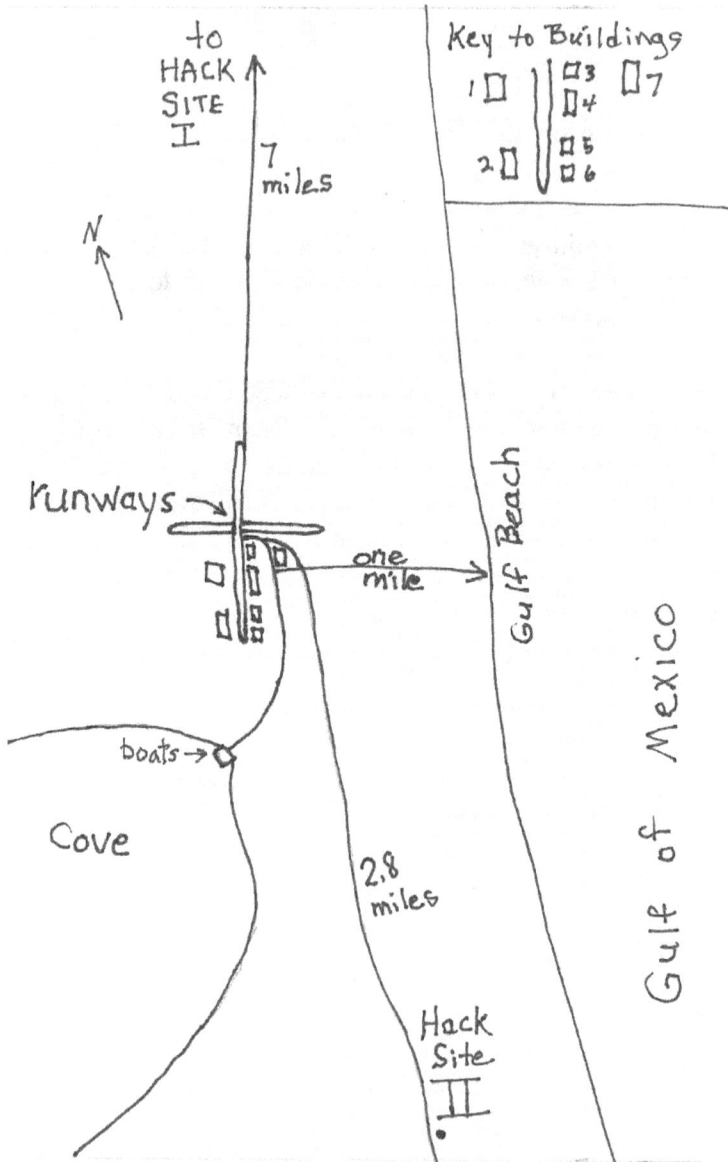

to HACK SITE I

7 miles

N

Key to Buildings
1 □ | □3 □7
        □4
2 □ | □5
        □6

runways →

Gulf Beach

Gulf of Mexico

one mile →

boats →

Cove

2.8 miles

Hack Site II

Matagorda Island Unit of Aransas NWR, Building Complex: 1-hanger (vehicle storage), 2-workshop, 3-duplex, 4-office, bunkhouse, classroom, community kitchen, 5-Doc & Martha's house, 6-workshop, 7-historical ranch house from cattle ranching era

STAGES OF THE HACKING PROCESS

In the book my husband and I wrote, *Seven Summers with Peregrines: Finding Midlife Adventures*, we describe in some detail the stages of the hacking process, and I invite you to read that book to learn more. Here I will provide a brief summary of the steps that follow after the young falcons have been produced by captive breeding and reared until they are fully-feathered and almost ready to fledge, typically at about seven weeks old (range 31-39 days in the 1997 Matagorda falcons).

Installation
Several young falcons, typically 4-6, were formed into a group, banded, and flown from The Peregrine Fund's captive-breeding facility in Boise, Idaho, to Corpus Christi, Texas, and then brought to the Island by Coast Guard helicopter by arrangement, or by vehicle and boat. A Release Specialist or the Operations Manager from The Peregrine Fund, removed the young falcons from their travel-crate and placed them into the hack box.

At Matagorda Island Site Two, where I worked with JCW as my partner, two groups of young falcons were installed sequentially. The first group, consisting of two males and two females, was installed by Brian, the Release Specialist, on 26 June when I was still on duty alone at Site Two; the second group, which included four males and two females, was installed on 17 July. I assisted Brian with the first group, JCW assisted Bill, Operations Manager, with the second group. This involved climbing the tower, and operating the doors of the travel-crate and the hack box, as the expert handled the falcons.

The two women, MHI and IMI, who worked at Matagorda Island Site One, had two hack boxes on two separate hack towers to observe. They had started work before I arrived, with their first group of five young Aplomados being installed in one box and a second group of four in the other box, both installations taking place on 17 June. On 26 June and 17 July, two more groups were installed in those boxes, but these, groups #3 (five falcons) and #4 (five falcons) were older birds, each just over one year old. They had been intended for release in 1996, the year of the disease outbreak in the Boise breeding population of Alplomados. Despite being quarantined and not becoming ill, it was feared these falcons were carriers of the virus and might introduce the disease into the population in the wild, so they were held in captivity until summer 1997, when permission was finally obtained for their release. A fifth group, six young falcons, was installed on 17 July in the box already vacated by the older birds placed there on 26 June.

Me, climbing ladder to put quail on the tower for falcons, Hack Site Two. Note hack box, and branch perches.

Releases

Typically, the young Aplomado falcons spent several days to almost a week confined in their hack box and being fed quail via a food chute that concealed the fact that human hands were providing the food. Frozen quail were provided by The Peregrine Fund, but thawed before being given to the falcons. The purpose of this acclimation period was to give the young falcons time to recover from their journey and to observe their new location through the barred front of the hack box. On release day, Bill or

Brian came to the Island to open the door to the hack box to set the falcons free. The attendants observed and recorded notes as the falcons emerged from the box, hopefully ate some of the food provided, and took their first flights.

Observation Periods

During the weeks following each release, it was our assignment to observe the falcons, record their activities, and continue to provide their supply of food. The first two weeks after release of each falcon group were to be weeks of "intense observation," which I took to mean we should be on duty all the daylight hours, usually both attendants for most of those hours. In this way, it was hoped we would notice any problems, such as an injury, that occurred in the first days after release when the falcons still could not fly well or catch any of their own food. We were also to provide whatever protection we could. For example, we might, knowing that one falcon was on the ground, try to scare away an approaching coyote. In later weeks, we were permitted to relax our observation efforts, especially on any day after we had sighted and identified each of our falcons.

The older falcons that were released as groups three and four from Matagorda Island Site One did not remain in the vicinity of their hack towers, and in fact, none of them were ever clearly identified again after they flew out of the hack boxes on their release day, although I saw at least one of them at Hack Site Two. The younger birds, in contrast, having no real experience in either flying or hunting, generally made use of the towers they were released from as their food source for varying numbers of days.

At Site One, seven of the ten falcons in their groups one and two did well, while only one of the six falcons of group five was seen in the several weeks following release. MHI at that site, became convinced that a female falcon of group five was injured, but she had some difficulty convincing IMI (her partner) and our boss (by phone to Boise), so she asked me to take a look. I agreed that the falcon was injured, reported so to our boss, and Site One attendants were told to try to capture it. This they succeeded in doing on the morning of 5 August, and then it was necessary to call Boise to report the capture. This involved sitting around waiting for a return call with the flight information.

After Bill made the flight arrangements, he called and instructed MHI and IMI to cross to the mainland, with the injured falcon in its transport crate, and drive to the airport in Corpus Christi. The airport would house the falcon overnight and put it on a flight connecting to Boise the next morning.

The on-island refuge staff, three that day because one had come out to stay overnight, agreed to take the boat back to the mainland early in the afternoon to assure a timely arrival at the airport for the falcon. However, one staff member failed to show up at the island office at the agreed time. This was worrisome, the more so because she was expecting a baby and her coworkers had been trying to get her banned from working on the island until after she gave birth. The other staff members set off in search, one of them found her where her truck had become bogged down in sand, pulled the truck out, and they all returned to the island office. By this time, the intended early departure from the island had been delayed about 90 minutes.

Once they finally reached Refuge headquarters, the two Site One attendants set off with the injured falcon for Corpus Christi, where the second shift airport staff refused to take charge of the falcon. This necessitated another call to Boise, to the boss at his home. MHI and IMI booked a motel room for the night, smuggled the falcon in its crate into their room, and delivered it to the airport the next morning. The staff member who had caused the delay and overnight stay, arranged to hold the boat returning to the island that morning, waiting so MHI and IMI would not have to spend another night on the mainland away from their duties. The falcon was returned to Boise where examination revealed a very serious leg fracture; surgery was attempted, but the damage was not repairable and the falcon had to be euthanized, a blow to us all, but especially for the two attendants who had tried so hard to get help for it.

At Site Two, where I worked, releases occurred on 2 July and 20 July. Eight of our ten falcons did well, returning frequently to the hack tower to feed on the quail we supplied, and we were able to regularly identify them. Most interestingly, one falcon from our group #1 was not identified at the tower for a period of several weeks, yet somehow survived on his own, only to reappear at the tower 48 days after release, and then to remain in the tower vicinity to the end of the period. Keeping track of two groups of released falcons and identifying the individuals was not easy. Having more than one group released at each site, effectively cancelled the chance to relax observations on the first group because by then, we were in the midst of the intense observation period for the second group.

Dispersal

Dispersal for a released falcon is defined as that falcon leaving the hack tower area and no longer taking quail from those we supplied. If the falcon had hung around the tower and taken quail for about three weeks, it was considered reasonable to assume it was then capable of successfully hunting on its own. To encourage dispersal, quail were provided only every other day at the tower for the seventh week after a release. Again, this usual procedure was rendered impossible by there being a second group, so alternate-day feeding could only occur in the last week after the second (or last) group's release.

Further complicating our Site Two observations, one falcon from the first group released at Site One, began visiting our tower and this behavior was eventually copied by six other Site One falcons. At least one of our falcons visited Site One in return. By mid-August all of the young falcons that had not yet dispersed were being seen only at Site Two and quail were provided only at that tower thereafter. At this point, IMI, one of the attendants from Site One, left Matagorda, and the other, MHI, came to help JCW and I observe at Site Two. We were thus able to divide the relaxed observing effort into shorter shifts.

Since I had a contract for a full-time teaching job at the University of Wisconsin-La Crosse for fall semester 1997, to start on 25 August, I left the refuge on the 19th, a few days before the job would end on 30 August. Another attendant was sent by The

Peregrine Fund to help with observations during the last few days, though none of the rest of us thought that was necessary.

Unusual Sightings

Raccoons ascended a tower at Site One, killed and consumed a young falcon. A trap was set under the tower that night, and subsequently, electric fencing was installed around the bases of all three towers. A Barn Owl began frequenting one of the hack boxes, and continued to visit the tower after the box door was closed to prevent the owl from considering the hack box as a suitable nest site. Turkey Vultures came to Site One and consumed quail, but since Site One falcons had begun frequenting Site Two, discontinuing supplying quail at Site One solved the vulture problem.

About the time the first group of falcons were to be released at Site One, a subadult male Aplomado began to frequent the towers and take quail. Newly-released falcons are not instantly expert fliers, so the subadult was a threat to them at first and the attendants were advised to chase it away until the young falcons gained more skill at flying. The subadult's leg band identification code was relayed to Boise; from the records there, it was identified as having been released on Matagorda Island the previous year.

At Site Two, a Great Blue Heron perched on the tower on 8 July, flushing the young falcons. A coyote ran under our tower on 23 July with four falcons following it closely, even stooping (diving) at it. Because of the falcons' behavior, I could tell where the coyote was even after it entered the tall grasses. Seven wild hogs were sighted on the trail leading to the tower on 2 August. These were descendants of feral pigs that combined their genes with European wild boars, which had been released in Texas in the past for hunting.

On 30 June and 9 July, visiting environmental education groups came to observe the falcons at Site Two, and Doc McAlister asked me to address them about our work. On 15 July one of our falcons chased a Scissor-tailed Flycatcher directly toward the observation shelter where JCW and I were seated; the frightened flycatcher took shelter with us under the canvas shade tarp, hiding first behind my chair and then perching in front of JCW on her spotting scope until the falcon gave up and flew away.

Environmental Education class visiting Hack Site Two to see the falcons and learn about our work

Of course, some of our best sightings were of the falcons themselves. On 26 July I noted that we had seen and individually identified 13 falcons at Hack Site Two, the highest such total for a single day. On the 27th of that month we saw a falcon eating a small bird. We assumed it caught the bird itself and wished we could have observed the process of that successful hunt. On other, earlier, occasions we did see falcons capture and consume insects such as dragonflies.

Reports
We were required to produce two reports for each hack site. The
report that would be published in *The Peregrine Fund Operation
Report, 1997*, had to conform to a standard format, with the
following sections:
Personnel at Hack Site
Description of the Site
History and Details of Young, including a chart with five columns
of information for each group of falcons released at our site
Pre-release Details
Release Details, with a six-column chart for each falcon group
Hunting Behavior
Roosting Behavior
Pattern of Dispersal, showing the last date seen for each falcon in a
five-column chart for each release group
General Evaluation of Falcons
Unusual Incidents
Acknowledgements

The second report would not be included in the annual *Operation
Report*, but was intended to provide useful information for The
Peregrine Fund, about the site and our experiences. It included
sections on:
General Evaluation of the Site, Marking Method and Release
Procedure
Suggestions for Improvement
Agency Personnel and Other Interactions
Visitors (a list with dates, names, affiliation, and addresses)
Lists of reptiles, mammals and birds identified on the island by
attendants, including relative abundance designations for each
species
Personal Statement on the value of the experience

From a letter: Tuesday, 8 July 1997
*The behavior of these young Aplomado Falcons is both like, and
different from, the behavior of the young Peregrines we've worked
with. They eat much less, the mid-day heat brings on a more
pronounced siesta, they land on the mowed area and walk around
hunting insects (and catching them sometimes already). They*

perch and lay on the towers and poles in the same ways, but also perch very lightly, with wings out, on thin mesquite branches Brian provided on the perches made of salvaged driftwood from the beach—they are so much lighter in weight that they can do this. They don't look much different in size or shape when flying, have the same color on backs, wings and head, but the markings differ somewhat, are orangish rather than buff. The upper breast is brown-streaked orange and the belly is orange. The breast has a wide dark-brown band, and there are narrow white bands on wing and tail flight feathers. They are very beautiful birds.

Because I would have to leave a few days before Site Two would be closed down, my partner and I worked diligently to write and type our reports, print, proofread, and correct them before my departure. Although we could type the reports on the island, we had to print them at the mainland office, another example of how working on an island made things more difficult. We did make some revisions before I left, but thereafter JCW would have a few details, such as last date of sighting of each of the falcons still frequenting the site, to add to the final version of the main report, and the final proofreading, editing, and typing to do.

Leaving early meant I lost control over the final version of the main report, and I am still chagrinned that it went to publication with several mistakes. Nevertheless, I had a three-day drive to reach home, and a university teaching job to prepare for as soon as I got there, so I could not delay. I had started Site Two alone since JCW was a week late in reaching the island, but she did not have to complete the final ten days at the site alone; Site One falcons were frequenting our site and they were being fed with our falcons. MHI thus could share observation duties with my partner at Site Two, and an extra attendant was also provided by The Peregrine Fund for those last days.

Shade-shelter at observation point, Hack Site Two

COMPLICATIONS OF LIVING AND WORKING ON AN ISLAND

This was my first experience of living by the Gulf coast, and though I found it interesting, I hope never to repeat it. It was hot and very humid, temperature ranges were 88-93° during the daytime, and 78-83° at night; it was mostly or entirely sunny every day, but generally breezy. I put on shorts and shirt or tank-top when I got up in the morning, my standard outfit every day on the island. My skin always felt sticky and I had to sit on a towel on my lawn chair to absorb the sweat. Ugh. Sitting in shade and a breeze on the screened porch with an iced drink, I was fine, but when out in the sun and moving, it felt like I was in a blast furnace. We were told how fortunate we were, however, that the summer of 1997 was exceptional in its low mosquito population.

The salt air and brackish dishwater corroded everything of metal that they touched. By the time I left, my watch had died, my pocket knife had fused in the closed position, and the aluminum handle of my favorite paring knife was pitted. I was concerned about my cameras, but they continued to function, though camera batteries had very short lives in those conditions. The salt air also created a scum on the vehicle windshields and our optics that we could not see through—we had to clean these surfaces at least twice a week. Another problem was that ink pens ran dry much faster than usual.

From a letter: Wednesday, 23 July 1997
I've been reading about Gulf Coast Texas refineries and chemical plants as major air-pollution sources—maybe the scummy film on vehicle windshields and optics isn't caused by the salt air at all?

Our work was on Matagorda Island and that is where we lived for the summer. However, the uncertain electrical supply based on an aged generator, and absence of Refuge personnel most weekends meant it was necessary to keep the freezers of quail that were the food supply for the falcons at Refuge headquarters on the mainland. This meant that twice a week supplies of quail had to be transported in coolers from the freezers on the mainland, by boat out to refrigeration on the island. From there, attendants took a few quail each day to each hack tower.

There was a cell phone in the office on the island, but we could use it only for emergencies. The required twice-weekly phone calls to Boise to report on our falcons and ourselves had to be made from the mainland Refuge headquarters. Further, we always checked for personal mail in the cubbyhole assigned us in the mainland headquarters office, and had to wait until we were on the mainland to call home, do laundry, and to go to Rockford for any supplies we might need. I was loaned a key to the mainland Refuge Visitor Center to go in and use the phone (with my calling card) to call home on Monday nights when I was on the mainland.

Matagorda Island's weather was very stable that summer, never disrupting the schedule of regular boat movement back and forth between mainland refuge headquarters and the Island Unit. My notes remark that a dark cloud on the afternoon of 1 August caused us to cease our observations early. At 5:00 AM the next morning we did have heavy rain, the only incidence of such weather while we were on the Island. We were there during hurricane season, but fortunately, no hurricanes occurred in the vicinity that summer.

The solution for all of these off-island needs was for one attendant from Site One, and one from Site Two (me) to ride the afternoon boat back to the mainland with refuge staff at the end of their work-day on Monday, and return to the island with the staff on the boat on Tuesday morning. The other two attendants, again one from each release site, rode back to the mainland with refuge staff on the Thursday afternoon boat, and returned to the island on the boat on Friday morning. While on the mainland, we called Boise, picked up the mail for all attendants, did our laundry, called home, and took care of any necessary shopping or other errands. In the morning, we had to load a supply of quail from the freezer in a mainland refuge building into 1-2 coolers, and be ready with the coolers, our clean laundry, mail, purchased items, and whatever else, to ride along with staff in a refuge truck to the mainland boat landing for the commute by boat to Matagorda Island.

Refuge boat at mainland dock; staff commuted eleven
miles across the intracoastal waterway to the island

Aransas NWR management had arranged for us to conveniently do
our laundry in a vacant residential-trailer on the headquarters
compound and had designated a mailbox for us in the office
building; as routines developed, the Refuge staff who regularly
came to the island on weekdays, began to bring our mail over with
them, and were usually willing to take our outgoing mail back to
the mainland on the afternoon boat. We were also provided shaded
parking spaces for our personal vehicles, and a small apartment
(with air-conditioning!) where we stayed overnight on these trips
to the mainland. Each week when I arrived on the mainland on
Monday afternoon, my first acts were to turn on the air-
conditioning in the apartment and put a can of soda into the
refrigerator. Next, I would call The Peregrine Fund office in Boise
to report on our falcons, and then collect the mail. Finally, I would
start my laundry and read my mail, call home and eat supper. On
these weekly mainland visits, I saw deer, armadillos and peccaries
as I walked from one part of the refuge complex to another to
accomplish these tasks.

The above system sounded good in theory, but in practice there was a serious problem in that only two of us had vehicles—I did, and one attendant from the other Hack Site. Because I was already very experienced in the difficult logistics of supply while working several weeks far from good shopping places, I had come well prepared, and had purchased a few additional fresh foods the day I arrived.

When my first turn came to make the round trip to the mainland, I traveled over with the vehicle-less attendant from Site One. After being on the island for a week, I had a list of a few items I wanted, and took the other attendant along to Rockford in the evening so we could both do our shopping. However, I made it clear to her that I was not willing to make that 120-mile round trip every week, so she needed to stock up well, and thereafter ask the other attendants to buy things for her. Adding to the difficulties, two of the attendants were committed vegetarians, which meant they consumed larger quantities of fresh foods than I did, and thus needed to shop more frequently. I had brought with me quantities of home-dehydrated foods, and canned goods—prepared or purchased in advance back home where prices were more reasonable—foods that were easily transported and stored.

From a letter: Tuesday, 8 July 1997
IMI and I got back from Rockford after 10 PM, seeing coyote and deer on the road and several frogs, two of which I inadvertently squashed—shades of the Cane Toad movie, which both JCW and MHI have also seen. In the apartment, we found a lizard behind IMI's bed and she was shooing it into the closet, when I said, "Wait," staying the broom with my hand and reaching down to capture the poor thing, now moving much slower from harassment. "Oh!" she said, "You are brave. I would never..."

Whoever's turn it was to make the mainland trip, had to remember to take a quail cooler, another cooler for groceries if planning to shop, to gather outgoing mail all the attendants had ready, take along wallet, money, phone card, dirty laundry and detergent, address book, an overnight bag of clothes, personal items, even food in my case, since I usually did not intend to go to town. One of the attendants not making the trip, would drive us down to the island boat landing, or we could ride with staff headed back to the mainland for the night. In the morning, we had to be ready to catch a ride with staff to the mainland boat landing. I carried the cooler of quail and all my stuff a block from the apartment to the Refuge office building, where, at 7:30 AM I met the truck going to the boat landing, which was located several miles away from the headquarters complex.

Because of my careful advance preparations before leaving home, I spent only $69.41 on food, from 23 June, when I arrived in the vicinity of Aransas and stocked up on fresh foods, and 19 August when I started away from the Refuge for the trip home. I spent more than half again that amount ($39.10) just before I left the refuge, purchasing books and other items from the Refuge gift shop as keepsakes and gifts. On the subject of expenses, we can add about $100.00 for three motel nights, several dollars for convenience items for the duplex—a clock, fly swatters, ant poison and traps—several dollars for postcards and postage, and I had to purchase ink pens, and batteries for my flashlight and cameras because pen and battery-life was much reduced in the heat, humidity and salt air.

The small mainland apartment where we stayed on these overnight trips was very comfortable. Partly to have something to do, since I seldom went to Rockport for shopping, and partly in thanks for the privilege of staying there, I spent time cleaning the apartment. My favorite memory of that apartment is the night I found a small gecko climbing the wall above the mattress that I slept on, and watched it.

Small apartment on Aransas NWR, used by Hack Site
Attendants during weekly trips to the mainland

I also remember, albeit somewhat less fondly, the trees and the
wild muscadine grape vines that formed a "roof" over the parking
spot where my pickup sat all that summer. The shade over my
vehicle was very desirable in the hot, humid Texas summer
weather conditions, especially since I kept many of my food stocks
and other supplies in my truck, only bringing them to the island as
I needed them. However, as the grapes began to ripen, they fell
onto the roof of my pickup's cab, and on the aluminum topper that
covered the cargo part of the pickup. When I discovered the mess
the grapes were making, and became concerned about their juices
and rotting fluids damaging the paint or metal, I had to do a big
clean-up job. Between the cab and topper, I had installed an
inflatable "boot" that allowed me to leave the topper's screened,
side windows partly open, and the windows open between cab and
topper as well. The air movement made possible by this
arrangement moderated the temperature in both cab and topper, but
the boot collected a pile of fallen grapes that I had to clear out of
the space between cab and topper.

The cell phone in the office on the Island meant that we could call the mainland Refuge headquarters, if needed, but the island office was closed after the Refuge staff returned to the mainland by boat, typically about 4:00 PM on weekdays. It was also closed on weekends, but Doc had a key. Though we could contact the mainland in an emergency, you could not just suddenly make a trip in either direction. The Refuge boat that made the regular Monday-Friday day trips back and forth was partially enclosed and good-sized for the conditions of a 30-minutes salt-water trip in any ordinary weather. There were two boats for the island, and when Doc was gone with one, and a refuge staff member had come to stay overnight, it was normally arranged that there would also be a boat left at the island. This required planning and coordination so that day staff could go home, one staff member could stay, and there would still be a boat at the island overnight. I remember being especially cautious on the single occasion when events conspired to prevent a boat being left at the Island.

There was a small "fleet" of assorted vehicles on the Island for the staff to use in their work, as well as for access between the island boat dock and the island office. The salt-laden air was very hard on vehicles and we were told that other national wildlife refuges sent the older, almost worn-out vehicles from their fleets to Aransas for the last part of their useful "lives." The maintenance shop on Matagorda was well equipped to maintain the structures, the diesel generator, the water pump, and the old vehicles used by refuge staff who worked on island. Each team of Hack Site Attendants was issued one of these island vehicles so we did not have to walk back and forth each day, from the duplex where we lived to our hack sites. Site One was located seven miles north of the complex of buildings that included our duplex; Site Two, where I worked, was 2.8 miles south of our residence.

Each day as we prepared to go on duty, we loaded the vehicles with a bag of quail to put out for the falcons that day, a cooler and thermos bottles with ice from the ice machine to keep our lunches, snacks and beverages cold, our binoculars, spotting scopes, tripods, observation notebooks, pens, and whatever else we needed for the day. These vehicles were constantly failing us. The first pickup

JCW and I were assigned was a tan-colored Dodge, 2-wheel drive, automatic without a spare tire. I was on duty alone at first and Doc said if I had a flat to walk "home" and someone else would deal with the problem. Sure enough, I had to have him help me out one day when one of the tires on "my" assigned vehicle was very low.

In the first week I was there the Dodge failed to start for me or JCW five times, and finally they had to give us a different vehicle. I learned later the Dodge had a bad battery, bad battery cables, a failing alternator, and very worn V-belts—no wonder it was so hard to start! Sometimes one of us had to go get one or two of the other attendants if they did not return when expected. Convinced that I would eventually have to walk back to the duplex in the dark, I added my big D-cell flashlight to the gear I carried with me each day, and packed my most essential items in a small backpack. I wore hiking boots to "work" each day in case a vehicle failed and I had to walk "home," but we wore sandals during our long hours on duty in the observation shelter because of the heat.

As part of my gear, I had brought to the island a Rubbermaid Action-Packer™, a hard-plastic storage container with a tightly-latched lid, which allowed JCW and me to leave a few items overnight in our observation shelter. The four of us kept track of each other, and if one woman was overdue to return to the residence, one of the others would drive out to find her, or lacking a functioning vehicle, ask for help from Doc. He came to the duplex every evening to check on us and forbade us to go off exploring without telling him which way we were headed so he would know where to look for us.

The second truck JCW and I were assigned was a red, much more recent, hard-sprung, propane-powered Ford flatbed 3/4-ton truck! I found a good length of new 3/8-inch manilla rope on the beach and the Release Specialist helped me dig it out of the sand and clean it in the gulf. JCW and I used the rope to tie the coolers on the flatbed truck. Later, we had a more dependable white, standard-transmission 2WD pickup, but all four of us seemed cursed to endure several more stints with the old Dodge. Once, while maintenance was being done on the white pickup, we got the

Dodge back temporarily; it had a new alternator and fan belts, but then its transmission "locked up" on us. Another annoying experience with the Dodge occurred when IMI's assigned truck failed to start, causing her to take the Dodge to meet her partner who was returning on the morning boat. Both attendants went to Site One that morning, but IMI liked to come back to the duplex for lunch. After she ate, that old Dodge wouldn't start for IMI, so she hiked out to Site Two since it was closest, and took our vehicle to drive the seven miles to Site One to relieve her partner on duty. MHI kindly came out to our site in the evening to give JCW and me and ride back to the duplex.

We also had a diesel, automatic, 4WD Chevy Blazer for a while. The Blazer had air-conditioning but was hard to start so I kept the A-C off. The tan Dodge's gas mixture had been set so high it would go 25 mph in Drive with no foot on the accelerator. By contrast, the Blazer had to be "tromped" to go at all. What a range of driving experiences, from automatic to standard, 2WD to 4WD, two gas-powered vehicles, one diesel, one propane, several different brands, and various sizes!

Vehicles and other large equipment items and supplies were brought to the island via occasional trips made by a barge. Access could also be gained via the ferry to Matagorda State Park on the north end of the island, but the long road from the state park on the north end to the refuge on the south end of the island was gated at the border of the park. Thus, we never had unexpected visitors.

Alligator nest: eggs buried within the mound of decaying vegetation are "incubated" by the heat of decay processes

Hack Site Attendants on Matagorda Island by the "Danger Alligator" sign

TIME-OFF ACTIVITIES ON THE ISLAND

In the first weeks after each release of falcons, we had little time off, at least I did not relax from observation duties even though the other three were a little more willing to do so. However, after the two weeks of required "intense observations" following our second release at Hack Site Two, we could officially relax our efforts. Three weeks after release, The Peregrine Fund believed the young falcons were probably capable of hunting for themselves. From that point on, one of us observed singly for a half day, went back to the apartment for lunch, and the other took the truck and went out to observe during the afternoon. If my observation shift was in the morning, I might even walk out to O.P., and walk back for lunch.

If I had time off during the hottest parts of the day, I spent it sitting in the screen porch with a cold drink, reading, or writing letters. In the cooler hours of early morning or early evening, I often took long walks for exercise and/or went birding, when I was not on duty in the later weeks. After we got past the period of intense observation duties, I managed walks of 2-6 miles nearly every day. One evening I saw two poisonous snakes on my walk on the runways, but I always carried my snake bite kit with me and told one of the others where I was going, or left a note with that information.

There were two old 3-wheeled bikes in the shop on the island, and JCW got permission for us to use them for little explorations. She oiled the chains so we could ride to the beach or the cove. JCW had brought a drum and drumsticks to the island and liked to march up and down the road near the shade-shelter, practicing. Her boyfriend sent her a set of "devil sticks." I had never heard of the form of "gyroscopic juggling" for which these sticks are used to promote exercise, coordination, and timing. These activities were a distraction to me, but at least the devil sticks were quieter than the drumming.

I enjoyed trying to identify the island vegetation, especially wildflowers, and my partner was also interested in the flowers. Unfortunately, there were not many species in bloom when we were there, perhaps because it was already full summer and very hot.

Besides being a personal hobby, birding was partly business on the Island for me as our Internal Report to The Peregrine Fund was supposed to include lists of reptiles, mammals and birds identified by the attendants; these lists would provide information about potential food species for the falcons when they could hunt on their own. I listed 12 species of reptiles, which included American alligator, three kinds of lizards, two species of turtles, and six kinds of snakes, three of them poisonous: massasauga, Western diamondback rattlesnake, and cottonmouth. The five species of mammals we sighted were black-tailed jackrabbit, coyote, raccoon, feral pig, and white-tailed deer. The list of 77 bird species was due mostly to my efforts, since my partner was not much of a birder.

We learned quite a lot about island wildlife while we lived there, and tried to identify and list the species we encountered. We even located a place where nine Wild Turkeys usually roosted at night in this nearly treeless place.

From a letter, Wednesday, 23 July 1997
I found out why whistling-ducks are so-called—they really do whistle. We have Black-bellied Whistling-Ducks here and they whistle beautifully. See if you can find an audio online, or on the software I purchased for teaching Ornithology classes.

The cove and salt marshes were especially productive places for birding. In my first days on the island, I thought the salt marshes stank, but after living on the island a while, I just thought they smelled like salt marshes. My Life Bird List was enriched by several species during my summer on Matagorda Island. I observed Magnificent Frigatebirds on the boat rides between the mainland and the island. My first sightings of a Scissor-tailed Flycatcher, Aplomado Falcon (the subadult—one is not supposed to count a newly-released, captive-bred bird), Gull-billed Tern, Sandwich Tern, Wilson's Plover, Barn Owl, Clapper Rail, and Crested Caracara all took place on the island, a total of nine new life birds. My annual bird list for that year gained 30 species in

Aransas and Matagorda. In fact, 1997 was one of my best birding years, with 17 new lifers (two in North Carolina during the banding study, five during a spring-break trip to Louisiana with Gary, one while visiting our daughter in Wyoming in January) with a year-total of 257 species.

From a letter: Wednesday, 6 August 1997
I walked down to the boat dock a little before 7:00 tonight. All the others are off watching falcons, but it's my night off and after having a couple hours alone at the house, I came here to prolong the rare opportunity for privacy. I have been down here before, especially enjoying the Black Skimmers as they forage across the surface of the cove, but also have tried to entice a Clapper Rail into view by playing a tape of their call. That worked twice, but in both instances, it was too dark for a good look. When I arrived this evening two raccoons were foraging and a rail was complaining, so I waited. To my delight, I eventually saw a Clapper—a life bird for me! And then, I saw three more together.

As I had on Peregrine Falcon jobs, I packed a box of reading material to bring to Texas knowing I would have time to read, even while on observation duty—the falcons were not always at the tower after the first few post-release days. On weekly trips to the mainland, I took back to my truck any books I had finished, and brought in more reading material. I also spent a lot of time writing letters and postcards to stay in touch with family and friends, and to encourage my mother as she recovered from hip surgery.

Some of us also brought materials for craft activities. My partner, for example, did beadwork. On the long solo drive to Texas in June, I had an idea for making oil lamps. After being introduced to the mainland Refuge maintenance man, I asked for scrap copper wire and he found some for me. Pounding a nail into the shade-shelter, I used a pliers borrowed from the refuge toolbox, coiled the wire around the nail to form a holder for a wick that I crocheted. The wire coil could be placed in the bottom of a shallow jar with an inch or so of cooking oil, and the wick lit as a primitive lamp. I made a jar lamp for each of the others, one for Doc and Martha, and one for myself to take home.

Office, classroom, bunkhouse, and community kitchen building on Matagorda Island (duplex at far right)

Other island adventures and concerns

The resident naturalists told us about a nearby active alligator nest, so the four of us went to see the large mound of soil and vegetation the female had accumulated to cover her eggs, up to 60 in number (average clutch about 35). The rotting vegetation provides heat to incubate the eggs, but the female remains near her nest to guard it and the young, which hatch after a couple months. As we approached the nest and took a photo, we kept a sharp watch for the adult female, almost nine feet in length and weighing 200+ pounds, who was always on alert somewhere in the vicinity.

On one occasion when a refuge staff member stayed on the island while Doc and Martha were away, he told me about his wild hog-hunting activities—these animals were a problem on the island because they dug up native vegetation—and refuge personnel who liked hunting were encouraged to kill them. We were told we were welcome to shoot them if we got permission to have a gun, in fact they would loan us one! He did shoot several hogs that evening and came to the duplex to show me a 100-pound boar because I had expressed a wish to see one up close. I wondered what he intended to do with the dead animal and rode along when he took it in a refuge vehicle to one of the large bomb craters, which was a known lair of a big alligator—we dumped the hog into that big hole. For the next few days as we went by, we were subjected to an awful odor of decaying feral hog!

Feral hog crossing one of the runways on Matagorda Island, encountered on one of my walks

After sitting on observation duty all day, I liked to take walks in the cool of the evenings, though well aware of the island's dangers: the abundance of poisonous snakes, scorpions, alligators, and wild hogs for example. There were also coyotes and raccoons—probably not dangerous, but that did not mean I especially wanted to meet them while out walking alone just before dark—so I took my walks on the old Air Force concrete runways so I could see approaching dangers. I did meet Massasauga and Western Rattlesnakes, a big wild hog, and assorted other critters, but never went anywhere on foot on Matagorda without my snake bite kit.

Because of the snakes, our Release Specialist asked refuge staff to mow the grass around the towers, the observation stations, and the paths we needed to walk back and forth from O.P. to tower. Brian also bought a pair of tall rubber boots for each hack site to help protect us from snakes; we kept the boots in our observation shelter so we could grab them in a hurry if we had to go out into the grass to try to find a falcon if one landed in deep grass right after fledging. The mowing also benefitted the falcons since on their first flights they often landed on the ground, where snakes might be lurking if the grass was long.

As usual in fieldwork under wilderness or near-wilderness conditions, it was necessary for each of us to dig a small personal latrine in the vicinity of our observation shelters. Somehow this is a subject that is usually not mentioned, but it is a fieldwork reality. I borrowed a shovel from the shop, chose a spot about 100 yards from our O.P. but only ten yards off the road and hidden by a mesquite clump, covered the back-fill dirt pile with grass so it would not catch the eye of anyone driving by.

A Texas Gulf Coast island was an entirely new experience for me. The hot, humid weather provided excellent conditions for the growth of mildews and molds. These organisms had to be kept in check by diligent cleaning of the apartment and our equipment.

I have already mentioned the ants and our difficulties in keeping them out of our food and off our persons; vigilant cleanliness also helped against ants. Fire ants had the worst bite. Although there were few mosquitoes on the island that year, we did suffer from biting flies.

From a letter: Thursday, 3 July 1997
The most common fly, the local version of the "deer fly" back home, is golden-brown, double the size of a house fly and more elongate in shape, with bright yellow-green eyes. They don't fly annoying, buzzing circles around your head as the ones at home do, instead they get right down to business by alighting so softly on your bare skin that you don't always notice, and then they bite a big chunk out of you.

We also encountered huge roaches in the mainland apartment, and I tried to keep it clean on my weekly Monday night visits even though others were using the apartment on other nights. The communal kitchen on the island also was infested with the big roaches, but I did not feel responsible for cleaning that area since we were in there only to get ice from the ice machine. Other objectional island critters were the scorpions; one had to check for them before putting on shoes or boots, and under things that you lifted. I killed two in the house, one was under a cloth that I picked up; the other women got at least two more, and MHI got stung.

Hack Site Two area and path between tower and shade shelter, mowed to help falcons and attendants avoid snakes

Out at our O.P. shelter, we found huge mud-dauber wasps and emerald-jawed jumping spiders. The spiders lived in the structural joints of our observation shelter. The wasps were seen carrying mud pellets into one of the boots, which Brian had provided for our safety when walking through deep grass, after he encountered a 7-foot snake near our Site Two hack tower—not, he warned us, that the boots would help against such a big snake, as it would be able to strike above the boot! Between uses, we had kept the boots suspended upside-down under the canvas roof of our shelter, where the wasps found them desirable as a place to construct a nest. Fortunately, we heard sustained buzzing behind where we sat and noticed the wasps going in and out of the boot, before either of us put a foot into it! After dumping and scraping out the mud nest-start, we stored the boots differently. Then we discovered mud-dauber wasps building a nest under the dash of the refuge pickup we were driving at the time. We found a can of OFF™ in one of the other Refuge trucks and used it to spray underneath the dash of our vehicle, hoping to keep the wasps out of there. The wasps even tried to start a nest in the small hole in the end of the handle of my spotting scope mount—to foil wasp use of that location, I stuffed the opening full of toilet tissue!

I admit that JCW and I did take a form of revenge against the abundant island ant populations. There were a number of ant lion pits in the sand around our shade shelter at Hack Site Two. These are conical depressions in the ground, excavated by the fiercely predatory larvae of a type of insect that traps ants. If an ant happens into such a pit, it often has trouble climbing the unstable slope before the ant lion detects its presence and captures it. Sometimes, when we picked up an ant that had been crawling on us, we dropped it into one of the pits to see if it could crawl out before the ant lion came out of hole at the bottom where it had been lying in wait.

The most interesting creatures I encountered on the beach included a few ghost crabs—they can move fast, and sometimes go sideways—but they are mostly nocturnal and I certainly was not at the beach after dark. I also saw an occasional jellyfish stranded on the sand. There were gulls and shorebirds at the beach too, and these I identified for our island bird list.

From a letter: Thursday, 3 July 1997
Last night we left the tower to return to the duplex just before dark and encountered a two-and-a-half-foot long alligator on the road. JCW, who was driving, stopped the truck, and I got out to stomp on the road to encourage it to move off, but in a flash, it leaped and

spun 180° and threatened me with open jaws! I wasn't close, but it was startling. I retreated into the truck.

From a letter: Thursday, 14 August 1997
We've suddenly been seeing a lot more snakes. Last week, JCW saw a cottonmouth crawl under the plywood "floor" of our O.P.— she stomped on the plywood and it glided on out. She also saw a Diamondback a few feet from the O.P.

Not all island reptiles were dangerous, nor all snakes poisonous; we also saw speckled king snakes, ribbon snakes, and Texas horned lizards. I enjoyed seeing a slender glass lizard, the latter a legless species of lizard that you might mistake for a snake. They can be recognized as lizards, despite being legless, by their different way of moving, and because they have ear openings and eyelids, characteristics that snakes lack.

From a letter, Sunday, 29 June 1997
Doc just drove by as I was making my supper, and I saw him stop suddenly on the road, hop out of his vehicle, go into the grass and catch a snake. I walked over to see it: a speckled king snake like one I saw just the other night in that same area. This one appears to have four eggs in her—large symmetrical bulges in a series. He plans to show it to the current environmental class.

From a letter, Saturday, 5 July 1997
There are Texas horned lizards along the little road and we try not to hit them. I like watching as the Barn Owls hunt around the buildings. One date palm has fruit, another's flowers attract bees.

The feral pigs posed a danger, but could be avoided with caution. The other problematic island mammals—coyotes and raccoons— were more a danger to newly released falcons, than to Hack Site Attendants. Raccoons, though, could be attracted to the buildings and to the odors of foods and cooking at the residences.

From a letter: Saturday, 26 July 1997
Last night JCW and I had to get up and chase away three raccoons that were trying to break into the porch—fortunately, the bottom

three feet have hardware cloth over the screens! I think they were
attracted by the smell of our bucket of kitchen scraps so I went to
dump it by the incinerator this morning.

What about staying healthy while we were all far from home? The
other three were young and all of us were basically healthy,
however, there were a few issues of concern that summer.

From a letter: Thursday, 3 July 1997
When I arrived, I had small poison ivy blisters from being exposed
in North Carolina. Now what? Monday night I noticed a sore in
my mouth that looked like a cross between a canker sore and a
patch of white mold. It spread on Tuesday and Wednesday with
white skin flaking off the older parts like sunburn, or a popped
blister, and the area underneath was inflamed bright red. Not
knowing what this is, I used mouthwash more often, and gargled
salt water—today it finally looks better. Why does this weird stuff
always happen away from home? One day I woke from a siesta
with blurred vision and it took half an hour to dissipate. Another
day, I had severe foot cramps in the toe tendons of both feet and
had to take a long walk in the heat to get the cramps to release.

From a letter: Friday, 4 July 1997
MHI woke me early, being up and moving around three times. I
knew it wasn't her usual routine. She'd gone out on the porch, but
I couldn't hear her there and realized she'd gone over to the other
bathroom. When she came back, she flopped suddenly in a porch
chair and I went out to ask if she was okay. She isn't and we think
she has sunstroke/heat exhaustion. I made her promise to take the
day off and one of us has Gatorade™, so we set a cup by her bed
to warm to ambient temperature and urged her to <u>sip</u>, not drink it.
We'll go back to the house in shifts to check on her. We must
decide by mid-afternoon if she should go back on the boat (if there
<u>is</u> a boat on the 4th of July) for medical help. We haven't told Doc
yet, but will if MHI can't keep liquids down—she had thrown up
the orange juice she tried early, is light-headed and unsteady. I
laid out my thermometer to check for fever later. [Note: she
recovered well on a regimen of rest and Gatorade, but after that I
bought Gatorade to have a supply of my own available.]

Keeping in touch with our families and friends was important to all of us, hence our phone calls during mainland trips, and our correspondence. One attendant's parents lived outside the U.S., and when she did not call them for a period of three weeks, they emailed our boss and he got a message to her. She was embarrassed, but did call her parents the next time she was off-island, and more regularly thereafter.

Back then, the cell phone Gary and I had was the large "bag phone" type and although I brought it to the island, I did not offer to let the others use it—roaming charges for calls outside your home area were a dollar a minute back then. I turned it on for one hour most evenings as a "listening watch" in case Gary needed to reach me in between the Monday evening calls I made when I was on the mainland. He was very good about writing letters, and I was especially anxious to have reports on my mother's recovery, and about an impending housing issue for another family member. It would be hard to over-state the importance of mail while one is away from home for months for a fieldwork job, and the difficulties inherent in the conditions of working on Matagorda Island made communication even more important. I mailed 28 postcards, two greeting cards, and 27 letters; many of the latter remain to fill in the details of these experiences. I made only two calls home with the bag (cell) phone, but from the mainland I called Gary every week, daughters four times, my mom and sister once each. It was difficult being so far from home and loved ones.

From a letter: Monday, 4 August 1997
On the outside of one of JCW's letters from her boyfriend that I picked up today, was a message for me; "Tell Jean that Peregrine 1A "Stetson" is back!" [JCW's boyfriend was working as a Hack Site Attendant at a Montana hack site where Gary and I had worked in 1996; Stetson was one of the Peregrines released there 'on our watch' and I knew Gary would be as pleased by the news of Stetson's return as I was.]

Aplomado Falcon on perch Brian built from beach-scavenged lumber and mesquite branches

CLOSING COMMENTS

Having left the Refuge on 19 August, I started driving north later in the day in order to get around Houston at night, and slept a few hours in the cab of my truck in a rest area after I passed the city. It was a grueling trip, but I arrived at my home in Wisconsin in three days. It was immediately necessary to plunge into preparations for the fall semester at UW-L. One of the things I accomplished that fall was to prepare a study guide/lab manual for the indoor lab exercises I planned for my Ornithology students. I also wrote a grant for funding to improve the Ornithology course, which I had first been assigned in 1995. The $12,000 grant award I received allowed me to purchase more 35mm slides of Wisconsin bird species, a 35mm slide-projector and projector cart with extension cord, a laptop, and ornithology software. I hired an expert to prepare additional specimens for the bird specimen collection from birds that had flown into windows and been preserved in a freezer. With grant money, I also chose a field guide and purchased copies to be signed out to the students who enrolled each semester, and additional binoculars to be loaned to those students who could not provide or borrow one themselves.

I regret that Gary could not share these Aplomado Falcon and Matagorda Island experiences with me, but one of us was needed at home and he generously volunteered so that I could continue summer fieldwork as part of my career development as an ornithologist. I also carried feelings of guilt that I was not there for my mother and other family members who were encountering difficulties during the 72 days I was away from home in the summer of 1997. Gary, along with my sister, Patti, had done a kind and thorough job of assisting Mom as she recovered from a broken hip and the subsequent surgical repair. She was back in her mobile home, but no longer able to drive, so she required groceries to be purchased for her, to be driven to her clinic appointments, to have someone mow her lawn, as well as a variety of other assistance. Meanwhile, there were other decisions pending about family matters, and I was glad to get home to help with them. Together, Gary and I decided to purchase a double-wide house and place it as a second home on our farm.

Gary had resigned his engineering job in 1991 to do field work, but the success of Peregrine Falcon reintroduction was making it clear that Peregrine work would soon end. Rising family issues and monetary needs had brought Gary to the point of re-applying for engineering work. His several short-term engineering consulting contracts, along with my teaching contracts, had supported us adequately for six years, but would perhaps not provide sufficient income for the next several years as we prepared for early retirement. He did, in fact, go back in fall 1997, to work four more years full-time, as a corporate engineer.

These circumstances and decisions did not, after all, put an end to our fieldwork adventures as Gary's Wyoming Grouse Survey story in this book illustrates. In this book we have tried to cover several of our non-Peregrine field work adventures, without making this volume too lengthy. Yet untold, are the Greater Sage-Grouse and Ring-necked Pheasant projects on which we worked together in Colorado in 1994, and a variety of other smaller projects—too much material to fit into this book—so maybe we will write one more book of fieldwork adventures.

REFERENCES

Annual Report, The Peregrine Fund, Inc., 1994, 1995.

Operation Report, The Peregrine Fund, Inc., 1990-1997.

Website for Aransas National Wildlife Refuge:
https://:www.fws.gov/refuge/aransas/

Safe Harbor Agreements:
https://www.fws/gov/midwest/endangered/permits/enhancement/sha/index.html

General article about saving endangered species:
"The Road to Recovery" by Jim Clark; *Birder's World*; February 1999; pp. 32-45.

Whooping Crane Conservation website:
USFWS:Whooping Crane Reintroduction - Questions and Answers

Institute for Bird Populations website:
IBP - Banding Classes (birdpop.org)

Part 4 – Gary

Grouse Lek Surveys

Wyoming

2001 - 2009

Greater Sage-Grouse in their courtship display on a lek

85 Greater Sage-Grouse occupy this lek on a private ranch, (small white dots in short grass at mid-photo)

Finding Adopt-a-Lek

Sometimes the significant events or stories of our lives seem to originate randomly, apparently without a traceable cause. They just happen, or are a result of a personal whim. Other times, one can trace the origin, the seed, which caused a larger experience to develop. The seed for my performing nine years of springtime grouse monitoring in Wyoming was a cap given to me by the foreman of a large private ranch astride the Green River in western Wyoming. I was on assignment, alongside my life partner, Jean, working on Peregrine falcon reintroduction as a hack site attendant during the summer of 1993. John, the ranch foreman, gave me a cap with the logo of the Wildlife Federation of Wyoming emblazoned on it.

The cap was just a small gift, produced and sold by the Wyoming Wildlife Federation as a promotional item and modest income producer for the organization. John was a member. Jean and I were lovers of the Wyoming landscape and its wild inhabitants, and when we returned to Wisconsin, I sent in my fee to became a member of this Wyoming federation.

As I was reviewing the periodic publication, *The Pronghorn*, of the Wyoming Wildlife Federation in late 2000, I read with great interest their call for volunteers for a program referred to as "Adopt-a-Lek". The state federation was seeking volunteers to census and survey Greater Sage-Grouse at their traditional breeding grounds (leks) in March and April on public and private lands. The work would be done in cooperation with local resource agencies and landowners. The resulting data would be used to help assess Greater Sage-Grouse population trends.

Jean and I had thoroughly enjoyed monitoring over 100 Greater Sage-Grouse leks while we worked for the Colorado Division of

Wildlife in 1994. A project like this would give me the opportunity to participate in the study and preservation of a favorite species in one of our favorite states. Jean could not join me in the Adopt-a-Lek program as she had already contracted for a multi-year field study of grassland birds on a 315-acre private grassland in Wisconsin. This meant we could each be involved in a fieldwork project on birds in two very different states. With her support for my goal, I sent in my application.

My Role in the Adopt-a-Lek Program

In late 1999 the Montana Wildlife Federation developed a citizen science program called Adopt-a-Lek, which would involve volunteers in counting Greater Sage-Grouse on their Spring leks. Lek is a term for a specific area where males of a species gather to perform courtship displays to attract females for mating. Lekking species are polygynous; males of such species mate with more than one female. The males are in competition with each other, but it is the individual females that choose which male to mate. Surveys to count the number of males and females on a lek, are a standard biological method of censusing lekking bird species.

The program was launched in Southwestern Montana, with a trial run conducted in 2000, and then expanded to Wyoming and Nevada in 2001. Volunteers, organized and modestly funded by the state Wildlife Federation, were paired to state and federal wildlife agencies and the biologists of those organizations. The volunteers would assist the biologists in gathering information on Greater Sage-Grouse distribution and population through physical observation. Then, the responsible agencies would apply the data to hopefully stem the decline of this species.

I was one of ten volunteers accepted for the Wyoming Adopt-a-Lek program, somewhat uniquely, in as much as I was a long-time resident of Wisconsin. I would be driving from our home in Wisconsin to Wyoming to census leks there and participate in the Wyoming surveys for about a week each spring around the peak time of lek activity.

I had requested and been granted assignment in the Northeast corner of Wyoming because we were familiar with that area and had access to a remote cabin in the middle of ranching country. The cabin was privately owned, primitive (no running water or line-delivered electricity), and was several miles from the nearest maintained roads. We had vacationed there in that lovely, secluded spot each year since 1995, and I felt it would be a good base of survey operations. The area, north and south for 50 miles from the cabin, was the general eastern extent of Greater Sage-Grouse and their habitat within Wyoming. I would be the lone volunteer helping the state and national wildlife agencies in eastern Wyoming. The other nine volunteers lived closer to the areas of greater grouse density in central and southwest Wyoming and were able to range out on their surveys from their own homes.

The Wyoming Wildlife Federation was the coordinating organization and provided modest funding to cover volunteers' mileage costs while surveying, but our physical interface and assignments came from the local government agency which utilized the data we collected. In my case, those individuals were the Biologist for the Thunder Basin National Grassland (first year only) and the Biologist for the Wyoming Game and Fish Department (each year). I never actually physically met anyone from the Wyoming Wildlife Federation, but I had very informative and pleasant written feedback from them throughout my years of spring surveys. I provided written summary reports to both Wyoming Game and Fish and the Wildlife Federation at the conclusion of each season.

My assignments were quite varied from year to year and changed depending on the needs of the biologist involved. Compared to other volunteers, a major difference in my assignment was that I was requested to monitor and report on Sharp-tailed Grouse and Sharp-tail leks in addition to Greater Sage-Grouse and their leks, the major focus of the Adopt-a-Lek program. The other volunteers worked primarily in Greater Sage-Grouse rich habitat, whereas in eastern Wyoming the ranges of these two grouse species meet and overlap. This was personally exciting and rewarding to me as the cabin I stayed at had an active Sharp-tailed Grouse lek one mile to the west and several other Sharp-tailed Grouse leks within nine miles. I had long admired both species and relished the opportunity to see more of each of their lek displays, the similarities and the differences, while also helping out the responsible local Biologists.

I parked my pickup truck near a reservoir for a one-night solo
camp in the midst of prime grouse habitat

Two track road leading to good grouse habitat, the gumbo soil
gets deeply rutted if driven over when wet

Performing my Role

With the latest assignment and maps in hand, each Spring (typically in April) I would load up my pickup truck with spotting scope, binoculars, cameras, and a time proven assortment of camping gear so that I could camp out in the back of the truck, if need be. I drove 800 miles from Wisconsin to Northeast Wyoming but did not charge the Wildlife Federation for any miles going to Wyoming or returning to Wisconsin. Just like the Wyoming volunteers, I only charged for actual grouse survey mileage on assignment in Wyoming. And then I donated some of my earned compensation back to the Federation. Some nights I truck-camped near my starting lek. Other nights I would be at the cabin and then get up in the dark, about 3:45 AM, and race off to the first lek, generally 15 to 20 miles away, in order to be there just when it was barely getting light, around 5:30 AM, and I could begin to see or hear the gathered grouse.

My volunteer grouse work was very weather dependent, both for being able to see grouse on their leks in rugged and remote sagebrush country, and to traverse the primitive roads to leks with few human habitations nearby. Some of those roads, weaving over gumbo soils, would turn into the worst greasy, slimy, yet tire-accumulating mud one could imagine with the slightest amount of rain or snow. Amazing stuff. Without abundant caution one could easily become mired down.

Having a good forecast to plan my daily activities was essential, and it was rare to have more than two or three days in a row when viewing and access were most favorable. Perfect weather for the start of each censusing effort included already having had several days of dry weather in order to have firm roads. The best conditions for seeing and being able to hear distant lek activities were clear to partly cloudy skies with calm to moderate wind.

Needless to say, "perfect conditions" were seldom available, and many mornings a degree of hope and caution were needed. But on those mornings when everything met my hopes, oh, then it was a marvelous experience, and I cherish the memories.

Each night before censusing and surveys I would select which lek to start at and plan to be there just before dawn. Then it would be a race between myself and the clock as I drove to the next viewing location because within 2-3 hours the lek activities of the grouse would wind down. Thereafter they would disperse from the lek site to their individual feeding or nesting areas, sexual activities for the day being done. The grouse are vulnerable to predators, such as Golden Eagles or coyotes, when at the lek and there is a fine line between the need to breed and the need to survive.

My assigned observations included both the counting of grouse on known leks, whether they be Greater Sage-Grouse or Sharp-tailed Grouse leks, but also the scouting out of new leks or leks that might have moved since a previous census year. But even the discovery of a new lek, always an exciting accomplishment, required the grouse to be there and so I encountered the same time restraints every morning. By 9:00 AM or so any chance of seeing grouse on a lek was very small and my prime activity for the day was done.

By that time of the morning, I could then enjoy the luxury of a fine camp breakfast in the cab or back of my truck as it was parked in some beautiful but remote and secluded setting. On a few mornings breakfast might include a fresh donut or two, but finding donuts in good grouse country is rare, and you might have to drive 10 or 20 miles to then park at the perfect breakfast site. Most mornings involved canned juice and fruit followed by Grape-nuts™ with powdered milk, water and sugar, or, optionally, instant hot cereal prepared with my small backpack stove. Individually wrapped granola bars were always an at-hand supplement in case I was still hungry. Topping off the meal would be a relaxing cup of hot tea while I enjoyed the view of such unique prairie country, the preferred habitat for grouse and pronghorn antelope. Then it would be time for the 20-60-mile drive back to the cabin or to the next camp site.

On some mornings, after my breakfast break, I would hike out to a newly discovered lek to get the GPS co-ordinates (geographic position) of that lek to allow the Wyoming Game and Fish Biologist to enter it accurately into his records. Other mornings I might hike to an old, but documented, lek site to look for feathers or droppings which could indicate an active lek. Some mornings or afternoons, if the proposed survey locations were unfamiliar to me, I would drive the roads to the site to familiarize myself with the roads and landmarks I would encounter in the dark the following morning. And all this time, with or without grouse present, I would be engaged in one of my favorite activities, exploring and becoming familiar with sparsely populated, near-wild country, and seeing some of the natural denizens of the diminishing sagebrush "sea."

2001

I drove to Newcastle, Wyoming and met the Biologist of Wyoming Game and Fish department to review his needs and to receive some detailed maps showing the location of grouse leks. During the afternoon I drove out to the assigned Greater Sage-Grouse area northwest of town and scouted the roads to familiarize myself with the prime viewing locations for several known leks in the area. After spending the evening camping in the city park on the east edge of Newcastle I arrived at the overlook of the first lek in the early dawn of my first day as an Adopt-a-Lek volunteer, the coming daylight barely perceptible. I parked, turned off the engine, and hopped out of the cab. It was a quiet and calm morning. As my eyes adjusted to the dim light of the morning to come, I waited for the annoying clicks, ticks, and pops of a cooling engine to subside so that I might listen instead for the distant popping of strutting Greater Sage-Grouse males deflating their air sacs. There they were! I gathered my binoculars and peered toward the sounds, taking advantage of the light gathering and magnification of the binocular's lenses. Again, I was rewarded by having the clear image of grouse after grouse, bird after bird, come into focus as I scanned the lek, quickly spotting the grouse as they pivoted about, the whites of their tail and pendulous breast feathers framing and showing me where to look. I hadn't seen Greater Sage-Grouse on a lek for seven years and I took in a breath of excitement and wonder as I gazed at this natural seasonal phenomenon. Just me and the grouse, the apparent only occupants within hundreds of acres.

Feeling blessed by the outdoors I had come to enjoy I succumbed to the rational need to return to being a citizen scientist. Sweeping back and forth with my binoculars, and a bit later, the spotting scope, I counted and then counted again. Being involved in wildlife observations, the counting is automatic and one finds oneself counting over and over again, until you must declare you're done and it is past time to move to the next lek and count there. At the first lek of a morning's survey efforts it is tempting to linger a bit because the sky lightens allowing better viewing and the advancing time gradually may bring in a few more grouse to the lek you are watching.

That morning, in the prime grouse habitat of eastern Wyoming, at that lek, and several miles away from the invasion of established oil wells pumping crude, I counted a maximum of 57 males and 6 females (not an unusual ratio, the males must be on lek to secure mating opportunities, the females can come and go) or a total of 63 Greater Sage-Grouse. I was elated! It felt marvelous to witness that many birds at one viewing. At the same time, I recognized it was marvelous only in the context of changing times and changing habitat conditions and grouse populations. I was humbled and saddened then, to recall maximum numbers of Greater Sage-Grouse on productive leks not that many decades earlier had numbered in the hundreds. Everything is relative. That is why I was there that morning, monitoring populations for today's biologists and conservationists.

By the time the grouse were dispersing off the leks, I had surveyed two more leks, recorded the counts, and downed my breakfast where I had parked my truck in the middle of rolling plains and sparse, mostly untamed, country, not a human habitation in sight. This still left time for a long drive to Leiter, Wyoming, where I did some personal scouting for an antelope hunting trip I was hoping to engage in that Fall.

I camped that evening in Keyhole State Park, near Moorcroft. The following morning, I changed species and surveyed an automobile route which brought me past four Sharp-tailed Grouse leks, and on a later day hiked to the Sharp-tailed Grouse lek west of the cabin. I was pleased to find four out of five sites actively in use, the grouse dancing the Sharp-tail dance, a more vigorous jumping and fighting dance noted for its rather rapid cessation of dancing. After the momentary stop, and after apparently gathering renewed energy, the males would go at it again, cooing, displaying, stomping the ground, rustling their feathers, fighting one another. Delightful to watch. One site had up to 18 Sharptails on it at one time.

In that same April trip, I was lured to explore exposed rocks and short cliffs enveloping one end of a small valley within the Wyoming Black Hills. Elevation and steepness are deceptive when viewed from below but after a strenuous hike over hillocks and swales, occasionally grabbing trees and branches to pull myself higher, I came to the base of the short cliffs, about 20 feet below the top of terrain. I scrambled back and forth, weaving my way from boulder and rock onward to vertical rock faces intersecting with the more gradual slope of gravel and soil leading back to the valley below. There, light and shadow of the descending sun gave contrast to a message carved in the soft sandstone on a cliff face. I was not the first to have come to this picturesque location, sheltered from the eastern wind and open to the landscape below and west: buttes, escarpments, valley bottoms covered in new green grass, hilltops and valley sides decorated with Ponderosa Pine. The message inscribed on the cliff, "Heaven", was followed by two sets of initials with a plus sign joining them together. From my more recent perspective of the setting and scene before me, I had to agree with these apparent young lovers. The location was quite heavenly. I have no way to know if their love lasted, but I found comfort in finding their expression of it, on that rocky cliff, had by then lasted about a century, and I think, based on the depth of the excision of stone, it could still be visible several centuries hence. Not that I plan to let anyone know where it is.

During my 2001 lek-watching "season" I had the pleasure of seeing and recording 224 Greater Sage-Grouse sightings with the maximum number at any one site on any single day being 63. I saw 43 Sharp-tailed Grouse with the maximum number being 18. I was well pleased with the grouse and my experiences and knew I would be back in 2002.

In July of 2001, I enlisted the help of my Biologist spouse while we were on vacation at the cabin and she and I went back to Newcastle and the same lek sites I had surveyed in April. There we performed an extensive biological study using a documented protocol and a Daubenmire frame. Our data filled 10 pages of vegetative information gathered for the Adopt-a-Lek program of the Wyoming Wildlife Federation which they would utilize to correlate Greater Sage-Grouse density to measured habitat conditions.

After plotting four transects and recording their location, we measured and logged on the data sheets: percentage of sagebrush cover; percentage of grass, shrub, forb, bare ground; height of residual vegetation; height of live vegetation; height of sagebrush. What we remember best is our measurement day coincided with an exceptionally warm day with temperatures above 90 degrees. The sun was high above us in cloudless skies and we sweated profusely in the dry air of Wyoming in July. A tall glass of iced soda was a welcome and refreshing relief after we completed our work.

2002
In 2002 I repeated the survey route established the previous year for Sharp-tailed Grouse, and increased the maximum number of Sharp-tailed grouse observed at any single lek on any single day to 27 grouse. Habitat conditions are well suited for Sharp-tails on this route, but I am concerned that an increase in housing developments around local communities, and more sub-division of large ranches will reduce grouse numbers.

A new biologist was assigned by Wyoming Game and Fish Department to the Casper region this year and I met him outside a restaurant in Upton, Wyoming. The Casper region includes northeastern Wyoming and he gave me suggestions for how I could best help him in his grouse responsibilities for the area. In the afternoon we drove on the back-country roads through likely grouse areas as he showed me where to do my work.

Although the roads were dry that day, it seemed to me the local ranchers and hunters were totally unfazed by the potential of getting stuck in some of the gumbo soil conditions we saw.

Multiple very deep ruts were locked into place on dry, frozen ground until further traffic and erosion, or the next rain or snow, would reconfigure the road bed into a new quagmire for anyone attempting to drive through. I vowed to only drive these routes when they were dry, and to exit the area if the weather changed to rain or snow. My surveying opportunities in wet or snowy weather were limited by the recognition that if I got stuck, I would be solely responsible for extricating myself. When surveying active leks, given the sagebrush areas covered and wild habitat grouse preferred, I would generally be miles from the nearest ranch or other human habitation, and I would be out there alone.

After riding with the Biologist to explore my new assignment area, he returned me to my truck. I chose to camp in the vicinity to be up before dawn the next morning and camped on the edge of a high ridge south of Upton, Wyoming. I was 0.8 mile along the ridge from the nearest road, overlooking a view several dozen miles in circumference. The Black Hills were visible in the north and east during the day, the lights of Upton in the valley dotted the black screen of the night. The ridge dropped steeply on the north to a sagebrush pasture I would scout in the future. On the south side, the ridge flowed smoothly downslope to sagebrush and ranchland beyond. I would listen for grouse there before I left this campsite the following morning.

As an addition to my normal assignment of counting all grouse I encountered, I was to scout and listen for the sounds of grouse on unrecorded leks and then note location and numbers. This involved driving through likely, or what should be, grouse habitat, and stopping and listening. Every one-half mile or so, or at the next possible grouse habitat I encountered, I would stop the vehicle, turn off the engine, wait for the cooling sounds of the engine to subside, and then listen in all directions. Not trusting only my ears I would also take the binoculars from the truck seat and scan the surrounding vicinity for any white flashes of grouse displaying. With my experience in Colorado and Wyoming I knew the preferred dancing or display grounds would more likely be in bottom swales or more open areas and I paid the most attention to where grouse might be if they, in fact, were regular inhabitants of the surrounding area.

Experience, and knowing where to look for grouse, paid off well in the early morning. I located three new active leks and quickly drew a sketch of how the Biologist or anyone else might be able to locate for themselves these leks which held 29 Greater Sage-Grouse. I was able to add to the grouse data base for Wyoming and it made my 1600-mile round trip from Wisconsin well worthwhile, and personally satisfying.

The following morning, I was back at the cabin and arose as the interior began to lighten with the sun's approach to the eastern horizon. With abundant time to meet the grouse on their home turf, I dressed for a cool morning hike, grabbed binoculars, and a light-weight spotting scope kept at the cabin for just this type of occasion, and marched out the door to check the Sharp-tailed Grouse count on the nearby lek. Twenty Sharptails had already flown and walked into the lek by the time the lazy human finally arrived, the sun not yet over the eastern rim.

2003

I started the new grouse-viewing season by driving to the far north end of Crook County, Wyoming, and truck-camping just eight miles south of Montana. My camp was on Bureau of Land Management grounds hidden behind a screen of scrubby pines and brush, overlooking a sparsely-vegetated, large pasture of flat land. Even the sagebrush did not look healthy or abundant.

The following morn I hiked a short distance out from camp, listening and looking for grouse. Nothing. Based on the vegetation, I was not surprised. Then I hurried back to the truck to do an extensive survey for any possible grouse leks in the area, per my Biologist's request. I did as much driving and listening as I could in the few morning hours of prime grouse activity, but confirmed that, although the area could hold a few grouse yet, it was not prime habitat, and I did not find any leks or grouse. Even finding no grouse is important information for the wildlife biologists to know in order for them to approximate and delineate grouse habitat within Wyoming.

Next on my Biologist's survey agenda was the area north and west of Devils Tower National Monument. The prairie dogs were already active in the dog town at the monument and I enjoyed, as always, their antics on my way to the monument's campground. Early in the tourist season, I was one of the few campers there and truck-camped that night to be close to the roads I planned to follow the next morning. I was pleased to confirm that an historical lek of Greater Sage-Grouse was still active, and I located one new, previously undocumented, Sharptail lek before the day was too far advanced to warrant any further scouting.

I had time to fill before driving to Upton, Wyoming, to prepare for grouse work the following morning, so I dropped in on a neighboring rancher we knew in the area of the cabin. There I found he and a few of his friends and neighbors engaged in a small roping and branding rodeo. He graciously invited me to attend the excitement and watch. This rancher acquaintance had the misfortune to be born 100 years too late in terms of the life he wanted to engage. Although he had the equipment and means to run all his new calves through a confinement system and branding chute to speed the job and minimize the risk of human injury, he preferred to do one batch of cattle in the old manner. The friends

337

he invited had the same weakness and deficiency in adapting to modernity and relished the opportunity he gave them to practice old skills they had all learned on their fathers' ranches.

I stood there, camera in hand, to gaze in gawking amazement as several participants mounted their horses and made ready with their lariats. A small huddled mass of calves was in one corner of the large corral, horses and men and a good cow dog in the opposite corner. Several fellows took their turn as the "throwers and branders," tending a wood fire built on the ground inside the corral fence where the branding irons were heating.

At a shout and direction from the ranch owner, the action commenced. One rider lassoed the head and neck, another a hind foot (how is that even possible??), and the bawling, struggling critter was dragged over to the fire, tipped on its side if it wasn't already, and a hot iron placed on the hide, hair burning away, skin instantly roasted, the odor of burnt hair floating on the gentle breeze. The animal was now permanently marked with the chosen symbol of the owner.

Brands can still be an important characteristic of cattle operations in many western states where ranches may cover thousands of acres and have common access to open range land. These unique markings minimize ownership questions during normal movement or shipment of the cattle and in sales transactions. The state of Wyoming has official Brand Inspectors and an office to administer the choice and usage of brands, operating under the auspices of the Wyoming Livestock Board.

After joining the cowboys and ranchers in a delicious ranch meal hosted by the rodeo's organizer, I drove 20 miles south to meet the ranch owner on whose private land I was to survey grouse the following morning. This rancher was a personal acquaintance of the Biologist I worked for, and was an excellent example of those ranchers who willingly work with the Wyoming Game and Fish Department and advocate for the preservation of natural resources and wildlife. The rancher and his wife shared what they knew of grouse and conditions on their ranch after I explained my role in the effort of grouse surveys. They very kindly granted me permission to roam about on their ranch, to discover what I could, and allowed me to camp that night in a setting of my choice on their ranch land.

I was ever so glad to have already met the kind, friendly people who owned the ranch the minute I turned into the long ranch lane winding to a few buildings and a concrete bunkhouse about a mile in. Because the minute I passed through their gated entry, the first sign I saw, large, professionally painted and hand-lettered, mounted on a sturdy post and easily viewed from the ranch lane through the windows of my truck read. "Warning – Trespassors will be shot, Survivors will be few." The second sign I saw, the same easily-read and official-looking sign as the first, about midway to the ranch buildings, stated "Anyone found here at night will be found here in the morning". The third and last sign was posted on the door of their cabin/bunkhouse and told me "There is nothing in here worth your life." I was impressed. These Wyoming ranchers had an interesting approach to a security system.

Perhaps needless to say, I slept soundly and securely that night, my truck parked on a rise of land overlooking their ranch and ranch-site buildings below, a quarter moon casting enough glow for me to climb into the back of the truck after I turned off the flashlight. The next morning, I surveyed the entire ranch and nearby state land and was able to confirm one Greater Sage-Grouse lek, which the Biologist hoped still existed.

The following day found me back at the cabin awaiting the arrival of my spouse, Jean, and her friend, Patricia. They were driving from Wisconsin on a pre-planned birding tour of several western states and this would be their first stop. I had offered to put them onto several Greater Sage-Grouse leks and the nearby Sharp-tailed Grouse lek to give them a positive start on their quest to see several new species for their yearly bird lists. Rain clouds had moved in over the Black Hills in the night and impinged on the perfect conditions every birder hopes for. But, in the continuing sprinkle of rain drops the following morning, we were able to hike to the Sharp-tail lek and found enough birds there for viewing and tallying, the mating ritual more important to the birds than staying dry.

Back at the cabin, we gave up on a leisurely breakfast, and instead opted to quickly load the off-road all-terrain vehicle, before the two-track trail leading to the cabin got significantly wetter and possibly trapping us there until conditions improved. The rain continuing and pounding harder and faster, we successfully drove and maneuvered our way the four miles back to a hard-surfaced road, the tire treads fully loaded with greasy red gumbo mud of remarkable tenacity, adhesion, and slipperiness. At intervening cattle gates our boots picked up the same gumbo and easily more than doubled their weight and size. Some of the mud would sling off our footwear if we kicked vigorously. And then it would build up again when we dealt with the next gate. Very tiring and messy.

Thankful to have made it back to our highway vehicles, we transferred our gear and bid one another thanks and good luck. I drove back to Wisconsin, another Spring lek survey successfully under the belt, and appreciative of having good adventures in the open landscape of Wyoming. Jean and her friend drove to Newcastle and were able to see the large numbers of Greater Sage-Grouse on lek following the map I had given them. From there they traveled on to Colorado and Kansas and added several new species to their life and year bird lists.

2004

Earlier in my part-time career as a Field Biologist I had attended a prairie grouse conference and had met the State of Nebraska Biologist whose specialty was the Greater Prairie-Chickens of north central Nebraska. In 2004 he generously offered to arrange for me to witness a booming ground (lek) on a large private ranch on my way to my volunteer grouse work in Wyoming. I met him at his office and he guided me 20 miles south to the gently ranging contours of dry land farm and ranching country, a vast area of few people, few trees, and a feel of silence and far distance. With my profound thanks, after he showed me the location of the booming ground, he left me there to ponder my good fortune, good weather, and the decision of where to camp.

As prairie grouse are wont to do, several male Greater Prairie-Chickens were at the lek late in the day, after sundown, practicing their moves for the females the next morning. I elected to camp several hundred yards east of the display grounds on a slight rise overlooking an area of crop fields yet laying fallow, small groups of a few scattered trees in the low lands, and large acreages of native prairie grass fields, this land deemed too dry and low quality for anything but the grasses growing there. In other words, near perfect wild chicken country. I was elated.

I prepared a light supper in the back of my truck, some hot chocolate, and dined while perched on the tailgate, while witnessing the natural flight of a prairie chicken or two as they sought their own supper and resting spot for the night. Sometimes, just like in our chickenyard back home in Wisconsin, I could hear the occasional cluck and chuck of prairie chickens muttering to themselves and others of their kind.

With the quiet night and full moon rising in the east, I had waited until well after sundown when I believed all the prairie chickens on the booming grounds would have roosted or gone to a nest. With the abundant light of the moon, I took the blind I had brought and walked to the grounds to set it up ready for my occupancy the following morning. Even that late, I bumped into an errant Greater Prairie-Chicken or two that were driven to be near the booming grounds at first light. In this case perhaps hoping the early bird gets the sex.

I slept well, the few coyote cries bringing a drowsy smile as I rolled over, appreciative of remembering where I was. Rising out of my sleeping bag just as the eastern sky was beginning to brighten, I grabbed my tripod with scope, binoculars, and my camera and hurried down to the blind. Too late! Several male Greater Prairie-Chickens were already at the booming grounds and strutting about, muted chicken clucking emanating. But climbing into my blind and seating myself comfortably on the folding chair, I settled in for a three-hour show. It was a grand show of numerous male and female Greater Prairie-Chickens going about a hormonally-driven and evolutionarily-determined dance of the ages. Females would come and go but the males were very intransigent in their willingness to stay until the sun, fear of predators, perhaps hunger and thirst, and other survival needs shut down the action and I could at last exit from the blind. I had been determined to outlast them in order to not disturb their ritual.

Returning to the truck, I drove on to my first Wyoming grouse survey of the new season, being extremely pleased with my experience with the Greater Prairie-Chickens of Nebraska. I knew my memories would last and the many pictures I took of the birds would remind me of my time with them and of their value in the grassland ecosystem.

I camped two nights, once at a reservoir east of Upton, and once at last year's private ranch with the intimidating signs, and performed Wyoming grouse surveys each morning. After the second morning's survey I drove back to the cabin, accessing it by a shortcut involving parking my truck, and then walking in across a mile of state land containing a prairie dog colony. The process saved a rugged drive along a four-mile two-track road but didn't really save any time. I enjoyed lunch at the cabin and hiked out again for one more night of truck-camping and one more morning of grouse surveys. On the vacation property, walking through Ponderosa Pine forest 100 yards east of the cabin, I discovered elk droppings, the first positive sign that elk had returned to that area of Crook County. It is probably hard for any city dweller, inexperienced with rural or ranch living, to understand how excited and pleased I was to find elk poop that day! Perhaps even more difficult to comprehend, is my reason for taking some of the dried pellets of scat, putting them in a container, and saving them at the vacation cabin to show the rest of the family when next we all might visit there again. But I did.

Sharp-tailed Grouse in their display on a dancing ground,
note out-spread wings and tail feathers held up in a point

Another isolated truck camp, near the end and edge of a
high ridge south of Upton, WY

2005

Envious of Jean's western bird watching tour in the Spring of 2003, I started my 2005 season of Wyoming grouse work by first driving to the Cimarron National Grasslands near Elkhart, Kansas, hoping to observe Lesser Prairie-Chickens on the booming ground Jean and her friend had visited. In the early morning, still dark, I awoke from my bed in the back of the truck and hiked to an established blind, built for visitors' use by the Grasslands. The only human there as the day brightened, I was able to observe the antics of these chickens, a unique species but related to the Greater Prairie-Chickens, which I had observed in Nebraska the year before. It was a wondrous experience to witness their own dance of the season and to know it has been going on for centuries in essentially the same location. Will it continue to be so? Only if humans allow it.

As I closed the door of the topper on my pickup truck bed after my camp breakfast, the pneumatic cylinder failed and the door slammed shut, breaking the glass into a thousand tiny shards. What a mess! Little glass pieces all over the back half of the truck bed and a gaping hole in the back of my truck. I swept up the former window and bagged the glass fragments for later disposal. Driving to the nearest town, I engineered a solution, bought some plywood and copious amounts of duct tape, and fabricated a water-resistant and wind-proof closure to replace the glass lift gate of the pickup topper.

From there, I followed Jean's recommendations and drove to Gunnison, Colorado, where I was able to add another "life bird" to my species list. After camping nearby in a private camp ground, I joined several other parties at a public blind the following morning to view the Gunnison Sage-Grouse, another unique species of grouse. I was very interested to note the subtle differences between it and the Greater Sage-Grouse of Wyoming and Colorado.

Next, I drove to Loveland Pass in Colorado, but I and a fellow bird watcher there were unsuccessful at finding the White-tailed Ptarmigan we both hoped to add to our life lists. Proceeding on, I camped at Pawnee National Grasslands north of Denver for the night before resuming my normal Spring grouse duties in Wyoming the following day.

As I was scouting my assigned survey route for the year north and east of Upton, I encountered an older car with two scruffy-looking occupants. Twice, in different locations but on similar back country and seldom used dirt roads. I was acquainted with the ranchers of that sparse country and what they drove. I had encountered Wild Turkey hunters on occasion in previous years and was familiar with their routines. But I had only spotted a single vehicle at a time roaming these roads in other years, and then not every year. To find this car in two different locations at two different times of the late afternoon on roads very seldom utilized was highly unusual.

At home in Wisconsin, I receive the Crook County weekly community newspaper and had read of several "meth busts" and arrests for possession near this area of the state. Being cognizant of this information and taking into account my normal safety and security precautions I could only wonder and surmise a possible explanation. My meetings with local ranchers and hunters had always been brief, and usually just in passing, but had always struck me as cordial. It seemed to me the car and occupants' actions could be explained as meeting for a purchase, or setting up a drop of illicit drugs. The looks on their faces as we passed one another on the road could have been the same as mine when I saw them: we regarded each other as an unwanted invasion of our privacy.

At that point I decided to change my planned campsite from anywhere near the strange car's prowling area and instead went to another of my favorite area campsites for the evening. As was generally part of my solitary camp requirements, my camp that night offered a location for my truck that could not be blocked from access, as well as having an alternate escape route, a "back door" exit path. Early in our camping years in Wisconsin we had learned the value of selecting such a site when we were rudely awakened at 2:00 AM one morning and had to deal with a drunk and his three pals. While we were inside our tent, they had driven past our tent close enough they struck our tent poles with their out-stretched hands, yelling and driving erratically. We bolted from our tent and held a heated discussion with them from the safety of our locked truck.

I did not normally travel with self-defense weapons when camping with my family or wife in high occupancy, well used, vehicular campgrounds adjacent to, or near, public roadways. But for my solitary truck camping in remote, semi-wild, primitive back-country I usually slept with a loaded firearm within easy reach, either shotgun or revolver, along with a reliable flashlight, and a can of bear spray. I never feared the four-legged predators, it is always the two-legged ones that are worthy of appropriate extra caution. I would load my firearm just before going to sleep and unload it and pack it away before breakfast.

I awoke early the next morning before dawn, pleased with an undisturbed rest, and drove out on my survey route for the day. I did some stop-and-listen survey work and also was able to see grouse on two of the known leks. One of these leks was previously unknown until I first identified it in 2002. Very rewarding to confirm its yearly use and occupancy.

I then met the Wyoming State Biologist in Upton, and we drove south to a large private ranch where he introduced me to the owner. This ranch was known by both the Biologist and the ranch owner to harbor a lek, large in both size and grouse count, and my Biologist wanted me to confirm its use and the number of grouse this year. The owner led the way in his old ranch truck, and showed us the access he wished us to use to get to the best viewing spot for the lek. I made careful mental note because the route went right past the owner's house and wound through an intricate set of turns and gates, some of which were electric wire gates, continuing on until we were about a mile west of the ranch entrance lane. My challenge would be that I would arrive in the dark and need to find my way to the observation point by myself without using the familiar landmarks that had been visible during our daylight visit.

After camping the night before on Thunder Basin Grassland property near a small reservoir 17 miles north of this lek, I drove with headlights on all the way to the lek, managing all the gates and turns correctly. The ranch owner was already up in the pre-dawn leaning against a porch railing, quaffing a cup of coffee under the ranch yard light and gave me a friendly wave as I trundled past. One has to rise very early each day in order to match a determined rancher eking out a good living in, what many would deem to be, harsh country.

Hoping to see a lot of grouse on a quiet, lovely morning, I turned off the engine and headlights, hopped out of the truck, waited for my eyes and ears to adjust, and was instantly granted my wish. They were out there! Binoculars at the ready, spotting scope set up on its tripod, camera out of the case, I began scanning the basin below me, focusing on its short grass center, the perimeter and beyond being thickly adorned with sagebrush.

The day brightened, the morning ticked away, my sense of time erased by centuries of ritual enacted on mornings such as this, at seasons such as this, by dramatic birds such as these. Would I drive 800 miles to see such a site? Would I give up a week of my time on a Wisconsin farm to witness sage-grouse on this lek? You bet I would! Before leaving the ranch, I entered the sighting of 80 Greater Sage-Grouse at the same time on that secluded lek in my log book, 70 males and 10 females. It was a grand morning.

One day later, while surveying for grouse and leks in new territory, I located an undocumented lek with 25 sage- grouse on it. The day after that I confirmed the Sharp-tailed Grouse lek near the cabin was still active for another season. In addition, near sundown, Wyoming permit in hand, I bagged a Wyoming Merriam's Wild Turkey, my first of this subspecies, in contrast to the Eastern Wild Turkey which we were familiar with in Wisconsin. I had no shortage of good excitement and fun wildland living on this trip

2006

An early start in 2006 did me little good. I arrived near the Wyoming cabin on March 29 but was halted by muddy, greasy, gumbo in the road, and a snowbank over the road, blocking the last mile of access. I cached some gear I had brought for the cabin near the trail, drove back out to park on firm ground at the neighboring ranch, and walked the four miles back to the cabin to spend a couple days of peace and quiet, listening to the symphony of the wood burner, and getting used to breathing mile-high air.

Two days later I drove into the ranch south of Upton where I first surveyed grouse last year, camped on the ranch overnight, and witnessed 85 Greater Sage-Grouse on lek the following morning. I had just enough time left in the morning to drive to a second lek, and was able to count 26 more Sage-grouse there.

In order to minimize wasted hours driving and hiking into the cabin before more grouse work the following morning, I spent much of the day in the Newcastle Library studying western literature and taking advantage of their computer to write an email to Jean. Then I drove 13 miles west of Upton and camped in a secluded draw below a low-use roadway, placing my truck out of the line of sight of all but the most observant drivers.

Awakening to the call of nature at 3:00 AM I climbed out of the truck bed over the tail gate, clad only in light sleeping wear, and plodded off several yards into the night. Gazing upward I saw the stars and moon plainly visible, over the sky haze of the lights of distant 24/7 coal mines near Gillette, and felt the open sky boded well for my grouse survey plans in 2-3 hours. I fell quickly back asleep and drowsily became aware of a light rain plinking on the thin roof above me. Oh-oh. When I awoke again at 5:00 AM I could no longer see any stars or moonlight through the rear camper window. The window seemed obscured, fuzzy, a wind was picking up, rocking the truck slightly. I sat up, snapped on the flashlight, shone it on the tailgate window, then opened it for a look outdoors. What the ...? The tailgate window was thickly coated with sticky snow, as was the ground surrounding me, and the air was filled with fat, thickly-falling snowflakes, glistening in the flashlight beam. Sneaky Stuff! After the noisy rain drops had turned to soft snow flakes, I could no longer hear their impact on my camping rig, and it was past time to either get out, or get stuck, here in the base of this little now-white vale.

Back in the truck cab I locked in four-wheel drive, started up and was able to creep up to the main road. The term "main road" gives it too much credit. It was in fact, the only road I had for the next few miles, and under the deluge of snow, it too was becoming treacherous. Back roads in that area do not receive much gravel or maintenance unless they service more than a few ranchers or households and carry at least a little "regular traffic." The gumbo soil of the road had turned to grease with the precipitation and I felt like I was driving on a bed of roller bearings, and proceeded slowly and with great caution for the next few miles until I came to a genuine gravel road offering me traction and safety from worry.

I stopped and reviewed my maps to find the best route back to a paved highway. Although it was just getting light, snow continued to fall. I knew the known leks and any new leks to be discovered would all be on lesser-traveled roads. Between road and weather conditions I knew any possible grouse work was canceled for the day and plotted the best use of my time and perceived obligations to my grouse work.

In 2006 I had no access to the instant and good weather forecasts now available on universally-used cell phones. But I pieced together the best forecast available then through the previous day's newspaper in a truck stop, and boringly putting up with an endless stream of commercials and country-western music on the truck radio as I waited for the weather forecast of the day. After dining on the luxury of a fresh donut from the truck stop and the rest of my breakfast in the truck cab I drove to and spent the bulk of the day at the Gillette Public Library. Libraries are wonderful places for biological field workers to spend the day in inclement weather: dry, warm, filled with free knowledge, and quiet.

With all my favorite remote camping spots now under snow and difficult to access, after dark I drove to the large parking lot at the east Moorcroft truck stop gas station and confirmed I could sleep there in my truck. In my younger days I used to try and park in a remote corner of the public interstate rest areas and commercial truck stops to try and minimize sleep interruption from the noisy giant diesel engines pulling in and out all night long. Through hard experience I found I could actually sleep better parked right next to a huge rig with its engine running through the night. Once a person gets used to the steady rumble and roar of the closest engine and you fall asleep because you are finally THAT tired, then you can no longer hear the other diesel engines coming and going. You've got your very own "white noise" blocking out all other sounds. Granted, it is a loud white noise, but it works for me. It got down to 30 degrees that night, but I was cozy in my sleeping bag and blankets.

Well before the sun rose, with little activity in town, other truckers all asleep in their rigs, the parking lot dark, I rose and emptied my bladder at the deeply shadowed, weedy edges of the lot and drove out of town. Much of the snow had melted, road conditions were passable, and the weather was favorable for stop-look-and-listen surveys. In spite of my best efforts, I could find no grouse or active leks on the 20 miles of roads I surveyed that morning.

To assure my exit back to Wisconsin in a few days, I parked on the neighbor rancher's house yard at mid-morning, and walked in to the cabin, skirting the snow banks and muddy holes of the trail in my waterproof hiking boots. My grouse work for the season was shorter and less productive than some years but it felt good to have the survey completed. I enjoyed two days of wood heat, hot meals, a little whiskey, and the opportunity to read and write under the sighing Ponderosa Pines, before weather drove me out once again. I left one day early because rain, wind, and snow were predicted that evening and all the next day. As I drove down Interstate 90 and crossed the Wyoming border into South Dakota, headed to Wisconsin and home, I could see in my rear-view mirror the black storm front moving in with flashes of lightning.

Clay gumbo soil packing my truck's tire treads

My "Cedar Knoll" camp on Thunder Basin National Grassland property

<u>2007</u>

I left Wisconsin in the early morning hours, before daylight, and arrived in Wyoming with several hours of light left. Never knowing the condition of the local roads, I drove directly to my survey area and found my route to be passable. This allowed me the luxury of looking for a new camp site within Thunder Basin National Grasslands that would offer a different view of the wildlands I had come to appreciate and a faster launch point to start my grouse work the following morning. As is often the case on these lands, I did not hear or see a single vehicle during the night nor the next morning while I checked my leks.

I confirmed occupancy and usage of three leks by sage- grouse and saw a total of 87 birds before the morning slipped away. It always remained a challenge to cover the rugged and barely-drivable roads and still get to the leks before the birds dispersed for the day. In order to get accurate counts, utilize my optical equipment, note the time, and record the data: time, temperature, number and sex of each bird, I would often spend at least 15 minutes at each stop. And the leks covered this day were separated by at least 25 miles. Every survey was always a race between me, the sun, and the birds.

Two mornings later I drove a new survey route down County Road 18 known locally as the Raven Creek/Popham Road, the moniker referring to a drainage basin and a large ranch of the area. One lek, which I had never seen before, held 52 grouse in an old short grass pasture near a windmill, which brought my total number of individual Greater Sage-Grouse for this season to 139, my second highest count for any of the nine years I participated as a volunteer for Wyoming.

On my way back to the cabin on a hard surfaced highway, I pulled several miles off on a familiar dirt trail and parked on an overlook of one of my leks to have a quiet breakfast in my truck cab and admire the view of sage, sparse grass, and rolling swales amidst gentle hills. I was the sole person in the middle of at least six square miles of short prairie grasses and sagebrush. Halfway through my powdered milk and instant hot cereal, the local county Sheriff's Deputy pulled up in back of me and walked to my window. Like any good, red-blooded, family man and American citizen I immediately had two thoughts: "Has something dreadful happened to a member of my family?" And "Why does he want to arrest me?" Both of which tumbled through my brain simultaneously, fighting for supremacy, for the next few seconds.

Reaching my window, the pleasant member of the law enforcement community merely asked if I was having any trouble and if everything was OK. I explained I was a volunteer for Wyoming Department of Game and Fish, doing grouse survey work, and that I had stopped for breakfast and some hot tea. He seemed very interested in my work for Wyoming and we had a good, brief discussion on conservation of natural resources. In retrospect, I speculated he had perhaps stopped to check on me because of my out-of-state Wisconsin license plate. A "normal tourist" would have little incentive to be parked in such a remote location.

2008

Spring was always a busy time at our farm in Wisconsin. Having retired from active crop and livestock farming, we were engaged in establishing native prairie species, both grasses and forbs, in appropriate locations on our farm. Annual burning to encourage the prairie species worked best for a few precious weeks at that time of year. Our tractors needed conversion from Winter functions of snow removal, to Spring and Summer functions of mowing. As I drove the 13 hours to Wyoming, trading one week of Spring in Wisconsin for one week of Spring in Wyoming, I pondered how much longer I wanted to spend doing grouse surveys.

I left a trailer-load of deck materials, intended for the remotely-located vacation cabin, at the neighbor's ranch yard, since the access road was impassible. I then drove directly to the Moorcroft truck stop to spend the night camping in the back of my pickup at 22 degrees amongst the semi-trucks. I knew many of my favorite camp sites would be difficult to reach because of mud, but by starting my first night out on a firm gravel parking lot, I would be able to get in a long survey the following morning.

I was able to cover four leks the next morning, finding grouse at each, with my maximum count being 32 at the new lek I had just seen last year. The trail to the cabin was still too muddy to drive so I hiked into the cabin for the day, four miles in, four miles out, and drove to a reservoir near Upton at dusk. The evening was pleasant and as the sun slipped behind the ridge, several mallards on the pond were soft-quacking their way to darkness.

Driving old roads and new, searching for new leks and observing old leks, I had rather poor results the next day, but birds are where you find them, and there were few to be found that morning. I met my Wyoming Biologist at his Newcastle office and we swapped a few wildlife stories before I drove back to Sundance and visited the rancher neighbor lady in the nursing home. I was sad to find her there but she had always been kind and friendly to us. She was impressed with our self-care individualism and once told us, "Why, you folks are like Greyhounds, walking all that way into and back from the cabin up on the hill."

I camped out the next night at what I referred to as The Cedar Knoll camp. It was secluded while still offering the two routes of access referred to earlier and had the vista views that I like.

I did find a few grouse the next morning, but my highlight of the day was carrying in some Plaster of Paris to make a cast of a cougar track in mud on the road to the cabin. The cast came out well, with fine detail of the toes and pad, and still sits on a shelf in the cabin, reminding me of the wild reasons I like to visit that area of Wyoming, hoping I might yet, one day, see the live animal.

2009
Due to Wyoming weather, unmet obligations at our farm in Wisconsin, and tasks at the vacation cabin, my grouse work for Wyoming Game and Fish in 2009 proved to be limited. I was forced to question my priorities for what I could get accomplished in this Spring and future years, but I told myself to take the coming year to think it over.

Muddy roads and terrible observation weather prevented any level of routine access to Greater Sage-Grouse leks during the spring of 2009, but I was able to hike west from the cabin three mornings to survey the Sharp-tailed Grouse there. I found the Sharptail population quite robust, and recorded my highest count of the nine years of official surveying, 27 birds. Obviously, the habitat and seasonal growing conditions, whether for animal life or plant life, had worked in their favor. With this Sharptail lek being in the middle of a major tract of large private ranches that receive limited and gradually reduced grazing and ranching intensity, I have optimistic hopes it will long persist.

With rural roads still in poor driving condition, and many of my favorite remote, but lovely, campsites hidden in a veil of lightly falling rain and fog, I stayed my last night in Wyoming on this trip in the Upton Motel. Starting out the next morning with concrete under my wheels, and determined to get in at least one thorough grouse survey, I was able to cover four leks but found two leks with grouse, two without, a total of only 20 grouse.

The engine-check light of my Ford had come on while still in South Dakota during my drive out. But I had found that by babying the engine and transmission I could still attain 60 miles per hour speed. It just took a little longer to get to that speed and I could not count on fast passing performance. I was a little trepidatious starting out on my drive back home but, with care and the advantage of double lane traffic on the Interstate, managed to keep chugging along for the next 13 hours of driving, vehicles occasionally piling up behind me. I breathed a sigh of relief to arrive home at our farm and back in the land and convenience of my normal auto mechanics who could resolve the engine problem.

As I drove back home to Wisconsin, I was admittedly a bit dejected by the results of my effort for the season. Yet, I knew on a rational plane, that is life in the wild when dealing with wild critters. Normal population cycles, the weather, travel limited to the roads that exist, not roads where you wished there were, and the ever-present march of time and obligations all have an impact on biological surveys. And I knew the grouse, the coyotes, the antelope did not have one whit of any obligation to myself, but were gamely living the life they have always had, as best they could. I wished them and the sagebrush country I had come to love the best of a natural and permanent existence.

Conclusion

By February of 2010, after due consideration of my life goals and accomplishments to date, I decided it was time to resign from my volunteer grouse survey work. Each Spring, for nine consecutive years, I had made the 1600-mile round trip to Wyoming. I wrote to each of my two main contacts, one the Biologist at Wyoming Game and Fish, the other, the Adopt-A-Lek Coordinator at Wyoming Wildlife Federation, and explained my rationale, and thanked them for the opportunity. Each had been unfailingly complimentary of my efforts each year and in response to this conclusion of my efforts. I was proud to have assisted their work in the preservation of Sharp-tailed Grouse and Greater Sage-Grouse. I will long cherish the experiences and memories of my time at the grouse leks, the magic of the sounds and displays of the dancing birds.

During my nine years of grouse survey work I had observed 820 Greater Sage-Grouse, the number derived from a total of the maximum of male and female grouse seen at any one site on any one day. The highest number of Greater Sage-Grouse observed at any one time was 86 birds.

During the same years I had also observed 307 Sharp-tailed Grouse, the quantity was derived in the same manner as above. The highest number of Sharp-tailed Grouse observed at any one time was 27 birds.

From 2001 through 2009 I drove 2880 miles on local roads to perform my assigned surveys. This figure does not include the approximate 15,000 miles I had driven back and forth from Wisconsin to Wyoming each year.

I had camped out alone 19 nights in the back of my four-wheel drive Ford pickup in addition to sleeping in the vacation cabin as appropriate to schedule requirements.

I was reluctant to leave the now normal spring-time ritual of these yearly grouse surveys. They had become another precious addition to our series of outdoor adventures.

The authors are retired from their vocational fields, Jean as a biology and ornithology instructor at the University of Wisconsin-La Crosse, and Gary as a Professional Engineer. They live in a rural area of Wisconsin and actively farmed for 20 years. They have resided on their farm for more than fifty years and are restoring native prairie grasses to portions of it while utilizing the whole as a place of quiet refuge. Gary and Jean are proud of and enjoy the love and nearby companionship of two daughters and a granddaughter.

The authors' previous books include:

A Memoir of Holstein, An Engineer Traces his Origins by Gary G. Ruhser

Seven Summers with Peregrines: Finding Midlife Adventures by Jean C. Beyer Ruhser and Gary G. Ruhser

For Love of Nature by Gary G. Ruhser and Jean C. Beyer Ruhser

Our daughter, Gayle C. Edlin, has published two novels: Here & Now, and Between.

The above books are available from Amazon, or can be ordered from your favorite bookstore.

Find Jean and Gary online at: garyandjean65@gmail.com
And at: garyandjean65 (Facebook)